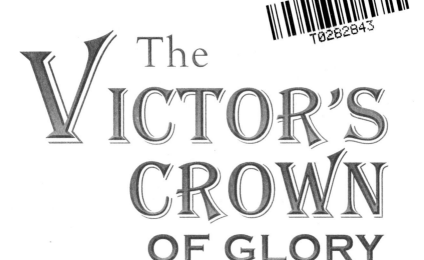

The VICTOR'S CROWN

OF GLORY

True, Miraculous Stories of God at Work in the
War-Torn Middle East and North Africa

As told by John Samara
By Dorcas Hoover

ananias (A) house

Good Books

New York, New York

Because of their inspiring example of selfless service to God in the crossfire of the Syrian war, this book is dedicated to two of the most courageous warriors of the Cross we have ever known—Abraham and Amalee Samara.

"The people living in darkness have seen a great light; on those living in the land of the shadow of death a light has dawned."

Matthew 4:16

"Don't be afraid of what you are going to suffer. . . . The Devil is going to throw some of you into prison so that you may be tested. . . . Be faithful until death, and I will give you the victor's crown of life."

Revelation 2:10 (ISV)

"Blessed is the man who is steadfast under trial and perseveres when tempted; for when he has passed the test and been approved, he will receive the [victor's] crown of life which the Lord has promised to those who love Him."

James 1:12 (AMP)

"Then, when the Chief Shepherd appears, you will receive the victor's crown of glory that will never fade away."

I Peter 5:4 (ISV)

CONTENTS

PART III. IN THE CRUCIBLE OF CONFLICT

PART IV. I AM A POOR WAYFARING STRANGER

PART V. FRONTLINE WARRIORS

FOREWORD

Meeting the frontline warriors in the Middle East and North Africa risking all to follow Jesus revolutionized my life. I will be forever impacted by the pastor kidnapped by the radicals, the sheikh whose son had the encounter with the Man in the glowing white, the teacher of the Qur'an whose daughter was miraculously healed, the pastor who escaped from ISIS beneath a burka, the leader who endured the siege of Aleppo on the battle lines of ISIS, fearless Pastor Abraham, and dozens of others.

In my interactions with the men and women of the MENA region (Middle East and North Africa), as they rise out of the ashes of the past, struggling against all odds, I marvel at their maturity. I am impressed and humbled by their strong faith and tested lives, finding myself to be walking among giants.

These Believers are not rudimentary in their Christian life but living in a maturity of devotion rarely seen in the established Western church. The price of being a Christ-follower there is high, and when they count the cost of not loving their lives dear to themselves, their spiritual moorings are anchored deeper in Christ than many of us in Western society who grew up attending church all our lives.

"Do not focus on our suffering, rather focus on the Joy of our Salvation" is the rallying cry of these brave Soldiers of the Cross, receiving death threats and staring down gun barrels as the bombs explode around them.

Their daily lives are marked with uncertainty of life and liberty. Yet they discreetly, but boldly step into their day, asking, "Will this be the day I die?" while offering the only message of Hope that can change their desperate surroundings.

The Kingdom of Jesus Christ is forging a radical transformation in the MENA region through the efforts of these faithful men and women as they offer material relief, education, and share the Good News of the

Gospel. Every time I interact with these amazing individuals, I am challenged on what it means to be a follower of Christ.

We share these stories as a testament to the Eternal Flame of God still burning in the regions of the Early Church. Every miracle documented took place as described while the names of the courageous warriors who risk all to follow Christ have been changed, to protect their lives. Abraham Samara and his family retain their original names in this document.

Read on to meet courageous heroes who seem to step right out of the book of Acts. I am confident your life will never be the same.

Soli Gloria Deo!

Ervin Barkman, pastor, missionary, and teacher at

Ananias House MENA pastor's conferences

July 29, 2024

INTRODUCTION

When my great-grandfather encountered a missionary stranded in the Syrian desert in the early 1900s, he didn't know the divine appointment would change the trajectory of the lives of his descendants and, in fact, impact the Middle East and North African regions as well.

Since Cain's murder of Abel, whose blood cries out from the ground, the blood of hateful conflict has drenched the Middle East. Despite the relentless violence in this region, the Lord has maintained a remnant of hope through all the wars and deaths. The lifeline of hope flowing through the church since the time of Christ pulses with vibrance, swelling today, still offering healing and the promise of the resurrection for the Middle East and Muslim nations.

I am eager to share the stories of the journeys of the Christian believers and of the church in the Middle East today.

Discovering the missionary and his Ford stranded in the desert, my great-grandfather moved stones, carving a path for Dr. Freed's Ford to reach the remote village, enlarging the paths made for camels and donkeys. Dr. Freed shared the Gospel with my great-grandfather. My father, in turn, spent more than five decades serving the Lord in the region, walking alongside others, spreading the Gospel in the Middle East and North Africa.

It all started with the story of one faithful, committed missionary braving the scorching desert with its perils. Today we see thousands of commitments to take up the Cross, and the faithfulness of Christians despite the hardships they face.

These are the accounts Ananias House organization introduces in these next pages. They are not our stories, but God's stories. We are sharing our part in *God's* story:

- The stories begin with my father Abraham, a fearless man of God, who lives with his ear to the heart of God, and his knees on the floor.
- Stories of miraculous answers to my father's prayers, including prayers for 5,000 Bibles.
- Stories of my sister facing barrel bombs in the school yard surrounded with crying students.
- Stories of my friends getting abducted.
- Stories of miraculous healings in the refugee camps.
- Stories filled with God's presence, direction, and deliverance on the front lines of battle, bringing hope that God is working powerfully in the twenty-first century, even in the most difficult of situations, just as He worked in Damascus in the days of Paul, 2,000 years ago.

And yes, the first story tells of my own arrest.

John Samara

August 2, 2024

Part I

Damascus Light

"I am the light of the world. Anyone who follows me will never walk in the darkness but will have the light of life."

John 8:12

"Darkness cannot drive out darkness; only light can do that. Hate cannot drive out hate; only love can do that."

—Martin Luther King Jr.

HANDCUFFS

(Middle Eastern Border Crossing, 2007)

"Romans 8:17 says if we suffer with Him, we will be glorified with Him, combining suffering with glory. Paul knew his mission was to suffer severely for the name of God, but he also saw the glory at the end."

—Rami Ibrahim

"You can only grow in jail what you take with you. You can only grow in persecution what you take into it."

—Ripkin, *The Insanity of God*

Should a university student need to sit in a Middle Eastern prison cell for carrying a Bible in his backpack?

John didn't notice the glint in the border guard's eyes as the sweaty fingers rifled through his backpack. After pawing through the neatly pressed shirts, the toothbrush, the comb, the guard lifted out the carefully typed conference notes. And his Bible.

The Syrian youth could almost smell the sizzling lamb at the shawarma stands just beyond the diesel fumes of the muggy customs line. After the months of intense study in cloudy, cool England, John's muscles relaxed under the welcoming caress of the Middle Eastern heat.

John signaled a thumbs-up to his University of Manchester classmates in line behind him, flashing his characteristic wink. Other years, it was John's father, Abraham Samara, the godly, courageous Syrian pastor, who traveled to speak at Middle Eastern conferences.

"Guys, you have no idea how much this will mean for students from England to care enough to travel so far to invest in the youth at the rally."

"You've told us so many stories of what they endure. . ." John's friend dropped his voice, visualizing the beatings, kidnappings, and threats the Syrian, Lebanese, Egyptian, and Turkish Christian youth endured.

"Hey, we're every bit as excited as you are."

"For sure. And falafels. Freshly squeezed pomegranate juice. Bring it on!"

"Feels like the capstone of my life, guys. Like all my studies and experiences have been leading up to this moment . . ."

John's voice died away and his eyes grew large as they focused on the soldier flipping through the highlighted pages of the well-worn Bible. The hateful glint in the guard's steely, narrowed eyes curdled John's stomach with apprehension.

"What's this all about?" The border guard's greasy fingers held John's precious Bible by the back cover. Pages of notes fluttered to the floor.

"If you thought you could smuggle contraband into this country, you have another guess coming."

Ice slithered down John's spine. *Radical Islamic soldiers . . . Dear Lord.*

"A Bible is not contraband," John countered quietly, a flush rising in his cheeks. Every fiber of his body burned taut with emotion. Sweat beaded on his forehead.

"It is perfectly legal to carry one's personal religious book . . ."

"I happen to be in charge, not you." The guard's steely eyes narrowed with scorn. "This is how we deal with anyone trying to smuggle contraband," he snapped, yanking a pair of handcuffs from a drawer.

John's spine stiffened. He felt a clutch of panic in the pit of his stomach. He wiped his clammy hands on his jeans. *Please, Jesus!*

"You have no right to arrest me. Besides, I have dual citizenship—Syrian and American, in addition to being a British student." John struggled to keep his voice steady as he slapped his American passport next to his Syrian document.

"Hands behind your back! You can argue from your prison cell." With sinister flourish, the guard slapped the cuffs onto John's wrists.

How can this be happening? God, I'll miss the convention! The struggling youth have looked forward to this all year! My friends came all the way from England . . .

Tourists tipped back their straw hats, removing sunglasses for a better view of the clean-cut gentleman the guard shoved toward the door.

A hasty glance over his shoulder assured John his colleagues had vanished into the crowd.

"I need to make a phone call," John appealed as the door of the police car slammed behind him. "I am scheduled to speak at a conference."

The icy glare told John smugglers didn't get privileges. Especially "infidels."

God! Why? Where are you? What's going on?

Imposing concrete walls topped with coils of barbed wire and manned guard towers felt surreal, but the clanging of the iron gates assured him the arrest was no illusion.

None of the professors at Mount Vernon nor the courses he studied for his master's at University of Manchester had prepped him on how to survive in a foreign prison cell. Under Islamic guards.

Inside the prison, the soldier roughly stripped John of his backpack, his wallet, his belt, and his shoelaces as well as any remaining fragments of self-respect.

The guard thrust a key into a cell door and unlocked it, shoving John into a small, dingy cell reeking of human waste with flies buzzing around smelly piles on the filthy floor. "Make yourself at home!" The guard cackled cruelly as the door clanged shut. A key turned in the lock.

Footsteps echoed down the cavernous hall, seeming to sneer mockingly, "You're finished! You're finished! You're finished!"

The weight of his predicament crashed over him like the neighbors' slimy dish water disgorged from the sixth-floor apartment above Mama's courtyard. John gently massaged his wrists where the handcuffs rubbed his skin raw.

"Don't be afraid. You are a God-fearing man," a voice rasped from the shadows. "He will not let go of you."

John's eyes blinked in the shadowy darkness, focusing on the silhouette of his cellmate crouched in a corner, elbows resting on the robe flowing over the knees. Gnarled hands grasped the checkered kaffiyeh covering the grayed head.

John scanned the cell mate inquiringly. The urgently needed message soaked deep into his heart like a warm salve from the hand of God.

I will need those words.

A guard unlocked the door of the cell, gesturing to the cellmate. "Hustle buddy, you're out of here tonight."

As the cellmate hobbled stiffly down the hall, John stared after the unique messenger. *Do angels sometimes dress like Muslims?*

"Thank you, Jesus, for the unique greeter you arranged to encourage me!"

Surveying his wretched surroundings, John crouched in the corner that appeared to have the least human waste.

What do I do now, Lord?

Night fell, draping a heavy shroud of darkness over the prison. Holding his hand in front of his face, John could not see his fingers. The rank odors intensified in the blackness. Small paws scuttled around him, but he could not see the rats. He smacked at the bugs scampering across his ankles. A few stars flickered sympathetically beyond the barred window the size of his hand.

In exhaustion, John leaned his head against his knees. He could not coax sleep to grant him a reprieve.

Does anyone even know where I am?

My future just vanished. . . . It's gone. Destroyed!

If only I could pace to release the stress. But he couldn't see the feces, the reeking toilet hole, or the vermin, so he remained slumped against the wall.

Is this where I will spend the rest of my life? God! I thought you were leading me to train prospective leaders here in the Middle East. What's this all about?

"*Lord, I choose to trust you,*" he whispered hoarsely, lifting hands in surrender toward the tiny window.

Slowly, John submitted to the new reality of life in prison. His taut muscles began relaxing. *I have Jesus. It will be okay.*

My dad heard your voice. You've answered more prayers for my baba than those stars I can see from this window. You are a living God. Will you speak to me like you spoke to my father? Like you spoke to the ISIS prisoner?

What would it be like to experience the dynamic presence of a living God?

Baba told me the story so often with such passion, I can almost feel the trembling of the building. . . .

DIVINE ENCOUNTER

(Damascus, Syria, 1959)

"But Saul, still breathing threats and murder against the disciples of the Lord went to the high priest and asked him for letters to the synagogues at Damascus, so that if he found any belonging to the Way, men or women, he might bring them bound to Jerusalem. Now as he went on his way, he approached Damascus, and suddenly a light from heaven shone around him. And falling to the ground, he heard a voice saying to him, 'Saul, Saul, why are you persecuting me?'"

Acts 9:1-4

"If we are abandoned to God, He works through us all the time."

—Oswald Chambers

Draped in the mantle of darkness, the walls and roof of the dorm shuddered under the dynamic Presence. The windows rattled and shook as if about to explode from the uncontainable, awe-inspiring aura of the Divine visitation.

Damascene high school boys dove beneath the bunks. They flung blankets over their heads to hide from the magnificent Power. Wretched, helpless awe of a Force beyond anything they ever encountered seized the quivering hearts.

"Abraham!" a dynamic voice pierced and echoed through the darkness. "Abraham! You are My son. I am calling you to be a minister of the Gospel."

Beyond the quaking windows, Mount Hermon rose majestically, etched against the dark sky, standing guard on Syria's southwestern border, as it had three and a half millennia before when biblical Abraham's camels kicked up Syria's desert sands. Melting rivulets from its regal

8

snowy cape trickled down the dark slopes to the clear Barada River. Moonbeams glistened on the rippling river threading through apricot and pomegranate orchards, flowing on toward the stone walls of Old Damascus. The shadowy outline of the battle-scarred citadel guarded the city, hinting at the battles it had seen in its 1,000-year reign and of sieges yet to come.

Towering mosque minarets pierced the night skyline. The green hue they flung across the ancient city hailed the seventh-century conquest of descendants of Hagar, biblical Abraham's mistress. Beneath their olive glow, corroding memorials to Saul's encounter with the Divine light lent Damascus the air of an ancient mausoleum.

The sign APOSTLE PAUL BAR dangled in an alley. All that remained of the Christianity once blazing through these ancient alleys seemed to be cold, decomposing monuments.

In the secret closets of Damascus, a flame inched along a fuse about to detonate a government coup d'état. . . .

But the God who flung His blinding light upon Saul the Persecutor had reached down to the ancient city once again.

As the Divine Presence vanished into the night, the trembling subsided in the Damascene school dorm. High school rebels known for their bravado and troublemaking crawled out from beneath their beds, wiping the cobwebs from their dazed faces.

You are My son. . . . You are My son. . . . I am calling you, you, you. . . . The echo of those life-changing words ignited the Syrian schoolboy's heart with courage to follow where God led.

Abraham Samara pedaled his bike to the Muslim villages and suburbs around Damascus every weekend, sharing the Light of the Gospel. Obeying the Voice.

"Abraham, we feel God is asking you to preach next Sunday," the church elders informed the student a short time after the Divine encounter.

"Me? I'm too young!" he balked. "I'm just a teen!"

"God told us you are to preach," the elders insisted.

I have called you, Abraham remembered the Voice saying.

"I will not argue with God," Abraham relented.

This remarkable lad knows his Bible more fluently and teaches with more passion than any other man in church, the congregation observed.

When the church's minister died a short time later, the Damascene congregation commissioned Abraham as the church's official pastor. Syria's sparse Christian populace allowed few options for pastor selection and training.

The Divine encounter catapulted the lives of all of Abraham's buddies in that dorm from mischief to a trajectory of lifetime service for God's Kingdom.

Meanwhile, a whirlwind coup d'état blasted through Syria in 1963, followed by a second coup three years later. With the new Syrian government's desperation for international recognition came alignment with the USSR, refashioning the Ba'athist party with Marxist theology.

"Don't mention 'his' name in public," the citizens whispered after Hafaz al-Assad's power grab. "If you don't want to end up in the Mukhabarat torture chambers, use a nickname when referring to the president in public. His Mukhabarat secret police are omnipresent."

How long will the regime manage to quench the smoldering sparks of Sunni majority's resentment toward the Alawite government? the world wondered.

Purging any potential opposition, the new regime expelled foreign missionaries. In a panicked exit, Old Damascus church and school facilities fell into the hands of Marxist teachers.

Lord, your church! Abraham grieved as he watched the takeover. *Your facilities! Stolen . . . Teaching Marxist philosophies in facilities dedicated to the advancement of Your Kingdom?*

During the government transition, Abraham graduated from high school and studied for a mathematics teaching degree, while evangelizing Saturdays and preaching Sundays. And he vowed his love to Amalee, a pastor's daughter with an elementary teaching degree.

Two thousand years after Paul's Divine encounter near Damascus, the Creator of the universe once again visited this ancient cradle of religion, transforming a rebel into a dynamic frontline leader to advance His Kingdom.

How great is our God!

Behind the block walls and metal bars, John asked, *God, where are you?*

Baba often said, "God has a factory in heaven where He takes what the enemy plans to use for evil, transforming it for an ultimate good."

It's not about me, it's about Your glory. John's weary muscles relaxed as he sensed God's hand over him.

God, I know you are real.

Goosebumps popped up on John's arms. *Where did I hear those words before?*

ISIS PRISONER

(Syrian Desert)

"That you may declare the praises of Him who called you out of darkness into His wonderful light."

I Peter 2:9

"God! I know you exist!" Prisoner 69 cried from beneath the black hood covering his head. "I know you exist!"

An ISIS guard bellowed out the identification numbers of the captives destined to stand before the court that day. He called each number in sequence, in ascending order, every dawn. Each morning, the announcement of the day's fated numbers injected paralyzing terror into the hearts of the ISIS prisoners in the desert. Every day, the gap narrowed between the numbers called and number 69.

The echoing tramp of approaching boots, the jangle of keys, and the shuffle of shackled feet always followed the chilling pronouncement of the fated numbers. The captive heard the rapid panting beneath the black hoods of the doomed prisoners shuffling past his cell to the formidable ISIS court. The court with no hearings. No witnesses. No mercy.

Sixty-nine heard muffled pleas, shouts of "Allahu Akbar" mingling with pleading screams. Staccato gunshots. Thuds and groans.

And none of the prisoners ever returned to the jail cells. Not one. And none walked out of the prison gates.

Blindfolded by black hoods to intensify the air of terror and hopelessness and to secure the anonymity of the faces of the captors, the prisoners huddled in their cells smothered by stifling heat and the oppressive darkness. But far more terrifying than the physical blackness was the palpable spiritual darkness. The hatred. The despair.

Beneath the hood, one could distinguish night from daylight by the variation of noises. While the shroud of darkness remained constant, the pleas, screams, cracks, and thuds of execution faded, morphing into the scurrying of tiny feet, the scuttering of roaches, groans, desperate prayers, sighs, and the smothered sobs of the night hour.

As each night faded with the scampering of the rodent paws, as the groaning of the gate announced morning's arrival, the prisoner tensed at the shouted daily roster of numbers. Mentally, he recalculated the days remaining until the guard would call "69," tabulating the hours left until the guard called him to stand before the ISIS court. The ISIS sword or gun barrel. Or worse.

As the moments dragged like a chained body behind an ISIS Toyota, "69" wrestled with the irony of his dilemma.

I am a Muslim.

My ISIS captors are Muslim.

I am a Sunni Muslim.

So are my captors.

I pray to Allah.

They pray to Allah.

I read the Qur'an.

My captors read the Qur'an.

But in the name of that same Allah, quoting the same Qur'an I read, they will execute me, screaming, "Allahu Akbar! Our god is great!" What kind of a god condones such barbarity?

"God? Who are you?" he wept, in a desperate, agonizing passion to know a Divine Being who could hear his cries.

The calculated execution date crept nearer like a desert viper slithering closer to its terrified prey. Sixty-nine's fear magnified with every passing hour. Restlessly, he paced the cell caked with human filth and smashed roaches, like a trapped animal, sensing the hunter's approach. He paced back and forth, back and forth, groaning, sighing, moaning.

His hood, damp with sweat and tears of desperation, reeked of the foulness of tortured sweat left by the fated prisoners wearing the hood before him. The odor tormented him with the awareness that whoever previously wore the hood no longer existed.

"God, I know you are there!" he kept crying. "Please . . . please . . . please, help me!"

The numbers crept higher: 49 . . . 59 . . . and then 68. As the calculated hour of doom approached, his heart muscles tightened. The compressing screw of a giant vise seemed to bear down on his heart with increasing force every passing moment almost beyond endurance.

"God!" he sobbed wretchedly. "I know you are out there! I need you!"

A brilliant burst of dazzling light flashed through the blackness of the hood.

"Don't worry, my son, you will be saved!"

A tranquil calm enveloped the prisoner like a child nestled in his father's lap. A sense of wonderment, a sense of the Divine.

"Please, help me!" he cried in relief mingled with frantic desperation.

"Don't worry, my son," the Voice replied, "You are saved."

Sixty-nine puzzled over the intense light filtering through the foul fabric of the hood; he pondered over the calm, authoritative voice.

God, who are you?

The night before his calculated execution, the prisoner tossed and moaned on the filthy floor.

Did I actually hear a voice? Did God speak to me? Will he save me tomorrow?

The creaking of doors, the thud of boots. . . . The young man huddled in the corner, clutching his knees, shivering despite the heat, too terrified to pace or even to move.

How will they execute me? Will I be tortured? Does one feel excruciating pain when a sword slices through his neck?

"God! I know you exist! I know you do! Please help me!"

"SIXTY-NINE!"

The heavy tread of approaching boots.

The panting beneath his putrid hood.

The screw of the vise ratcheted tighter over his aching heart.

And yet the calm sense of the Divine remained.

The rattling of keys. The weary moan of the cell door.

A boot caught "69" in the ribs.

"To your feet!"

The guard yanked his arms behind his back, slapped on handcuffs, and dragged him, stumbling, out of the cell. Unsteadily, the prisoner shuffled down the hall, the black hood obscuring his vision and concealing the terror in his eyes.

Each shuffled step took him closer to his fate. Closer to the court that called no witnesses and reviewed no evidence. Closer to the Khalifa, the ISIS prince who never bothered to glance through any files to read the prisoner's name, profession, family, or his charges, and who couldn't see the face of the condemned beneath the hood.

But it made no difference. The sentence was always the same. Without exception. The sentence was always "Death." The ISIS court never showed mercy nor permitted appeal.

The tramping of the guard's boots halted. The trembling captor sensed he stood in front of the ISIS Khalifa, the prince. Every muscle in his body tensed. Dread ran down his spine. His knees turned to water. His heart hammered with such intensity he felt lightheaded.

Please, God! I believe in you! Please, please, please help me.

He could not breathe beneath the suffocating hood.

God! Whoever you are! Please. . . .

He heard the rhythmic breathing of the Khalifa. The clearing of a throat. The squeak of a chair.

"Release this man!" a gravelly voice commanded.

"Release him??"

"Get moving! I told you to release this prisoner. Take him out to the desert and let him go. Next!"

The incredulous guard led "69" toward a truck, shoving him inside.

"Unbelievable! Unbelievable." The guard muttered as he started the engine and threw the truck into gear.

"I've never seen anyone released. No one, I tell you. The Khalifa couldn't even see your face."

The entire trip, the soldier continued to mutter.

"He didn't read your file. He knew nothing about you. What made him release you? Your God must really love you. Unbelievable."

Sixty-nine never said a word as the truck bounced over the ruts and the rocks of the Syrian wilderness, but he knew. He knew without a doubt there was a real and living, loving God who cared personally for him.

The truck lurched to a stop. The driver yanked the transmission into park, shut off the engine, and shoved the truck door open.

The soldier tied up the hooded captive in the position that ISIS called "folded in half"—his legs tied to his shoulders. Leaving him defenseless, blindfolded in the barren wilderness without water or food.

As the rumble of the truck faded into the desert, the young man relaxed into the toasty sand, weeks of built-up tension melting away beneath the warmth of the ground beneath him.

"God! You *are* real! You heard me! You see me! Please help me find you."

He twisted and strained, trying to wiggle out of his hood and to reach the ropes with his teeth.

He pictured the Levant vipers slithering through the desert sands.

Inexplicably, the knots loosened effortlessly. Yanking off the black, stale hood, he drank in the freshness of the gentle breezes, the brilliance of the cloudless skies, and the elixir of the golden sunshine.

"You are real! God, you are alive!" For a long moment, he just basked in the presence of an almighty, loving God.

And then he whispered again, "Help me find you!"

Surveying his surroundings, he noted the fresh truck tracks.

I will go in the opposite direction.

The released prisoner trudged through the wilderness, praying to the living God, looking for a sign of friendly inhabitants.

Eventually, the former captive made his way to the old city of Damascus, searching for a Christian pastor. God led him to Pastor Abraham Samara within the walls of the Old City of Damascus. The pastor with a shepherd's heart who seemed to carry about him the palpable presence of God.

"The glorious light of the loving Creator God reached down into the darkness, despair, and hate of the ISIS prison and set me free. And now, I choose to follow the Jesus of the Cross I once despised. I've counted the cost."

Within walking distance of Saul's encounter with God two millennia before, the former ISIS captive embraced the light. Within shouting distance of where Ananias had prayed for Paul and the wall where Paul later was lowered in a basket to elude his pursuers.

The same omniscient God who confronted the Apostle Paul with the brilliant beam of light still cared about drawing blinded men from darkness into the light and hope of truth 2,000 years later.

How great is our God!

If only I had a Bible I could bear most anything, John sighed. *Baba prayed for 5,000 Bibles, maybe I could pray for one.*

John could still picture Baba urging the church to pray for Bibles for Syria. . . .

FIVE THOUSAND BIBLES

(Damascus, Syria, circa 1989)

"For God, who said, 'Let light shine out of darkness,' is the One who has shone in our hearts to give us the Light of the knowledge of the glory and majesty of God. . . ."

II Corinthians 4:6 AMP

"The work of the church is not survival. She exists to fulfill the Great Commission."

—Brother Andrew

"We are not called to be successful in accordance with ordinary standards, but in accordance with a corn of wheat falling into the ground and dying, becoming in that way what it never could be if it were to abide alone."

—Oswald Chambers

"Let's ask God for 5,000 Bibles," Pastor Abraham suggested to the believers who had met to pray.

"There are Christians in this country who have never seen the Word of God. Syria desperately needs Bibles. We need to get a Bible into every home. Not just in every Christian home but *every* home in Syria. I have faith our powerful God can provide 5,000 Gospels for us to distribute, if we just ask!"

The congregants eyed each other with cautious, chuckling smiles.

Five thousand Bibles! This Islamic country doesn't even permit the printing of Scripture. Where could we find 5,000 Bibles? And how could we pay for them if we did locate that many?

At the back of the auditorium, an elder rose to his feet. "Our God is wealthy. He owns the cattle on a thousand hills. He owns the universe," he announced confidently. "Our God could provide 10,000 New Testaments if we asked Him! Why stop at 5,000 when the need is so desperate, and our God is so great!"

Smothered chuckles rippled across the auditorium. *Ten thousand Bibles! Utterly preposterous! Why not ask for the desert to freeze?*

And yet, why not ask? Still smiling at the far-fetched prayer request, the congregation knelt with their pastor. The grins faded into earnest expressions of intercession as the entire audience began to cry out to God for 10,000 New Testaments for Syria.

"Father, Syria needs your Word."

"We have seen your power. We have seen your miracles."

"It would be nothing for you to give Pastor Abraham 10,000 Bibles . . ."

"Amen!"

"Alleluia!"

Every believer prayed out loud simultaneously, storming Heaven's gates in a precious concert—earnest, passionate, pleading prayers in one voice. Their faith increased as the prayers crescendoed.

Twelve hours after that prayer meeting, the phone rang. Abraham lifted the receiver to hear crackling static alerting him the long-distance call originated in a distant country.

"We have several cases of Arabic Bibles we planned to send to Iraq," the caller announced through the crackling on the line. "Saddam Hussein's regime refused to let Bibles into the country. Could you possibly use 17,000 Arabic New Testaments and 1,000 Bibles?"

"Alleluia!" Abraham shouted, leaping out of his chair.

Could we possibly?! God, you don't waste any time, do you?

The miracle of the 18,000 copies of the Word of God was just another day in Abraham's journey with his miracle-working God in Syria. The divine interventions he experienced seemed as numerous as the stars looking down on the ancient walls of Damascus. He'd seen far too many miracles from the hand of his unlimited God to count or recall them all.

As the boxes of donated Bibles emptied, Abraham began to strategize. *Shipping Bibles into Syria involves red tape, challenges, and expense. Why not print Bibles within the country?*

Even beyond the legal challenges, printing Bibles in a Muslim majority regime would be a daunting venture.

But God. . . .

The persistent, passionate pastor researched, filled out applications, prayed, and hacked red tape with the confidence God would open doors.

In time, he received legal authorization to print Bibles in Syria. Believing the New Testament was friendlier to those unfamiliar with the Word of God, Abraham published tens of thousands of New Testaments, making the Gospel much more accessible in the Middle East.

Though Abraham worked with limited resources, God always provided finances for the visions He gave Abraham.

"Lord, help us get a Bible into every home in Syria," he prayed. The prayer eventually changed to "Lord, help us to get a Bible into every home in the MENA [Middle East and North Africa] Region."

"God's Word never returns void," the pastor told his congregation.

Abraham's vision eventually facilitated the distribution of more than a million copies of the Word of God in the Middle East.

Beneath the Alawite rule, the restless 74 percent Sunni Islamic population lay as dry tinder, waiting to explode in a conflagration of war. Only God knew the harvest those copies would produce when the flames of civil war raced across Syria.

"Please don't think of going to the Jihadi hotbed!" Abraham's friends pleaded. "If the radicals threw a priest out of the camp, who knows what they will do to you if you try to give them *Bibles*!"

THE JIHADI
STRONGHOLD

(Syria)

"Greater love has no one than this, that someone lay down his life for his friends."

John 15:13

"The Cross can point to suffering, but it does not symbolize suffering. The Cross symbolizes victory. The Christian life is not a difficult, suffering life. It is a good life, a wonderful life, a victorious life."

—Rami Ibrahim

"So, where are we going with this truck?" the hired driver questioned, maneuvering the rented truck out of Damascus.

"We are delivering blankets and Bibles for the humanitarian crisis up north," Abraham explained. With the Jihadi wars throughout the Middle East, Syria perpetually seemed a magnet for both refugees and Jihadists.

"The Jihadi hotbed!" The driver swerved onto the curb of the road with the screech of tires. "No sir, we certainly are not! That's suicidal! You're on your own, buddy!" A forceful slam of the truck door punctuated the driver's words.

Abraham hired another driver off the street, continuing on his mission unruffled.

Women in burkas, long-bearded men, and ever so many frolicking youngsters scrambled curiously from their makeshift homes to discover the new diversion from their perpetual boredom.

"I've brought you blankets," Pastor Abraham shouted with a

welcoming smile as he gestured to the stacks beside the truck. "Please take a blanket."

"And, if you want, you are welcome to gather around me. I would love to share with you about God's holy Book."

Refugees swarmed around him, clamoring for copies of God's Book and, to his amazement, neglected the stack of blankets.

A dignified elderly man stretched out his hands for a copy, his face etched with desperation. He beamed delightedly as he pressed the "Holy Book" to his forehead in grateful bliss.

"I have been searching for years to know what is in the Bible!" he cried, hugging and kissing Abraham tearfully. "I was a former English professor and always wondered about the Christians' holy Book. I've been searching for a Bible for years, and you just drive up and bring me one!"

How great is our God!

In the squalid, dingy prison, John tensed as footsteps echoed in the corridor. The rattle of keys. The creak of a door. "Samara, you are being transferred," a voice growled.

When radical Islamic guards transferred him to a third prison under the cover of darkness the next night, John knew, *They don't want anyone to know where I am. They are hiding me. . . .*

As John collapsed into the third cell, the shame smothered him, like a death shroud, once again. In the Arab culture of honor and shame, a prison sentence branded a man in the deepest disgrace. *Pastor Abraham Samara's son in jail!*

How will I ever teach again? Who will listen to me?

What girl . . . He shoved the dismal notion from his tortured mind. But the haunting thought ricocheted, returning forcefully.

Was Mero, the delightful girl from Latakia with the social work major, at the youth conference? What will she think if she finds out? And what will her father, a jet pilot, say if a guy with a prison term asks to date his daughter?

John shivered, hurling the horrid notion from him as if it were a live grenade.

If only I had a Bible!

Highlighted passages from his precious Bible scrolled through his weary brain. *". . . All things work together for good, for those who are called according to his purpose." Romans 8:28.*

Dear Baba. You were always so sure everything worked out for an ultimate good for those who loved God. You are turning the country upside down looking for me. Brave, fearless Baba. . . .

Sleep evaded John for three nights. The stench, the filth, the scurrying creatures, the cruel injustice, and the uncertainty made sleep impossible. His muscles felt like they'd been stretched on a torture rack. His weary brain seemed to flounder in a foggy swamp.

Mama, what I wouldn't give for one of your freshly fried kibbeh.

John could envision selfless little Mama with her round face crinkled into a smile, Baba with his neatly trimmed black mustache, and Nancy, Joanna, Silva, and Sila sitting around Mama's laden table in that tiny Damascene apartment in the Old City.

John could still picture the tear plopping onto Silva's flushed cheeks when his sister disclosed, "My friends were interrogated by the Mukhabarat."

Not even Mama's legendary kibbeh meat croquettes tempted her that night. . . .

THE SECRET POLICE

"We look not to the things that are seen but to the things that are unseen. For the things that are seen are transient, but the things that are unseen are eternal."

II Corinthians 4:18

"It is not about us being safe and comfortable. God is the center of the universe, not us. If He chooses to keep us safe, that's great, but if He chooses to allow us to suffer to bring glory to His name, then that's good, too. It is not about safety or comfort; it is about us bringing glory to God. And sometimes God receives the most glory when people see the grace of God shining from our broken hearts in response to suffering."

—Rami Ibrahim

Holding the shriveled, hard bread crust between his fingers in the dingy prison cell, John could almost smell Mama's famous kibbehs. His shrinking stomach rumbled as he pictured the savory ground beef, onion, and bulgar croquettes stuffed with pine nuts, fried beef or lamb seasoned with coriander, pepper, nutmeg, cinnamon, and cardamom.

The memory of the comforting aromas soothed John's heart as it always did when he walked into Mama's little kitchen with his torn jeans and a bloody nose once again.

Mama's delightful culinary creations and her generous spirit drew church family and neighbors to her table for tea and to stay for dinner nearly every day. Baba said the informal gatherings over Mama's treats forged stability, strength, and accountability in the church family.

John envisioned the tiny courtyard haven with a little swing, a laundry line laden with his sisters' home-sewn dresses, and fragrant, blooming cherry, loquat, apricot, and kumquat fruit trees.

He could picture the upper neighbors dumping their dishwater, potato peelings, and chicken bones from their balconies onto the courtyard, and Mama quietly cleaning them up. Dear Mama had the elasticity of a rubber band without the snap.

Mama made us feel loved and Baba always made us children feel secure and defended, John thought with a sigh. *All of us Samara children knew he would defend us and speak to our Islamic teachers when they treated us unjustly. . . .*

The block walls and bars faded as the childhood scene around Mama's table rose before John's eyes.

(Damascus, Syria, circa 1995)

"The Mukhabarat summoned Mariama and Elia to the secret police headquarters again," Silva whispered, her pale face looking down at her untouched kibbeh, eggplant, pita, and tahini as tears threatened to spill from her gentle eyes.

"Mariama is so stressed her hair is falling out by the handful. Their reputations are ruined. . . ."

"What would the Mukhabarat want with two 13- and 14-year-old girls from our church?" Abraham demanded, nearly rising from his chair, his dark eyebrows tangling in concern. The dark hair brushed back from his face, the groomed mustache, the glasses and his fit physique lent him the look of a dignified diplomat instead of a pastor and high school math teacher. "Girls from our church certainly would have no interest in scheming against the Assad Regime."

"You know they wouldn't, Baba!" Silva's taut muscles began to relax. Her fearless warrior Baba was a defender and a man of action, empowered by the passion of God's Spirit. He would not let the disgraceful injustice slide.

"Fasil had a crush on the girls and tried to get Elia and then Mariama to go out with him. Of course, Mariama and Elia would not be interested in a boy who is not a Christian. And they are too young for boy drama anyway!"

"Ah, so Fasil, the spurned lover, got revenge by lying to the Mukhabarat about Elia and Mariama," Nancy huffed, eyes flashing and brows knit.

"We must remember those who abuse us are not the enemy," Mama soothed, refilling the platters. "It is the spirit behind the abusers that is the enemy."

"I will personally look into this," Abraham declared. John and Sila exchanged gratified, knowing looks. That was their baba.

"You certainly aren't going to the headquarters for the secret police, Baba!" Joanna was old enough to understand the risks. "You might not come out!"

"I am and I will." And that settled the matter.

Baba did not need to say: "For me to live is Christ and to die is gain." His children all knew Abraham's life motto propelled him to live fearlessly as he followed the leading of God without faltering or fear. That verse coupled with God's direction was to Baba like fuel to a rocket, making Abraham Samara an unstoppable force.

Mama passed the kibbeh again. "Sila, did your homework survive today, or did the boys throw it into the mud again?" she gently questioned her youngest son.

"At least the gang didn't rip up my finished worksheets," Sila shrugged. "And the teacher is marking my grades more fairly since Baba spoke to her about it."

"Bring the soiled papers to me after dinner and I will try to wipe off the dirt and straighten them."

Jesus, I know you see what these dear youngsters go through for loving you, Mama often prayed. *Make a way for them to be faithful soldiers for you.*

"Silva, I am sorry you had to crawl across the playground. I suppose that was some unfair punishment because you are from a Christian pastor's family." A tender expression graced Joanna's fair face and petite features.

"I hope your teacher isn't targeting you because she knows you are the sister of Nancy and me. And I don't believe your teacher is marking your scores accurately. Everyone knows you are a star English pupil and earn far above the average scores she gives you."

Mama patted her youngest daughter sympathetically. It pained her to see her bright butterfly of a daughter like a wilted flower tonight. *What will the long-range effects of growing up in Syria be on God's precious heritage?* she secretly wondered.

"Mrs. Baghdadi knows I am the sister of Nancy and Joanna who spoke up for Jesus, and she doesn't like it," Silva sniffed. "Today it was hot, and the lecture was so boring. The whole class was restless. I promise I was not any more fidgety than any other student, but Mrs. Baghdadi looks sternly at me over those glasses and yells, 'Silva Samara, go crawl across the entire playground on your hands and knees. Maybe that will help you learn to sit still!'" Silva's sweet face flushed at the memory of the humiliating abuse.

Baba looked at Mama and made a mental note about the matter.

Like many Middle Eastern pastors and their wives, Abraham and Amalee realized, *We can endure the persecution, but what about the youngsters?*

Silva's recent cries as she burst through the door still scarred Mama's heart. "I did *not* convert to Islam!" the girl had cried as the story spilled out.

During a class break, the Islamic classmates had gathered around Pastor Abraham's youngest daughter, decking the lovely, petite girl with their hijabs and scarves. "Oh, Silva, this looks gorgeous on you! It just matches the hue of your eyes!" they'd gushed.

When they had her all decked in their Muslim garb, they crooned, "Now just say the Shahada,[1] say 'There is no god but . . .'"

As Silva innocently repeated their words: "There is no . . ."

The classmates gasped in shocked victory. "Aha, you became a Muslim!" the girls crowed triumphantly. "You said the Shahada, and now you are a Muslim!"

"Silva is a Muslim! Silva is a Muslim!"

Horror mounted in Silva's heart, spilling over onto her face as her hands flew to her heart. "No! No, I am *not* a Muslim! I didn't mean it! I am a Christian! I did not become a Muslim!"

Mama sighed deeply at the memory. And now Silva's teacher had publicly humiliated her.

John quietly rubbed his arm, relieved the shirt covered the bruise he received when Vergie knocked him to the ground yet again.

"Jesus sees how you children have been treated because of Him, Silva, John, and Sila. Always remember to love and pray for those who do not know the love of the Heavenly Father," Baba encouraged, laying his hand on his youngest son's shoulder and giving it a gentle squeeze.

"Maybe someday those who persecute you will become the proclaimer, just like Saul's transformation here in this city two millennia ago. But Ananias had to be faithful and pray for the persecutor when God asked him to, even though he didn't want to. History tells us his commitment to obey God eventually caused him to be stoned outside these city walls. But what if Ananias had not obeyed God and prayed for Saul? Would we be without two-thirds of the Epistles in the New Testament?

---

1 The Shahada is one of the five sacred pillars of Islam. The words are used for the initiation into Islam, declaring their belief that Allah is one God and Mohamad is his servant.

Children, pray for your abusers to become proclaimers. Be brave soldiers for Jesus."

Would Baba really dare to go to the Mukhabarat headquarters? his children wondered.

"THE BLOOD OF THE MARTYRS"

(Damascus, Syria, circa 1995)

"For to me to live is Christ and to die is gain."

Philippians 1:21

"Persecution, along with prayer and fasting, has been a powerful formula that drives the church to unity for generations—and it is through the unity of the body of Christ that revival happens."

—John Samara

"You children might be abused and beaten for loving Jesus," Baba told his family as they gathered in the living room for the evening hour of prayer. "But Nazir, the dear pastor who dormed with me at the pastor's conference, told me when we parted, 'I don't know how long I have to live, Brother Abraham. My life is at risk for teaching the Gospel here in the Middle East.'"

Amalee patted her husband's shoulder affectionately. "It's so nice to have you back, habibi. Tell the children about the pastors' conference."

Abraham's face brightened. "Ah, yes. What a strengthening time. You should have heard those Korean brothers pray." Abraham lifted his hands to demonstrate. "They all pray out loud at the very same time—like one big chorus of simultaneous intercession. Talk about powerful!

"The leadership conference is like a pastors' football huddle—we are all fired up to win the 'game' after hearing each other's journeys, praying, and encouraging each other, realizing we are not alone. We are so strengthened when we leave!" Baba's face glowed as he spoke.

"Oh, I wish we could have conferences here in Syria. If only Fawzi and Idris and the promising leaders I mentor could experience the encouragement like this. I will pray for that.

"Children, never forget, following Jesus is worth it all! And always remember, I lifted each of you up to God as newborns, dedicating you to Him—Nancy, Joanna, John, Silva, and Sila. You are His.

"John, God gave me a word for you before your birth. We had these lovely daughters, then God told me, 'You will have a son, and his name will be John, because he will be like John the Baptist, preaching and evangelizing.'"

"I hope they don't cut off my head," John quipped.

"There are things far worse than dying for Jesus, John. Far worse. Not being faithful to a call is much worse."

As the family knelt for the evening prayers, the phone rang. The intensity of Baba's voice shushed the children's chatter.

The family eyed Abraham's ashen face for a clue to his distress as he knelt with them to pray. No one spoke.

Abraham blew his nose into his handkerchief, silent for a minute, his face muscles drawn with a deep grief.

"Unbelievable. Just a couple nights ago we prayed and shared together. But Nazir, my roommate at the pastor's conference, never made it home. Someone stabbed him as he left the airport. His body was found on the sidewalk in a pool of blood, a knife in his back. . . ."

"Oh, Abraham!"

"Children, it will cost you something when you take up your cross and follow Jesus." Abraham's earnest eyes looked into those of each of his five children kneeling around him. "But never forget, each drop of blood you shed is like a seed dropping into the ground that will bring fruit and joy someday.

"Just think of the glorious welcome Nazir must have received at the pearly gates! Oh, the joy! Yes, a quick flash of pain. A life seemingly cut short, but children, think of it! Endless bliss with Jesus!"

Abraham placed his arms around his sons kneeling beside him. "And that, dear family, must be our focus, the *joy*, the *victory* at the end of the Christian journey, and not the pain."

The Samara family had much to pray about that night on the worn living room carpet as they lifted their burdens to an Almighty God and worshipped Him.

Mama led her favorite song: "Through wisdom you have the world in your control. The reins are in Your hands."

After the parents retired to their room and the three girls to the other bedroom, the two boys settled in their corner of the living room.

John tossed on the couch, thinking about Nazir, his grieving family, his church.

He pictured Nazir's body on the sidewalk with the knife sticking out of his back and the blood pooling around him. The cost, the risk, the rewards. . . .

What a man; he knew the risks but counted the cost and took them.

Baba's door creaked and his soft footsteps padded across the carpet. He knelt in front of his chair for his nightly hour of prayer with His Father.

"Baba?"

"You're awake, son?"

"Baba, I can't stop thinking of Nazir's courage. He knew following Jesus could cost him his life and he chose to follow anyway. And I want to go all out for Jesus too, no matter the cost."

"John, nothing could make me happier. But son, there will be a cost. If you go all out for Jesus, you can't be silent. You will testify to your friends, and they will beat you more than ever. It's not easy taking up one's Cross in the Middle East. Have you counted the cost and are you ready to pay the price for going all out for the Savior?"

"Baba, I know Vergie and the boys will beat me worse than before, but I have counted the cost."

Father and son wept and prayed together on their knees by the couch as the moon cast its glow about them.

Abraham placed his hands on the shoulders of his thirteen-year-old son and looked deep into his eyes. "John, it won't be easy, but it will be oh, so worth it. Never forget, son, the best retaliation will be prayer, and love. The drops of blood will bear fruit of joy. It really is true; the blood of the martyrs is the seed of the church.

"And John, we are bulletproof, knife-proof, and missile-proof until God says it's time to come home!"

Don't let the Mukhabarat imprison Baba, John prayed as he walked to school. *We need Baba. The church needs him. Syria doesn't have many pastors . . .*

CONNECTIONS
IN HIGH PLACES

(Damascus, Syria, circa 1995)

"Not by might, nor by power, but by my Spirit, says the LORD of hosts."
Zechariah 4:6

"Carrying the Cross does not mean carrying a burden, but it represents death to our will, and a willingness to die physically as well if needed."
—Rami Ibrahim

*G*od, *be with Baba when he goes to interrogate the Mukhabarat.* The thought made John smile. That's what would happen. His father would interrogate them about why they were harassing girls from his church. *Be safe, Baba.*

John glanced nervously around him. Fretting over Baba's safety had momentarily made him forget his own troubles. But now, exiting the school doors, John's muscles tensed to flee. Attending a school of 3,000 Muslim students was like running the gauntlet of fists and shoes every day for the Christian youth. He glanced nervously about to check where the gang might be hiding. And then, he was flat on the sidewalk beneath their fists, their spit, and their muddy shoes.

As a member of the Orthodox church, Vergie made sure he got his blows on John so the Muslim classmates wouldn't turn on him. He always took precise aim to kick where it would be sure to send John doubled over in pain.

John couldn't even walk into the ice cream shop without being spit at and the nasty saliva dripping onto his treat. But he never retaliated.

"Jesus bore the blows, the spit, and the mockery in silent humility, keeping His eyes on the joy set before Him," Baba encouraged. "And in the end, He was the victor."

Instead of revenge, John prayed for his abusers.

When John led his friend Darien to the Lord, the boy had to flee the country so his father wouldn't kill him to restore the family honor. John grieved deeply. "Baba, how can I lead friends to the Lord when they have to flee for their lives, so their father doesn't kill them? I ruined Darien's life!"

"John, this life is not the end. You aren't ruining his life. In eternity having to flee for his life will be a sacrifice he lays at the feet of Jesus. It will be worth it all."

Help me go all out for you, Jesus. Help me be a witness to my Muslim classmates who don't know you, John prayed every day for three years as he walked to school, dread curdling his stomach and tensing each muscle. *And please, please don't let Vergie kick me. Don't let the guys beat me today. . . .*

Driving home from school, Abraham noticed his third daughter, Silva, and the notorious teacher, Mrs. Baghdadi, walking along the sidewalk ahead of him. He pulled over, calling out: "Care for a ride?"

Riding in Baba's car was such a treat. Before he had the car, Baba rode the bus to preach at churches across Syria each weekend, always at the mercy of the bus schedules and routes. Trying to be as efficient and effective with their precious weekend hours as possible, Mama and Baba decided to live on Mama's third grade teaching wages one year, saving Baba's salary to buy a little car.

As Abraham chatted with Mrs. Baghdadi and Silva, he casually remarked, "Mrs. Baghdadi, Silva is a very brilliant girl." Meeting Mrs. Baghdadi's eyes in the rearview mirror, he smiled, adding, "I have great expectations for her future!"

Silva stared incredulously at her father as her teacher stammered, "Uh, yes, Mr. Samara. Uh, yes, your daughter is, uh, a good student."

In Syria parents ask *the teachers how their children are doing, they never* tell *them!* Silva's heart felt as though it had been hugged. She tucked the precious life-giving words into her heart to give her the dynamo to hurdle roadblocks she'd face in the future.

Silva proudly watched her father's confident strides as he left for the Mukhabarat headquarters to intercede for her two traumatized friends. *Dear Jesus, please bring him home.*

Abraham tossed the crisis of the two maligned, threatened girls around in his mind. He assessed it from every angle and dialogued with his Heavenly Father.

Everyone knew the shadow world of the Mukhabarat slipped even into the churches. Rumors said they assigned priests and pastors scripted sermons to preach. Recently, two mukhabarat infiltrated the congregation, pretending to be zealous Christians while ripping the church apart from the inside.

Abraham agonized in prayer and fasted about the disturbing dilemma as the church attendance dwindled. Unexpectedly, one of the secret police relocated, and the other died suddenly.

God is the One to be feared, he told himself as he faced the notorious building with its torture chambers. *Not the Mukhabarat.*

With quiet confidence, the pastor turned the door handle of the infamous headquarters, not knowing if and when he would walk through those doors again.

"I need to speak to the general," Abraham announced authoritatively as a frightened young man was fingerprinted and led away into the shadows.

"Follow me." A soldier directed the pastor down the steps and through a dark maze of alleys in an unfinished dungeon. Cries and shrieks echoed from somewhere in the cavernous darkness. Shadows of shaking, broken girls huddled in the corner, rocking and moaning. Scenes that could have been ripped from a horror movie branded themselves onto his heart.

The rumors of the underground terror chambers must be true. The electrical shocks, blindfolded interrogations, fingernails ripped out by the roots, fingers crushed by pliers, beatings, and mutilations. Disappearances. Unexplained dead.

What am I getting into? Abraham fretted as the immensity of the risk of confronting the Mukhabarat weighted his heart like heavy fetters. *I could become their next victim.*

With firm steps despite his throbbing heart, the courage of God pulsed through his veins as he picked his way through the damp slime in the dank semidarkness.

Shown into the general's vast office with endless filing cabinets standing like steel sentries behind the massive desk, Abraham extended a hand, confidently. "I am Abraham, the pastor of Mariama and Elia, young girls from Damascus accused of speaking against the regime," he announced, looking sternly into the eyes of the official.

The general flipped silently through the files.

"Do you actually think two young girls would dare to speak against the president?" Abraham demanded with calm authority, standing erect and fearless. "And do you believe a couple of teenage girls could cause any unrest in our country even if they *did* speak against our president?"

As he began presenting the case, Abraham felt the hand of God come over him, emboldening him with power and courage.

"You know what you have done to their reputations by listening to the lying accusations of this spurned lover and summoning them to this office!"

A frown drew his eyebrows together as he pressed on before the general could interrupt. "Sir, I don't want you ever again to bring one of the girls from my church here. If you have a problem regarding any of the women or girls from my church, I want you to come and speak directly to me," he ended forcefully. "I don't expect this abuse to happen again."

The Mukhabarat general—one of the most feared men in all of Syria—blinked at Abraham with astonished awe.

"Mr. Samara, I can tell you have connections in high places," he stammered.

"You are certainly right," Abraham gazed deep into the official's flitting eyes. "I do have connections in high places. In higher places than you think. I have connections with God.

"And, my friend, you too can have connections in high places." The steel evaporated from Abraham's voice as he gently proceeded to share the Gospel with the head of the Syrian Mukhabarat.

"I doubt the Mukhabarat will ever bother your friends again," Baba told Silva when she met him at the door.

In Baba's life, every time circumstances seemed impossibly hopeless, God exploded into the scene in a powerful miracle, John realized.

Like with Baba and the stolen church facilities.

John hugged his knees to his chest in the muggy prison cell, resting his weary head on his knees, shutting his bleary, red eyes. *God help me to pray with the faith and persistence with which my father prays.*

THE GOD OF THE
APOSTLE PAUL

(Damascus, Syria, circa 1986)

"What then shall we say to these things? If God is for us, who can be against us?"

Romans 8:31

"Our prayers can go where we cannot . . . there are no borders, no prison walls, no doors that are closed to us when we pray."

—Brother Andrew, *And When God Changed His Mind*

Retrieving the stolen church facilities that held the key to Abraham's dreams to impact Damascus for God would be no walk in the pomegranate orchard, he knew.

"You have legal right to the building," the lawyer assured him.

"But you will never get the property back," he was warned. "The school principal collects money from mission organizations. She uses their donations to bribe officials and the secret police in order to keep the building in her clutches."

Five thousand years of history sprang to life in the world's oldest continually inhabited city as Abraham strode down the cobblestone street toward Bab Sharqi, the Gate of the Sun, and the last standing Roman gate of the ancient Damascus wall.

He could almost hear the clopping of the camel hooves on the flag-stone streets. He could envision the grand entrance of the beasts laden with ivory, tortoise shells, animal skins, apes, silks, and myrrh and frank-incense, accompanied by manacled slaves shuffling through the eastern arched stone entrance still flanked by a pair of pedestrian gates.

Saul must have been led into Damascus onto Straight Street from this vantage point after being blinded by the Divine Light, he couldn't help but think each time he strode through the stone pedestrian arches.

An air of mystic romance emanated from the walls of the Damascene mansions along with the gentle music of the water droplets splashing into the courtyard fountains carried on jasmine-scented breezes. Fuchsia bougainvillea spilled from balconied apartments suspended over the Roman columns, above the souks and shops wafting the scents of exotic spices.

Black-coated, veiled women, burdened with bulging shopping bags alongside robust, mustachioed men in kaffiyehs, strolled along the flag-stone streets polished by centuries of sandals and hooves. "Buy Arabian coffee!" souk tenders urged beneath the coolness of the vaulted iron roof of Souq al-Hamidiyyeh as sun rays stole through the stone and bullet holes overhead. "Your money is like the desert! As good as boundless!" merchants teased.

A call to prayer floated from Sheikh Nabhan Mosque just ahead. *"Who are you, God? Whooooo really are you?"* The troubled cry seemed to wail like the caller's ancestor Ishmael and his mother Hagar must have cried in the desert 4,000 years before.

Another mournful prayer cry wafted from Isa (Jesus) minaret near Umayyad Mosque in the Old City, near the arch of Jupiter. *"Where are yooouuuu, God?"*

Lord, help this country discover the love of the true Isa—Jesus!

Strolling past the souks, mosques, and minarets, desperation perco-lated in Abraham's chest as he prayer-walked in the shadow of the Umayyad Mosque complex above the layers of history.

"Abba Father, fill this city with your presence once again! Father, we need the church that was stolen from us."

Abraham envisioned layers of history beneath the mosque courtyard stones: dust of a temple to a pagan storm god beneath the ruins of the Greek temple to the god of thunder, covered by the remains of the Romans' temple for Jupiter, eventually replaced by a Christian cathedral confiscated and transformed to a mosque in the seventh-century Muslim conquest. Somewhere in the seven layers of history beneath the great mosque lay the remains of the house of Judas, where Ananias had prayed over Saul, the former persecutor of the Jews.

"Lord, You came down with Your blazing light and called the most influential leader of first-century Christianity," Abraham prayed, walking through the cradle of religion, past dark, empty cathedrals where liturgy and form replaced sparks of light and life.

"Father, send your divine presence to Old Damascus once again!"

You are just as alive and powerful here as You were two thousand years ago, he prayed, strolling through a labyrinth of alleys better designed for donkeys than cars.

The calls of the merchants in Bab Touma's souks and the scent of sizzling lamb, shawarma, and cinnamon spices wafted through the alleys. On he walked, past ancient walled stately mansions transformed into boutique hotels and restaurants or maintained as private residences, the fruit of prosperity.

And there, ahead, stood the ancient, arched double wooden doors, just as he remembered, guarding the entrance to Abraham's dreams. Beyond the massive ancient stone walls of the former mansion lay promise and hope.

Father! Do you see this facility, once dedicated to training men and women for God, now being used as a hub to teach godless propaganda? You know, these facilities could provide a strategic base for evangelism, ministry, and training!

What possibilities. What roadblocks. But God. . . .

"Legally, that facility belongs to your church," the attorney said. "And you have legal grounds to regain possession. Go to the office of the Under Secretary of the Minister of Education and fill out a form to regain the property confiscated from the church."

Abraham filed the required paperwork. And then waited and prayed. Weeks passed with no response.

The pastor checked back at the office. "Has my request been processed?"

The Under Secretary huffed an annoyed sigh. "The application must have gotten lost. You will need to reapply."

Abraham refiled the application. Then he waited, inquired, and refiled again. And waited. And prayed. And inquired.

Each inquiry met the same indifferent grunt: "Your application must have gotten lost. You need to fill out a new form."

The Marxist nest courted connections with influential government officials. They would never surrender this prime real estate in the Old City of Damascus, Abraham knew. And certainly not to a church organization.

"The buildings belong to the church," Abraham told other officials, including the Minister of Private Education. "What can we do?"

"You are absolutely correct," the officials all agreed, reviewing the documents. "You have every legal right to the facility which has been taken from your congregation. You just need to have the seal of approval on your application."

The determined pastor gathered the courage to return yet again to the office of the Under Secretary. "I have filed dozens of forms, and I haven't gotten one response. What is going on?"

"Let me tell you something, Mr. Samara," the official scowled. "You have the legal right to that facility. You've filled out the correct paperwork. But I am telling you, you will *never* be given the authorization to reclaim the building. Don't *ever* come back!"

Abraham stumbled out of the office, grieving deeply for God's stolen facilities.

Father! What a loss of potential for teaching and training future leaders for You! Lord, I take this lack of progress personally. What have I done wrong? The church desperately needs its former facilities! Our children need a school!

Shoulders slumped in discouragement and emotional exhaustion,

Abraham closed his bedroom door. Falling on his face, he cried out to God. "Lord, I am bankrupt. There is not a thing I can do. If You want the building to be used to worship You, to train Your heritage again, *You* will have to restore it to us. I can't do it."

Abraham's children eyed each other silently with concern as they heard their father weeping. Then all was silent.

In the stillness of that room, God came down with a powerful presence, ministering to the broken pastor. Abraham dried his eyes that brightened with courage as he absorbed the words from Psalm 20 God was giving him:

"May the Lord answer you in the day of trouble! May he send you help from the sanctuary and give you support. May he grant you your heart's desire and fulfill all your plans! He will answer him from His holy heaven with the saving might of His right hand. Some trust in chariots and some in horses, but we trust in the name of the Lord our God."

A tidal wave of joy and hope lifted his despondent spirits from the rocks.

Abraham strode out of his room, his hair neatly combed, tall and erect, wearing a confident smile. His voice carried an edge of victory.

"Amalee, gather the children and pray. God strengthened my heart with a Psalm. I am going back to that courthouse and going to the Minister of Education himself to get to the bottom of this problem and find out what is actually going on."

Amalee gathered Nancy, Amalee, Silva, John, and Sila about her.

"Oh, Jesus, protect our brave Baba. Hear his prayers. Bless him with wisdom. Lead him to the proper officials. And move their hearts!"

Heading to the courthouse, the words of Philippians 1:28 came to Abraham's thoughts: "Not frightened in anything by your opponents. This is a clear sign to them of their destruction, but of your salvation, and that from God."

The pastor strode into that courthouse with an air of joyful confidence.

At the other end of the hall, an official recognized Abraham. "Pastor Abraham!" he hollered, running toward the pastor, waving a rolled document. "Look, Pastor Abraham! I've got it!"

"What do you have?" Abraham pressed, his face masking the hope rising in him as he smoothed the wrinkled paper the official thrust into his hand.

"Pastor Abraham! It's the approval for you to reclaim your church facility!"

"You can't be serious!"

"I am totally serious; look at the stamp!"

The pastor looked down at the official stamp and signature still legible between the creases in the paper and then looked up at the official, his eyebrows raised questioningly.

"What . . . How . . . ?"

"Pastor Abraham, I was in the office of the Under Secretary of Education when he was out of his office. I had no business there but had this strange urge to go to his office. Out of the corner of my eye, I noticed crumpled papers behind the bookcase. Curious, I pulled out one of the papers, uncrumpled it, and found your stamped, signed approval for the return of the church property, but the signature was crossed out."

The official paused to catch his breath, then blurted out indignantly, "Now that's illegal for the Under Secretary to refuse to carry out the decisions of the Minster of Education. I fished out the other papers stuffed behind the bookcase. Every last one of the crinkled papers carried a signature and the official stamp giving you legal permission to occupy the buildings again!"

Abraham lifted his dark brows in surprise, his lips parting and heart racing and skipping as he processed the words.

"And so, I personally took your papers to an official, asking if the form is valid. I was told, 'Absolutely! One hundred percent!' So, I carried the form through each processing step, and here you are!"

"Alleluia!" Pastor Abraham exploded with joy, flinging his arms wide in praise, not caring who heard.

The official looked confused. "Ollie who?"

"Thank you, Jesus!"

Only God.

Abraham threw open the door of his home, waving the document, shouting, "'Some trust in horses, some trust in chariots, but we trust in the name of the Lord our God!'"

How great is our God!

ONLY GOD

(The Old City of Damascus, Syria, circa 1986)

"No weapon that is fashioned against you shall succeed, and you shall refute every tongue that rises against you in judgment. This is the heritage of the servants of the Lord and their vindication from me, declares the Lord."

Isaiah 54:17

"One man with God is a majority."

—Brother Andrew

As Abraham placed the key in the lock of the heavy wooden arched doors, his heart thrilled with the miracle and the potential God had unlocked.

The doors swung open revealing thick stone walls, balconies, courtyards, and neglected garden beds all evidencing the aristocratic history and the resilience of the spacious buildings.

"This was the chapel," Abraham pointed out to his children, opening a heavy door. "They built a wall to divide it into classrooms, but we will deal with that."

That first Sunday, Jiddo and Taita, Baba's parents, were among those who joined Abraham, Amalee, and the five children in the reclaimed Jesus of Nazareth chapel. Their voices echoed through the spacious stone-walled rooms as they lifted their praises to God for His marvelous gift. They asked Him to cleanse the buildings, to use this compound. And they dedicated the recovered facility back to God.

"I forgot to mention, the facility is yours, on two conditions," the official warned Abraham, with a hint of a smirk as he finalized the deed for the building transfer. "We are returning the school to the ownership of the church on the conditions that the school's sizeable debts and its staff go with the school."

The pastor laid down his pen and straightened in his seat, staring at the official speechlessly.

"It's nonnegotiable. Take it or leave it."

Finding himself saddled with debt and atheistic teachers tamped down a measure of Abraham's euphoria. But his omnipotent God had orchestrated so far and would continue to work out details.

The Marxist principal and her colleague shared none of the pastor's vision for the school. Working against him, they taught godless philosophies clashing with the Biblical truths Abraham believed, undermining everything he tried to accomplish.

The principal and her collaborator swindled funds from the school account. The two viciously maligned Abraham to the parents, encouraging the patrons to withdraw their students from the school.

Patron after patron withdrew children from the school. The school seemed about to fold.

"You can't fire those teachers," officials warned Abraham when he reported the unprofessional behavior. "There's not a thing you can do."

But Abraham could pray, and he did. Approximately a year after regaining the facilities, he spent a day fasting in desperation. He clung to the "horns of the altar," pleading with God to intervene.

At 8:00 in the evening after the day of intercession, the pastor knelt on the floor of the school once again.

"Lord, I can't go on. My hands are tied! The school cannot prosper. We've got to have those two women out of here. But You know we can't fire them! I'm depending on your help to remove those crooked teachers."

Rising from his knees, Abraham left the burden in the hands of God.

The following day, he walked into his office, picked up the papers placed on his desk, and scanned them.

The resignations of the principal and her colleague!

"Alleluia! Thank you, Jesus!"

"Pastor Abraham, I don't understand!" the secretary stammered. "I thought such devastating news would upset you!"

"This is exactly what I've been praying for," he replied calmly, thrilled to begin operating the school for God's glory.

Only God.

"The Home of the Word School." The Word. Nothing could be more precious, impactful, lasting, or central to education than the Word of God.

"You are absolutely crazy for leaving your posh position as a math instructor at the UN academy!" friends raved, learning he was quitting the job to go into full-time ministry. "With the equivalent of a US salary, that job is a teacher's dream, and you are quitting!"

"When we follow God, He will take care of us." Abraham smiled.

The Samaras felt God leading the family to live on Amalee's third-grade school-teaching wages while Abraham administrated the Home of the Word School, led the church, and planted churches and discipled leaders across the Middle East, preaching in five churches each weekend.

Abraham recruited volunteers to teach at the school, including his daughters Nancy and Joanna, who attended seminary in Lebanon.

Who could have dreamt the Home of the Word School would become a headquarters for massive relief distribution during refugee crises and the Syrian War? Or that hundreds of Iraqi Muslim refugee students would learn Bible verses in these classrooms? Or that countless discipleship training conferences would be held on the site?

Who could have foreseen that in a short time, ISIS missiles would crash through the roof and into the alleys?

No one could have envisioned that before long, the chapel, stairwells, and courtyard would be packed with searching Syrians, requiring as many as fourteen services a week to accommodate the crowds with hundreds of baptisms in this courtyard.

Only God.

How great is our God!

As the hours dragged by in the putrid prison cell, John recited nearly every verse he ever memorized.

"Blessed are those who are persecuted for righteousness' sake. . . . Blessed are you when they revile and persecute you. . . . Rejoice and be exceedingly glad, for great is your reward in heaven. . . ." Matthew 5:10–12.

In desperation, John knelt, tears falling onto the dirty floor, not caring if the guard who sat outside his cell heard his anguished cries or not.

"Jesus! I need your help! You see me here in this prison cell. . . ."

He glanced up to see the eyes of the guard upon him.

"I see you praying. Tell me about your God and what you are saying to Him."

"I am praying to Jesus, the Son of God. I am asking Him to get me out of this jail so I can teach people about His love."

"Don't worry, John, your God will answer."

And then, a bit later, "John, who is Jesus? You talk like you have a relationship with Him. It must be nice to have a God you can have a relationship with. A God who hears you. . . ."

John's startled eyes met the guard's searching ones. "It is such a privilege to be able relate to the Creator of the Universe, to feel His love, and to experience Him speaking to us, giving us Divine wisdom and direction."

John read a longing in the guard's eyes.

God, what is your purpose in all of this? John sighed. *How can I get out?*

Neither question seemed to have a reasonable answer. His thoughts went round and round, agitating endlessly like Mama's wringer washer.

And there was no rest. He prayed. He quoted more verses. He tried to figure out a plan. But his mind felt wrung out.

"Hey Samara," his guard called. "Why do Christians worship a God who allowed himself the shame of being bullied and killed?"

John cleared his dry throat. "Well, let me ask you, would you rather serve a God who sacrificed His life for you, who teaches us to love even our enemies, or a God who commands violence and slaughter?

"Listen, friend," John continued. "It's not Christianity versus Islam. It's life versus death. Freedom versus slavery. Jesus came to set the captives free. God is not wanting slaves; He is wanting sons and daughters. The way to really know God is not through some religion. It is through a personal relationship with Him," John finished as the guard pondered in silence.

John recalled the words of a pastor who had felt the steely barrel of a gun against his temple. "The only way you survive the uncertainty of death and prison, is to realize you are not in control. You are not in control. The soldiers are not in control. God *is* in control, even when He seems not to be.

"And when you embrace this concept of God's hand over every other hand, you can endure anything."

He was spot on, John realized, looking up the light rays flowing past the bars of the tiny window. In a precious restful, awe-filled moment, he seemed to sense God's hand over him imprisoned unjustly in the dark, wretched, putrid cell.

Nothing else matters. Only God being glorified matters. It's all about God. God's glory, God's purposes, and not my safety or comfort.

That must have been what helped Baba survive those nights at the Mukhabarat headquarters. He lives with his ear against the heartbeat of God and somehow he knew it was time for us children to leave Syria. And only God could arrange for Nancy to meet the one person in 2,500,000 people in Damascus who could help us. . . .

ONE IN TWO MILLION

(Damascus, Syria, 1986)

"... On Him we have set our hope and He will rescue us ..."

II Corinthians 1:10 (AMP)

"You can't avoid your calling if you are a child of God, just be close to God and the doors will open."

—John Samara

During John's teenage years, on nights when Baba didn't come home, the boy knew his father had been taken by the Mukhabarat for questioning yet again. *Will Baba come home tonight? Is he being tortured?* John worried as he tossed on his bed on the couch listening for the turn of the door handle. Mama hadn't told him his father's life was in danger, that one of these nights he might not come home. But John sensed it.

And then, long after midnight, John would hear the comforting scrape of the key entering the lock and the door squeaking open. And John could sleep.

As the threats on Abraham's life increased, the pastor and his wife cried out to God on their knees, "Oh Father, we need guidance for our precious children. Where can they be safe and be equipped to serve Your Kingdom?"

After another night of uncertainty and threats, Amalee met her husband. "The time is here, isn't it?" she managed, her eyes pools of anguish.

"The time has come, habibti." Abraham took her soft hands in his. "We must look at the future, not the present. Always, the focus is on the joy before us, the victor's crown. But between now and then there are some intense battles. But we must focus."

"So true," Amalee bravely agreed, blinking back a tear. "It's the high schoolers—Silva, John, and Sila—whose lives and faith are more at risk. Joanna and Nancy are in more stable circumstances."

"The girls have their diplomas and are in a good place at the seminary in Lebanon," Abraham agreed. "Amalee, I know in my heart Rami Ibrahim keeps praying year after year that Nancy will change her mind and say yes. He's a brave boy.

"And Pastor Caleb told the medical student he needs to learn to know Joanna. Those girls will be okay. But we need to take Silva, John, and Sila to the US this summer." There was something in his tone that told Amalee he knew more than he said.

"God will open doors for where they should live." Amalee nodded through her tears. "We just need to go in faith. He will guide one step at a time. And God can take better care of our children than we can."

Amalee and Abraham flew with the children to the United States, having no idea where their children would stay or go to school, but praying for God's continued guidance, and to open doors. Trusting God to guide, as He always did. *Please Lord, let them stay together.*

As the Samaras travelled to the States, the Shaheens flew from Ohio to Damascus on a mission. While the Samaras wondered how God would provide lodging for the teens, Mrs. Shaheen and her teenage son stopped Nancy on the street for directions.

As always, Nancy injected a phrase about Jesus into the conversation.

"You are a believer in Jesus!" Mrs. Shaheen's eyes sparkled with delight. "Imagine running into a Christian in this Muslim country!"

The two laughed and shared, connecting deeply.

"I've enjoyed this immensely. I would love to connect with you again before we fly home."

"Me too! Why don't you stop by our home tonight?" Nancy invited, writing their address on a scrap of paper.

As the women shared that evening, the guest revealed, "You know, Nancy, we are here on an unusual mission. We felt very clearly God calling us to travel to Syria to adopt a couple boys. Our home is prepared, but now that we are here, we have no clue where to find the boys God wants us to have!"

Nancy's eyes grew large as she absorbed the startling words, sitting in silent awe for a moment.

"Well, that's quite intriguing. My parents, my two younger brothers, and my sister just flew to the US and are searching for a place for my siblings to stay while they attend school in the States! When my dad's life was threatened, my parents decided the younger children needed to leave the country for their safety."

"Let them live with us!" Mrs. Shaheen urged. "That's why God sent me to Syria!"

"How generous, Mrs. Shaheen, but you realize there are three youngsters. My brother John is your son's age, and Sila is just younger than him. My parents really want them to stay together and haven't found a place that will take all three."

"We want them. That is the mission God sent me to Damascus for, I know it is. Please let them stay with us! We will fly back to Ohio and meet them. The rooms are all ready."

Dear Mama cried every day that first year, praying day and night for her precious children. She could tell her children felt lost in the new culture. Syrian youth attending high school in Canton, Ohio, braved many cultural challenges, often feeling like exiles or refugees away from home.

The three Samara youths persevered, tooling themselves for future usefulness for the Kingdom. Silva and Sila earned degrees from Malone

University while John graduated from Mount Vernon Nazarene University, and then England's University of Manchester.

Yet while John languished in the filthy jail cell with no communication with the outside world, any future impact seemed to have vanished with the rats that disappeared at dawn.

John's British friends traveled to Damascus, reporting to Abraham that the border guard had taken John. The Samaras grew desperate when they could not locate him. Pastor Abraham called every office and consulate he could reach, but every official insisted, "There is no record of John Samara ever entering the country."

"John is an American citizen," Abraham informed the ambassadors and officials he spoke to. "Your country will have to answer to the United States government if they mistreat him!"

"We have no John Samara in custody in the country."

But Abraham knew John had to be in a prison somewhere within those borders. He made sure the British ambassador knew about John. Friends contacted the British government, who investigated and reported John Samara was *not* in the country.

I will find my brother, Nancy determined. She surely was "that lion's cub," as the Syrian proverb said, as fearless and persevering as her father.

Nancy traveled from prison to prison asking about John.

She had a special spot in her heart for her younger brother, whom she had babysat when Baba and Mama held Bible studies or visited the sick.

At every prison, she received the same response to her inquiries. "We have no one by the name of John Samara," the wardens told her.

Until the last prison. . . .

"John."

An electric current surged through his body as he twisted in his rumpled clothing to make sure he was not hallucinating. Only one person spoke his name in that tone.

"Nancy!" he gulped, staring through the bars. "Nancy!"

"John. . . ."

His sister's lovely face puckered as if she were about to cry. She flung her unruly curls from her face, taking in his rumpled clothing, the chaotic hair, the shadow of a beard, stringless shoes, and the purple bags under his bleary eyes in the horrid, smelly cell behind the bars.

John had seldom seen the "lioness" moved to this extent. Her compassion soothed the torment.

"Nancy!" He should have known his tenacious sister would find him. "How . . .?"

"What can I bring you, dear brother?" Nancy quavered, blinking back the tears at the sight of her brother in a prison cell.

"A Bible. If I just had a Bible, Nancy, I could endure it."

"Bibles are absolutely not permitted!" the guard groused.

But Nancy found a soldier she persuaded to smuggle her personal Bible to John along with a bottle of water.

Nothing had ever tasted more refreshing. Nor had the Word ever been so encouraging.

The sleepless nights, the stress, coupled with the lack of nutrition and water absolutely sapped his strength. But hope flickered in his heart. His family knew his location. Nancy would turn the Middle East upside down to get her brother released, he knew.

And Rami Ibrahim will be right there with her. Three years was a long time to keep that warrior of a man waiting. His quiet strength complements her passion . . . .

"Hey, Samara!"

John cringed at the voice of his guard and pretended to be asleep.

"So how do you explain the trinity? Three Gods?"

Maybe this guard really is serious. God, I will make a bargain with you. If I share the Gospel with the guard, will you release me?

My friend Omar would have evangelized the whole jail if he were here, John realized. *I have so much to learn from you, dear brother.* John tried to visualize the zealous, young evangelist from church in a prison cell. It wasn't hard to imagine, because Omar had been a prisoner. More than once. John would never forget . . .

MISSING

(Damascus, Syria)

"The weapons of our warfare are not physical. . . . Our weapons are divinely powerful for the destruction of fortresses. We are destroying sophisticated arguments and every exalted proud thing that sets itself up against the [true] knowledge of God . . ."

II Corinthians 10:4 (AMP)

"Even though the church is suffering in many locations around the world right now, and many Christians are prepared to die at any moment, what helps us press on and endure the suffering is seeing people get saved for the kingdom of God."

—Rami Ibrahim

An uneasiness twisted his gut when John read the name on the caller ID of his vibrating phone on one of his visits back to Syria.

Omar's wife.

This is not good.

Has that fearless soldier of the Cross taken one risk too many?

"Omar never came home last night," the young evangelist's wife sobbed softly into the phone.

"Do you have any idea where he was headed?" John forced himself to breath slowly to stay calm while his mind raced a million kilometers an hour. *Probably evangelizing the Druze . . .*

"He talked about going to the area you asked him not to go. You know, the area with the radical Muslims."

"That's far too dangerous! We've warned him often."

"I know. I told Omar the same thing. 'How can you put your hand in a hornet's nest without getting stung?' But he always says, 'The darkest places need the light the most.' And now he didn't come home," she wailed.

"Did you call the police station?"

"I did. He's not there."

"That means the Mukhabarat have him. Or the radicals."

If he's even alive . . .

"Let me call everyone to pray. And then, we can check with the Mukhabarat tomorrow. He's in the hands of God, sister."

The brothers and sisters from church fell to their knees, interceding and pleading for their precious, fearless—if stubborn—brother.

"No," the Mukhabarat secret police officer retorted forcefully when John inquired. "We certainly do not have a man by the name of Omar."

"That means the radicals have him," Abraham told John.

Why didn't you take our advice and avoid the radical Islamic area, Omar? Why are you so stubborn?

One couldn't find a better-natured man. And rarely a person more determined. Like the camels trekking the Silk Road for centuries, when inspiration struck, nothing could stop Omar.

But his persistence was advantageous when he defended his faith. Omar didn't back down or become intimidated. He knew the best questions and answers too, for that matter, in a debate with the best of Muslim scholars. Omar knew his theology like few pastors did.

"If Allah is a monad, a one god, is he relational?" Omar would reason. "Who was Allah relational with before he created man? So, you are saying the Allah needed man so he could be relational? Or relationships are not important to Allah, and so love is not important to his people either?

"If Yahweh is the greatest God, a God of relationship even before creation modeled relationship, then love and intimacy with Him and with others is important to His followers, too . . ."

But Omar must have gotten into one debate too many. Days passed, and there was no word from Omar. Not a clue.

The winsome evangelist had been in and out of prison numerous times due to his bold passion for the Gospel. But he had never before simply disappeared.

John worried about Omar. Such a firebrand. So needed.

If Omar wasn't evangelizing, he was interceding in prayer. John chuckled as he recalled Omar's prayer encounter in his friend's cherry orchard. Far above the heat and noise of the city, the mountainside orchard provided a refreshing haven to intercede.

The darkness also provided cover for theft.

Omar and the owner of the orchard strolled beneath the trees laden with lush ruby-red fruit, raising their hands over the city below, crying to God for a harvest of Syrian souls. They paced back and forth, lifting their hands to God in intercession, singing praises to Him, pleading for the salvation of the citizens.

The sun flared red on the horizon, dipping behind the Anti-Lebanon Mountains as the wailing prayer cries echoed through the Barada Valley. Below lay the twin roofs and dome of the Great Mosque punctuated with its green-lit minarets, the honey-colored citadel. The green lights of the minarets flicked on above the steep streets and yellow walls reminiscent of Italy.

A shadowy form slunk stealthily from tree to tree, a sack over his arm. The dark figure shimmied up the trunk, stuffing the cherries into his bag and his mouth. Before long, the bulging sack grew heavy.

The thief crouched on a limb to drop his loaded sack to the grass. Just at that moment, the two prayer warriors settled against the same trunk.

Refreshed by a handful of sweet, juicy ruby-red cherries and the cool night breezes, Omar and his friend continued interceding for their beloved country as they surveyed the twinkling city lights beneath them.

The thief shifted uncomfortably from time to time as the men prayed, sang, and waved their arms directly beneath his precarious perch.

Hour after hour, Omar and the owner of the grove lifted their hands in intercession, in praise, crying, singing, and yelling, claiming Damascus for God.

They interceded for the president, the army, ISIS, the Mukhabarat, the refugees, the church, their families, the churches in Sudan, Lebanon, Türkiye, Egypt, Iraq, and Morocco. They prayed for the Druze and the many, many searching open hearts among the Muslims all across the Middle East.

The intruder listened as the men prayed to their God like a friend and someone they believed would actually hear them and answer their petitions.

As the night passed, the thief grew wearier and more miserable in his awkward perch in the fork of the tree. He regretted his greed more every moment, wishing never to see a cherry again.

He leaned his head against a tree branch. His head began to drop as he relaxed and then began to doze off. The sack of cherries slipped from his grasp, and the thief tumbled out of the tree, rudely awaking as he hit the ground, smashing the cherries all over his clothing.

The two prayer warriors jumped to their feet, just as startled as their unexpected guest, pulling the thief to his feet.

"Are you hurt?" Omar asked with concern.

"I'm fine! I'm fine!" the humiliated thief insisted, uninjured except for his bruised pride and squashed cherries.

"Do you know Jesus?" Omar asked the thief, proceeding to share the Gospel with the miserable, cherry-stained neighbor who wanted desperately to run into the night.

John chuckled at the thought of Omar witnessing the wretched cherry-stained thief who was forced to be a captive audience.

Only Omar! And now, that precious, fearless evangelist had gone missing. The church continued to pray and to trust. But the leaders believed he must be dead. Hope ebbed away. They knew the Radical Muslims well enough. . . .

As John strolled through Damascus, he spotted the evangelist walking down the street, sharing the Gospel as he went. "Do you know Jesus?"

"OMAR!"

John sprinted down the sidewalk, grabbing his missing friend in a hug. "Omar! What in the world . . .?"

"I was sharing the Gospel when the radicals nabbed me."

"In the radical hotbed, where we advised you not to go," John countered sternly.

"In the area of the greatest need!" Omar contended with a twinkle and a mischievous grin.

"They put me in the Mukhabarat dungeon prison cell. The place was absolutely packed, John. Everyone wondered what my crime was. So, I started sharing the Gospel in that crowded jail, telling them why I was imprisoned—because I had been sharing the Good News of the true God who loves them."

John hung on every word, scarcely breathing as the story spilled out.

"And then guards took me for interrogation. The interrogators yelled at me. Threatened me. They intimidated me. So, I started preaching to them. And John, I shared the Gospel from Genesis to Revelation with the Mukhabarat! I talked as fast and hard as I could because I didn't know if I would ever have that chance again.

"And then the general of the Mukhabarat called me to his desk. He handed me his personal card and said, 'Omar, this is my personal cell number. If you ever have a problem, give me a call.'

"And that was it, John, they released me."

"Omar, that's absolutely unbelievable. Only you would share the Gospel in the radical hotbed with the prisoners and with the Mukhabarat interrogators. And only God could work things out so amazingly."

That prison stint never dampened Omar's enthusiasm for evangelism. He witnessed just as zealously, boldly, and passionately as ever to reach the lost. And with even greater confidence than before, in fact, for his wallet carried the personal card and cell number of the head of the secret police!

How great is our God!

"A MIRACLE, *PLEASE!*"

(Middle Eastern Prison Cell, 2007)

"And after you have suffered a little while, the God of all grace, who has called you to his eternal glory in Christ, will himself restore, confirm, strengthen, and establish you."

I Peter 5:10

"As Christ struggled up Calvary's hill and bled upon it, His aim was to eradicate self-love and implant the love of God in the hearts of men. One can only increase as the other decreases."

—Walter J. Chantry

*P*erhaps *the guard really is serious in wanting to know about God, and isn't just trying to harass me,* John realized, sitting up straight. *God, if I witness to him, will you let me out of here?*

The prisoner promptly gave the guard the most compact version of the Gospel he had ever given. "We all sinned and deserved to die, but Jesus took our punishment so we can live with God forever, but we must accept the gift."

Catching his breath, John ended with the words, "If you want to ask Jesus into your heart, pray this prayer after me: Dear God, I believe you love me. I believe you sent Jesus to set me free. I ask You to take away my sins. I want to be Your son."

John rushed on: "I believe you are the one true God. I give my life to You and invite You to live in my heart. In Jesus's name, amen."

"Amen!" the guard burst out with a broad smile.

Not sixty seconds later, another guard stopped in front of the cell, inserting a key, announcing, "You get to leave, Samara."

Hallelujah! Thank you, Jesus! Glory!

John strolled down the dark echoing corridor, brushing off his stained, wrinkled clothing. *What was that all about, Lord?*

With his belt and shoelaces in place along with a thread of restored dignity, John grabbed his sister in the biggest hug.

"Nancy, you are the best big sister ever!"

"You are out of prison, brother," she grinned, "but you aren't out of the country yet!

"I'd suggest you stay out of sight while I test the waters," Nancy advised at the border.

"What would happen if a John Samara showed up at the border to leave the country?" she asked the official, who searched his computer for a moment.

"We will take him into custody. He returns to jail!"

Nancy found John, taking him by the shoulders. "Brother, we need to pray for a miracle!"

The two found a quiet corner. "Lord, we are trusting you to come through and help us get safely back to Syria!"

Nancy lifted her chin, threw back her shoulders, and sauntered up to the border guard, with a glint of flint in her eyes.

"Sir, you know good and well you have no legal right to keep John Samara as an American citizen from entering Syria," she finished with a stern glare that would have withered her misbehaving students.

"Orders are orders, it's out of my power," he shrugged, about to turn his back on her, when his desk phone began to ring.

Strange. This is Sunday.

The guard casually picked up the receiver. "Border patrol."

Instantaneously, his eyes popped open wide. "Yes sir! Absolutely!" The guard's words nearly tripped over each other as they gushed out while he nodded his head emphatically. "Yes. Yes, of course! Yes, I understand! Immediately. Yes sir! Definitely!"

The guard replaced the receiver. "Uh, there's been a

misunderstanding," he stammered meekly, avoiding her eyes. "I have orders to give John Samara clearance to leave the country immediately."

Not one office across the whole country is open today—on Sunday, Nancy puzzled as she ran to find John.

"John, it had to have been the president! No one else would have that authority, John! And Baba made sure the president knew of your arrest."

Traveling back to Damascus, Nancy sized up her brother. "Did you ever think you could fulfill your calling better with a good woman at your side? I could think of a few . . ."

"All in God's good timing," John yawned. "But Nancy, what was that jail time all about?"

"It was for the Islamic guard that found the Lord," Nancy suggested. "And John, our greatest trials often equip us for our greatest ministries. In any case, it's an awesome feeling to know our great God has His hand over it all when things are out of our control."

When the war in Lebanon began a week later, John thought of his guard friend. *Has he been called to the front lines? Maybe God cared enough for a searching soul about to face the crossfire of battle to send him someone to share the Gospel message of salvation with him. Just in time.*

Please Lord, don't let Mero's dad be unimpressed. I was a prisoner for you . . .

The pages of the Qur'an fluttered shut. The lad's head began to nod in the warm rays of the rooftop sunshine.

In a brilliant flash, a tall being in radiant white stood before the startled boy. His heart thumped and a quiver ran down his body. The boy scanned the countryside in alarm. But cows grazed undisturbed beneath the clear blue skies in the shadow of the Aleppo Citadel. He shivered in awe of the purity of the powerful Presence. Yet his eyes were drawn irresistibly to the Being glowing with light. A loving warmth circled him, and he never wanted to look away. . . .

Part II

Acts of God

(2008–2013)

"Jesus was not a victim. He took the Cross willingly because of love.

We don't suffer as a victim, but we accept suffering because of our love for the Lord; and because of our love, we minister to people.

So we are not victims, we are victors of the Cross. Carrying the Cross is not a drudgery but a victorious journey with our focus on the goal and joy set before us."

—Rami Ibrahim

ISA—THE DREAM

(Aleppo, Syria, circa 2008)

"But God shows His love for us in that while we were still sinners, Christ died for us."

Romans 5:8

"Only one act of pure love, unsullied by any taint of ulterior motive, has ever been performed in the history of the world, namely the self-giving of God in Christ on the Cross for undeserving sinners. That is why, if we are looking for a definition of love, we should not look in a dictionary but at Calvary."

—John R. Stott

Ali blinked in startled stupor as he gazed up at the towering, splendid man in radiant white. The pages of his Qur'an fluttered shut beneath the tall man's luminous robes of the purest white he had ever seen. A tremor of awe surged up his spine in the power and purity of the majestic presence. He could not draw his eyes from the face of the tall, radiant Being.

"Your mother will have a son," the rich voice spoke. "His name shall be called Isa."

"Isa . . . Isa . . . Isa." The hills seemed to echo the majestic voice. And then the being vanished.

The boy's eyes flitted across the rooftop terrace to the cows and goats grazing placidly in the pasture in the shadow of the impregnable fortress of Aleppo.

He could see no trace of the tall, luminous, mysterious figure in white. *Who was the man in glowing white, and what had brought him?*

"Your mother will have a son. His name will be called Isa," the mysterious visitor had promised.

I was studying the holy book, so certainly, the message is significant, and the messenger is divine, he mused, scooping up the leather-bound Qur'an. *But a baby brother?! After seven sisters, I will have a baby brother?*

And how would the Man, whoever He was, know I will have a brother? Maybe it was simply a dream and not a vision.

But I know I did not imagine the vision because I would not have made up such an odd name. Isa.

Samira generously sprinkled the spices of Aleppo—allspice, pepper, nutmeg, cardamom, cinnamon, and ginger—over the ground lamb, minced onions, and grated cheese.

"Mama! I had a vision, and it was so real," Ali cried, bursting into the kitchen as Samira speared the lamb balls and cherries onto the wooden skewers.

"A tall glowing being in white came to me after I was studying the Qur'an and said, 'Your mother is going to have a son, and his name should be called Isa!'"

Samira dropped the skewer as she stared at her son in shock through her netted burka. "What?! I will have a son?! After seven daughters! How could this happen? I did not pray to Allah before dawn this Friday when he comes near to hear our prayer, so why would this blessing come? What honor will come to your father! But no, we already have seven daughters and a son. There will be no more babies!"

Samira stabbed another cherry and mutton ball with a skewer to emphasize her words. "The messenger was mistaken. Besides, such a name! We cannot name our son after the Christian's messiah, Isa! It cannot happen.

"Your father is helping Shada deliver her calf. See if he needs help, Ali, then tell him the kebabs are nearly ready. And we shall all hear what he says of your vision at dinner."

A glance at the window confirmed her son's friends were disappearing down the lane. Samira flung off her black burka and gloves with a flourish, a butterfly emerging from her chrysalis, free to be the queen of her house once again.

Samira's daughters whispered and giggled in amusement as they chopped the vegetables, patted the pita dough, and arranged the dinnerware.

"Just imagine! A baby boy!"

"What a strange name!"

As Samira rotated the sizzling, savory lamb kebabs, she glanced at the citadel high on the plateau, gilded in the last golden rays of sunlight. The ancient fortress lent an air of security, as it stood as a magnificent sultan over its dynasty of souks and mosques.

High on the plateau where Abraham once grazed his sheep, tourists watched the setting sun from palm-shaded cafes, savoring Aleppine pomegranate juice with a flavor as intense as the ruby color.

Aleppo felt as secure as the ancient battle-scarred magnificent citadel with moat and formidable entrance. Countless secret passageways and tunnels emerging in other parts of Aleppo added to the air of security and enigma.

For more than two thousand years, camel caravans from India, China, Egypt, and Europe trudged the Silk Road, stopping off at this natural commercial hub and crossroads to barter their treasure. Trains trailed 3,000 camels long in the most dangerous seasons.

At Souq Al-Medina, one of the world's oldest and largest covered bazaars, merchants watered their camels for centuries at caravansaries, bartering silks, wool, carpets, spices, gold, fruits, aged laurel soaps, and ceramics in the eight-mile labyrinth of scents and surprises.

Aside from the battle scars and embellishments of each succeeding empire, little had changed in one of the world's oldest cities.

The din of the braying donkeys, bargaining women, and shouts of vendors continued as they had for centuries. Merchants still served their patrons spiced tea and draped them in scarves, calling to them to buy antelope hair for the mistress.

Only the whine of the miniature Suzuki trucks replaced the clop of the camels' hooves on the cobbled alleys.

Yet, a blind man could still find his way through the eight-mile honeycomb of medieval vaulted aisles just by following the tantalizing scents from one stall to the next. The Al-Medina Souq housed specialized markets for everything from supplies for Bedouin camels to a woman's bridal market. The 1,000 shops of Souq Al-Medina displayed every imaginable novelty, it was said, but the desire to leave. Charmed, silvery tongues still echoed in the souks, where it was told that an Aleppine could even sell a donkey's dried hide.

Samira stirred cinnamon and lemon into the cherry sauce as she watched Abdul stride to the house from the barn. Such a warrior and businessman. Abdul always made her feel safe.

The eldest daughter minced the last of tomatoes, mint, and parsley into the bulgur, squeezing a lemon over top to create a delightful tabbouleh salad. Her sisters loaded the table with baskets of hot pita bread, bowls of fresh hummus, olives, grilled vegetables, and platters of golden rice as Samira ladled the spicy cherry syrup over the browned kebabs. Syrian cuisine effused flavors influenced by the Egyptians and Babylonians who fought over this land and the Persians, Byzantines, and Ottomans who tried to rule it.

The youngsters plopped onto the floor around the colorful spread of steaming bowls arranged on the brilliant cloth.

"What a blessed man I am! Shada has birthed another heifer calf, and I have a house full of women to cook for me!" Abdul boomed, appreciatively stroking his rich black beard, glancing at his lovely daughters surrounding the table like the jewels of a king's crown. A respected sheikh at the local mosque he helped to build, what more could a man ask for?

Abdul heaped his plate with golden rice and topped it with syrupy skewers of perfectly grilled lamb, loading it with all the goodness of Syria.

"And then a fine son to carry on my name." Abdul wiped the sauce from his beard with the back of his hand. "Tell me, my son, what have you learned from the Qur'an today?" Abdul questioned.

"It was not what I learned from the Qur'an, but what the man in the dream told me." Ali reached for the warm pita bread. "A Man in White told us we will have a baby boy . . ."

"A boy!" Abdul guffawed. "Your mother can't make boys! She only gave me one son!" he burst out in the graceless, clipped Arabic so characteristic of natives of Aleppo.

Aleppines speak like men and Damascenes like women, the locals proudly claimed. And Abdul was a true Aleppine.

Ali would not be intimidated. "I was studying the Qur'an when I fell asleep and had this vision. And the man in glowing white even told me what you are supposed to name him. His name shall be called Isa."

"Wullah! What a name! My son, we are Muslims! What good Muslim would call a son Isa after the infidel's prophet messiah, even if he was a good man and supposedly came out of the grave."

"And besides." Abdul rolled up his sleeve to reveal a tattoo on his muscled arm. "When I was in the military, I tattooed the name of my next son onto my arm. See here, it says Muhammad. If I have another son he will be called Muhammad, certainly not Isa!"

And that closed the subject.

Until Samira became pregnant six months later.

Definitely, the child would be another girl. But what if it was a son? Samira didn't dare hope for the honor of giving Abdul a second son! And to be called the mother of two sons!

But the Man in glowing white had said. . . .

But the name! Isa! It could not be.

Samira's flushed face glowed in pride as the midwife handed Abdul his ruddy, healthy, squalling son. *Now, I would not only be known as the mother of Ali but the mother of two sons! A second son after seven girls. And born after a divine vision. What a special child.*

But who was the Man in White?

And what about the name? Well, his father would have to make that call.

There wasn't a more dearly loved child in Aleppo, with seven sisters to snatch him from his crib at the slightest squawk, and an adoring older brother and a very proud, protective father. As the days passed, the entire family thought about the unusual name. They waited to hear what their father would decide.

"What is your son's name?" the visitors asked Samira as her daughters served another cup of thick, spiced coffee from the engraved copper pot brewing on the stove all day for the visitors dropping by.

"Ask his father," the mother wisely replied.

"His name is Isa," Abdul announced, crossing his arms decisively.

"Isa?!" The visitors sputtered over their coffee, recoiling in shock, horror, and amusement in turn.

"Isa!" Expressions revealed the thoughts they were too polite to utter. *Whoever heard of a Muslim family calling a child Isa?*

"His name is Isa," Abdul confirmed, mustering all the dignity of an Aleppine male. "My son Ali had a vision where a Man in White told him we would have a son, and his name was to be Isa, so we needed to listen to the divine messenger. Besides, even the Qur'an tells us Isa was a very good man, healing sick people and the blind."

Abdul had provided well for Samira since she left the familial Saudi Arabian mansion. And she had repaid him with nine children, including two sons! The oldest daughter, Dalia, married a devout Muslim and settled in Türkiye. What more could a woman desire?

How great is our God!

Shada would give the family a couple more calves before ISIS terrorists holed up in the citadel tunnels and the bombs began dropping on Aleppo to flush them out.

Only a few more peaceful summers until the ISIS Toyota roared up to the tranquil farm in the shadow of Aleppo accompanied by bone-chilling shrieks of "Allahu Akbar!"

GANGS AND FORCED MARRIAGES

(Damascus, Syria 2009)

"Therefore the Lord waits to be gracious to you at the sound of your cry . . ."

Isaiah 30:18

"We must live so in touch with Jesus and the Cross that everywhere we go, we reflect His love to the world around us, so when they see us, they see the Cross and see Jesus in us."

—Rami Ibrahim

Nancy stopped abruptly in the middle of the souk-lined alley of Old Damascus as refugee lads dashed past, overturning stands, escaping with their stolen loot as they dodged the shrieking merchants.

Every corner sheltered slouched youngsters smoking pot purchased with stolen booty. Behind the closed doors, survival forced the refugee girls into prostitution, or an early marriage often leading to trafficking.

"We've got a problem." Nancy tossed her curls over her shoulder, crossing her arms, bringing her lips together in a thin, determined line.

Rami's dark eyebrows raised with concern.

We have a problem?

He knew the first time he saw the spunky girl with the caramel curls, flashing eyes, and dynamic heart for God, that she was "the one." This rare, brilliant, gifted girl with a flaming heart for God would go far.

Unfortunately for him, no one told Nancy that Rami was "the one." He prayed. He fasted. He waited. He tested the waters. And she said "no thanks" or ignored him.

Rami persisted. There was an element of intrigue and manliness about pursuing a girl, even when she didn't seem to reciprocate. He admired her for the spunk to speak her mind, even when she said "no."

Even if Nancy wouldn't admit it, there was an alluring mystique about a man's patient pursuit. She respected the man who pursued, who persevered, in contrast to the boys surrendering to flirtatious advances, capitulating into a fragile marriage that soon collapsed.

When Nancy attended seminary in Lebanon, the dark-haired, sinewy mountain boy was there too. Rami's gentle eyes flashed fire when he preached in his deep rumbly voice. And he prayed with such passion.

"When we fast, we step out and God steps in," Rami said.

Perhaps God stepped in. Nancy began to realize Rami's calling aligned with hers. Their gifts complemented each other. And the personalities meshed in a unique balance as well. Rami was an anchor, strong but calm, balancing her dynamo.

Rami Ibrahim is a real man, Nancy began to see. *And a rare man of God.* Nancy's heart stopped resisting, and she fell in love with the man persistently praying and fasting for her for three agonizing years.

Like a well-matched team of draft horses quadrupling the pulling power of two alone, together Rami and Nancy pulled together for God.

"So, what is *our* problem?" Rami queried, his almond eyes, as Nancy called them, narrowed in concern.

"Look at all those refugee boys taking over Damascus. Bored. Nothing to do. No school. Just trouble brewing. And the girls! It breaks my heart to hear of yet another refugee girl scarcely in her teens forced into prostitution, premature marriage, or trafficking because her parents can't afford to support her."

Rami's eyes softened in relief. "So, Damascus has a problem, not us."

Nancy stormed on. "Look at all these children. A lot of them live and sleep on the streets. Think of it! Most are not in school, nor have they been for years! We can't just sit back and do nothing while this generation of children languishes and rots away in the alleys, losing their future. We have hope and we need to share it!"

A smile teased at his lips. This fascinating bundle of dynamo never ceased to intrigue him.

"Damascus has a problem, and you have the answer," he announced.

"Me?"

"Habibti, you are the teacher, your gifts are working with children. Have you thought about holding afternoon classes after the Home of the Word School dismisses? The children are bored. You have a wide-open door."

"Well, you might be on to something, Rami." Her voice grew softly thoughtful as she took his hand and the two walked through the souks amid the jovial shouts, the alluring aromas of rare spices and sizzling falafels mingling with the calls of hawkers offering shawarmas and freshly pressed citrus juices.

Rami and Nancy prayed over the desperate crisis among the refugee children. Both visionaries and catalysts for action, their dreams morphed into plans.

"If anyone can handle a couple hundred unruly refugee children, it's you, Nancy. I have total confidence you could do it. And I would support you."

Nancy and Rami spent hours praying over the prospective school. As they prayed, God gave them the name, "Acts of God." This was God's project. His plans. His work.

Nancy lost no time recruiting volunteers who modeled a loving discipleship of Christ to teach.

Those first weeks were brutal, chaotic, stretching, and dangling on the verge of hourly crisis. But the afternoon school called "The Acts of God" became a haven of love and the only home to many refugee children.

At Acts of God, many refugee children received their only meal of the day, the only hugs and loving words, the only family camaraderie, and the only hope for the future. Even outside of school, the older students looked after the younger pupils. "We stick together because we are family," they told their teachers.

The lessons and the love planted hope in the Iraqi youngsters' shattered hearts, convincing them that maybe there was a future beyond gangs, childhood marriages, and brothels.

Those youngsters played rousing games of ball and tag in the courtyard. They eagerly learned songs and recited Bible verses in chapel, learning reading, English, computer skills, and life skills in the classrooms.

The refugee children devoured sandwiches, learned to respect Miss Nancy, and absolutely loved their school. The school had become their life, their hope. Even gang members complied with school rules to attend Acts of God. "We'll cooperate, just let us stay," they pleaded.

Often, children came to school with bruises from beatings at home. "School is the only place we feel safe," many of the youngsters revealed. "It's our safe haven."

"How did you burn your hand?" Nancy questioned, gently bandaging the oozing blisters on the young boy's palm.

"My mom held my hand on the stove to punish me," the child stammered. A few tears squeezed out from between his blinking eyelids. Nancy's eyes stung as she taped the bandage and gave the child a hug.

"I had a visit from a delegation from the UN academy," Nancy told Rami, dropping a stack of books on the table one evening.

"Yes?" Rami raised his eyebrow. He envisioned the new state-of-the-art buildings the endless UN funds provided to try to rehabilitate the Iraqi refugee children. He had heard all about the splendid play yards, delightful classrooms with highly educated teachers providing fun activities and great food.

"You remember how some of my students switched to the impressive

UN school? And then they all returned within a few weeks, bringing their friends with them.

"Well, it seems the UN classrooms are emptying while those of the Acts of God overflow."

"Interesting. What was their agenda at the meeting today?"

"Well, it's like this: I'm told the community is taking note of the success of the Acts of God School in redeeming and rehabilitating unruly Iraqi refugee children and thieving gang members. They were all excited about this great idea of theirs.

"The chairman had the biggest smile as he addressed me. 'Mrs. Ibrahim,' he says. 'You have an impressive and most successful program. We would like you to help us with our school. Maybe we could work together and support your school as well.

"'We have been trying to figure out what you are doing that gets these kids so excited that they can't wait to come back. What would you say is the secret to your success in getting all these kids to attend day after day? And getting them to obey?'"

"I looked that official in the eye for a minute, then I said, 'Sir, the secret to redeeming these refugee youngsters is starting on a foundation of teaching the children about Jesus—His love, His character. . . .'

"Rami, you should have seen those smiles morph into disgust."

An intrigued grin spread across the young pastor's face as he watched his wife animatedly describe the meeting. *I would have loved to have been there and seen it firsthand.*

"'Mrs. Ibrahim. You don't understand,' says he. 'That will never work for us. We cannot teach about Jesus! Just help us run the school without Jesus. We can't put the religious element in, we just need to feed them, educate them, and provide activities. Please just help us with that.'"

"And then, Rami, my smile evaporated. '*You* don't understand,' I told the committee. 'Jesus is the focus, the basis of our education. Everything we model, teach, and do is built on the foundation of leading the children to Jesus. They feel the love of Jesus. The presence of Jesus. They learn to serve each other and to obey and respect because of Jesus. It is impossible to take God out of the equation and have the same results! Absolutely impossible.'"

An amused, admiring smile quirked the corner of Rami's mouth. "You are exactly right, Nancy."

What a princess warrior for God, filled with God's zeal for the advancement of His Kingdom!

The UN delegation returned to their impressive but empty facilities, eventually shutting their doors due to lack of attendance.

Acts of God School thrived, demonstrating God's power to the community through transformed lives, miraculous answers to prayer.

Former gang members found Jesus in Acts of God, laying their passions and leadership skills on the altar for Jesus. As these students emigrated to countries around the world, former gangsters became worship leaders, church planters, pastors, and teachers across the globe.

How great is our God!

Nancy and Rami followed news of the wave of Arab Spring protests rippling across the Middle East and North Africa, toppling long-standing regimes in the MENA region.

Surely, Syria won't be next. . . .

MISSILES IN THE NIGHT

"... Looking forward to the city which has foundations, [an eternal, heavenly city] whose architect and builder is God."

Hebrews 11:10 (AMP)

"Our Lord did not die to provide selfish men with eternal life while they remained serving themselves. But as he struggled bleeding and beaten up Calvary's hill, bearing the Cross on His shredded back, He intended that those for whom He was dying would redirect their self-obsession, into losing themselves in Him—thus in denying self would find the joy of fullness in God."

—Walter Chantry

"I, John Samara, promise to love you in sickness and in health," the trim, dark-haired bachelor vowed. John gazed into the hazel eyes sparkling with rapturous tears, never envisioning protecting Mero during a war. Darkening war clouds had yet to appear on his radar. All he could see was his bride's radiant face framed by the long curls escaping the veil as she smiled up at him in pure delight. God had led him to the lovely daughter of Eve, so perfectly complementing him. And God's hand would guide their next steps.

Despite the bride's meticulous planning, an electrical outage cut off the air conditioner, causing the audience to fan and sweat in the oppressive humid heat of the Mediterranean coastal town.

But Mero's blissful serenity evidenced resilience that would serve her so well in the coming years. The oppressive heat in the chapel and the droplets of sweat didn't ruin her day. She and her beloved John stood at the altar. Nothing else mattered.

Striding out of the church with his new bride on his arm, John's heart overflowed with dreams of a life of serving God together in Syria with this gentle, selfless, God-fearing social work major.

John met Mero at a youth conference in their home country of Syria, after earning a bachelor's degree in the US and studying for his master's in England.

Together, he and Mero carefully designed and planned every detail of their flat in the new housing complex in the suburbs of Damascus. John purchased the flat with the money he carefully saved while working in America. They designed the layout, chose the flooring styles, the paint colors, and the cabinet design. The two completed much of the labor themselves, dreaming of a life of ministry together in Syria as they hammered and painted.

Mero's vision to use her education to minister to children and families complemented John's focus on training young leaders and potential pastors in Syria.

The adventurous years of schooling abroad equipped John for his future. But Syria was home, with its snow-capped mountains, the molten snow flowing into the crystal rivers, and the lapping waves of the Mediterranean Sea. Syria was home, with the olive and apricot groves, lush vineyards, the ancient edifices, festive bazaars. Syria was home with its kibbeh, hummus, and hot pita bread. Syria, the country housing some of the warmest, most hospitable people on the globe, was home, and the launching pad for ministry.

An hour and a half south of John and Mero's suburban Damascus neighborhood, unrest simmered. Protests brewed. But life in regal, ancient Damascus continued as usual.

When John and Mero had swept the last of the sawdust and cleaned the paintbrushes, they launched their ministry, inviting the church youth to help celebrate their new flat.

After an evening of pizza, laughter, and prayers, they hugged their last guest goodbye with a euphoria of gratification. And hope.

Darkness draped its mantle across sunset's final glow as the couple stepped out onto the balcony overlooking Damascus. Refreshing breezes vanquished the last of the day's oppressive heat as flights of pigeons flew to their roosts.

Like diamond dust against the black velvet skies, stars glittered and twinkled over the ancient city spread out like a scattering of shimmering jewels emanating excitement, life, and hope. Among the glistening gold and pearl of the city lights, the emerald glow of mosque minarets dappled the bejeweled cape draping the bosom of Damascus.

The M5 highway flowed easily between the scattered gems like a sparkling ribbon. From Aleppo, just below the Turkish border, the highway wound south through ancient Christian Maaloula, a crowning oasis just above Damascus, on down to Daraa and the Druze community of Al Suwayda, near the Jordanian border.

Latakia fringed the Mediterranean Sea on Syria's western border with its graceful palms and warm sand beaches. Below Latakia's shores, the snowcapped mountains of Lebanon stood majestically engraved against the western night sky.

To the east, near the Iraqi border where the desert seared into the sky, lay Deir ez-Zor, known for its Christian monasteries and the end of the line of the Armenian extermination marches a century before.

Down along the southern border, the twenty-seven-mile strip of the Golan Heights separated southern Syria from Israel's Sea of Galilee.

"The house is finished, now we can relax." John leaned back on the balcony chair with a sigh of contentment as the heat of the day gave way to the cool night breezes beneath the stars.

"All that is left it do is unpack the wedding gifts!"

"And find places in the closets for the linens and dishes!"

"Hosting Bible studies around our table, inviting the neighbors, the family to our own pad. . . ."

"And rocking babies. . . ."

Like an assassin's dagger, thundering supersonic MiG fighters plunged down the runway below the housing complex, slashing through their dreams as they sliced through the night, trailing flaming tails against the black sky.

Fighters!

THE SPARK THAT LIT
THE FUSE

(Damascus, Syria, 2010/2011)

"Though an army encamp against me, my heart shall not fear; though war
arise against me, yet I will be confident."

Psalm 27:3

"If there were never any clouds (sorrow and sufferings) in our lives, we
would have no faith. God does not come near us without clouds."

—Oswald Chambers.

Rami Ibrahim cast a sideways glance at Nancy, one of his dark brows
raised questioningly.

"Why is Brother Andrew preaching on suffering again?" Nancy
whispered with a hint of annoyance. "Every session on suffering. He's
preaching dynamic sermons, but didn't he understand we wanted him to
speak on the power of prayer?"

Scarcely three months before Mukhabarat would arrest schoolboys
for painting graffiti on the wall, the audience tried to listen politely to yet
another of the Bible Smuggler's sermons on suffering. A restlessness simmered across the crowd anticipating hearing fascinating stories of miraculous answers to prayer Brother Andrew experienced on his travels behind
the iron curtain. Miraculous accounts of the Bibles the guards never saw.

Enough about suffering! As 2010 drew to a close, life was fairly comfortable in Syria, the fourth safest country in the world, as long as one
stayed in the good graces of the Mukhabarat. Syria was the only country
in the Middle East without debt, self-sustaining, producing all its food
and medicines, and home to some of the most highly educated citizens in
the Middle East.

"Persecution is an enemy the Church has met and mastered many times!" Brother Andrew said, impassioned. "Indifference could prove to be a far more dangerous foe."

Nancy sighed. *Our people came to hear how to pray more boldly.* Brother Andrew shared inspiring thoughts, but all this talk on suffering was heavy, and certainly not the anticipated inspirational topic.

Early in their marriage, as the two knelt for their morning prayer time, both Nancy and her young husband, Rami Ibrahim, simultaneously felt God saying: "Stop focusing on building your own kingdom—your own church, your own empire. Focus on building *My* Kingdom."

In response to that call from God, Rami and Nancy organized conferences promoting prayer and fasting the first three days of each month, inviting Syrians from across the nation to gather to intercede for Syria. They arranged the conventions in neutral locations so all would feel welcome, interceding together for God's Kingdom to come.

"Let's organize the largest evangelistic crusade Syria has ever seen," Nancy and Rami and the committee decided.

"Damascus Stadium has 30,000 seats!"

A phone call confirmed the stadium was available. And furthermore, the government offered the stadium free of charge for the event!

But a sense of unease floundered in their hearts.

I have other plans for bringing revival to Syria, God seemed to whisper. *My plans for reviving Syria are not through a massive revival crusade.*

The committee canceled the stadium.

What are God's plans to bring revival to Syria? the Ibrahims wondered.

A nationwide prayer conference at the end of 2010 seemed a reasonable place to start. Why not invite Brother Andrew, the Dutch Bible Smuggler, to be the keynote speaker? With all his miraculous encounters smuggling Bibles into the Iron Curtain countries, they thought Brother

Andrew must have a whole satchel full of exciting stories of answers to prayer to inspire the Syrians to pray more boldly for Syria.

But the Bible Smuggler spoke on suffering every session the first day. The second day of the prayer conference, Brother Andrew spoke on suffering again. Every session. Suffering, suffering, suffering! For three days. Suffering!

"Brother Andrew, we invited you to Syria to speak on prayer," Rami began gently in a voice that rumbled deep in his throat. "Every single session, you have spoken about suffering. We've not heard a single talk on prayer. Was there a misunderstanding?"

"I don't understand it myself," Brother Andrew faltered apologetically. "I prepared sermons on prayer. But when I get up on the platform, somehow, all I can preach on is . . . suffering."

At the close of Brother Andrew's final session on suffering, the 1,400 believers stood around the circumference of the large auditorium, holding hands, banding together in prayer, surrendering their lives to whatever lay ahead.

Three months after the "Prayer Conference" with Brother Andrew's unexpected sessions on suffering, a spark lit the fuse igniting Syria into a conflagration no one could extinguish.

Syria's history was fraught with tales of the sieges and massacres of the Assyrians, Mongols, and Turks. Local folklore claimed it was outside Damascus walls that Cain killed Abel, who, according to lore, was buried in the mountain with red soil spilling down its side, with Damascus said to be the original Garden of Eden.

Now, five miles south of Damascus, schoolboys in Daraya sprayed graffiti on the walls: IT's YOUR TURN, DOCTOR! FREEDOM! No one needed to explain that "doctor" fingered President Assad, an ophthalmologist.

Enthralled by the Arab Spring antigovernmental uprisings toppling

Egypt, Libya, and Tunisia, schoolboys signaled a message to the regime they felt had repressively ruled Syria for generations. Stoked with resentment and dissatisfaction, Syria lay as dry tinder waiting for a spark to set it aflame.

None of the schoolboys admitted to the graffiti, and no one wished to clean it up. When none of the students confessed, the Mukhabarat imprisoned fifteen random schoolboys whose names had been scrawled on the wall through the years. The monthlong imprisonment and torture of the preteens and early teens sparked outrage and demonstrations. Civilians thronged into the streets in protest.

On March 18, 2011, after Friday prayers in the mosques, the army shot bullets into the crowd of mostly peaceful demonstrators to quell the protests, killing two. Army tanks surrounded Daraya. Officials shut off the electricity, internet, and television. Instead of extinguishing the unrest, the oppression lit the fuse.

Syria would never be the same. The insatiable flames of anti-regime demonstrations blazed across the country, fueled by Sunni extremists pouring into Syria from surrounding countries. The al-Qaeda breakaway, soon known as ISIS, and its radical brothers hijacked the protests to advance their own agendas of Islamic global dominance.

Foreigners including the nationless Kurds, the Turks, Iranians, Russians, and Western factions fanned the flames, racing across the country to further their own agendas.

Across the country, ISIS radicals swung their bloody swords, shrieking, "Allahu Akbar! Our god is greater!" as heads rolled at their feet.

If Damascenes supported their harshly repressive regime, it was only because the rebel alternative lurking beyond the gates was more brutal still.

Roadblocks and sentry posts manned by assault rifle-toting soldiers blocked every other street corner with barricades of cement-filled drums and razor wire.

The unseen presence of the Mukhabarat intelligence added another stratum of tension.

Those first months of the war, the believers cried out to God in passionate prayer circles, "Please, Lord, end the war! Bring peace!"

Syrians fled the towns seized by ISIS to the relative safety of Damascus. They brought with them only their flip-flops, the shirts on their backs, gruesome stories, and tears.

"I was sharing the Gospel with five refugee families in a small two-room apartment," a brother shared with the church. "Every one of those refugees in the house accepted the Lord! The refugees lost everything, they are shaken by ISIS atrocities, and their hearts are open to receive the truth, like no other time before.

"'Who is Allah, who delights in killing the innocent?' they demand. 'I live a better moral life without such a god.'

"The Almighty God wrote the message of His love on their hearts. When the refugees hear of this loving, forgiving, generous God of healing who contrasts so sharply with the bloody Allah of hate, revenge, and anger, it resonates in their beings. They know this merciful God is the true God."

God is using the war to bring revival! the churches realized. The believers' prayers shifted from desperate pleas for the war to end, to "Lord, be glorified."

A revival far beyond anything Rami, Nancy, Abraham, and John could have imagined drew complacent so-called Christians and disillusioned Muslims alike to their knees. When everything they set their hopes on was shattered or robbed, all that remained was Jesus.

At the close of a service, the crowd packing into the chapel of the Jesus of Nazareth Church leaned forward to hear the words of the tall, dignified visitor.

"I was a pilot in the air force of my country. A respected general. Due to the turn of events, I had to flee the country. I lost my position as an air force general. I lost my family. I lost my home. I lost everything. And I have a price on my head."

The graying gentleman paused, looking down for a moment, and then he faced Pastor Abraham flashing a radiant smile, finishing triumphantly, "But I found Jesus! And it's worth it all!"

In the darkness of the night, each of the Christians wondered, *If the time comes to flee, how much notice will we have, and what will we take with us?*

ISIS IN THE COURTYARD

(Damascus, Syria suburbs, 2013)

"But we have this treasure in jars of clay, to show that the surpassing power belongs to God and not to us. We are afflicted in every way, but not crushed; perplexed, but not driven to despair; persecuted, but not forsaken; struck down, but not destroyed; always carrying in the body the death of Jesus, so that the life of Jesus may also be manifested in our bodies."

II Corinthians 4:7–10

"If the suffering of Jesus resulted in the most God-glorifying act in history—the resurrection and reconciliation between humanity and God—we can expect the suffering of true Jesus-followers, for his namesake, to echo this same glory. It is, in the end, a triumph."

—John Samara

"The chief aim of true Christian persecution is for the glory of God and the expansion of His kingdom—for His namesake alone."

—John Samara

The bullets, tanks, and missiles had seemed far from John and Mero's new home in the Damascene suburbs. Until tonight. Everyone believed the flames of the south would flicker out and die away, but they raced voraciously across the country.

Transfixed, the newlyweds watched the flickering lights flame across the horizon, hurtling toward apartment complexes, souks, and business towers. In a deafening roar, a pair of giant fireballs ripped open the heart of Damascus in a massive explosion. The wail of ambulances replaced the thunder of the supersonic jets fading into the night.

John and Mero sat in stunned speechlessness for a moment.

Fighter jets over Damascus!

"Lord, comfort the injured and the families of the victims! Guide the hearts of the government leaders!"

Retreating to the sanctuary of their new home, John shut the door against the smoke and sirens.

Perhaps dawn would return the sense of normalcy the bombers had snatched away. Their life in this darling flat had just begun.

Father! What does the future hold? the couple wondered, praying into the night, surrendering: *Our lives are Yours. All that matters is Your glory.*

Under the black mantle of darkness, two opposing rows of tanks crept toward battle lines drawn on along the M5 highway in front of the new housing complex.

Just as dawn began to lift the shades of darkness, stuttering machine guns and bullets drilling against the walls exploded into the couple's restless slumber.

"Allahu Akbar! Allahu Akbar!" The signature shout of the radical jihadists flung the couple from their bed. John drew Mero to the floor, shielding her with his body, tugging the mattress overtop of them. Any bullets would have to pass through him before they hit his bride.

Rapid bursts of machine gun bullets ripped into the brick walls, smashing through vehicles and apartment windows. The thunder of artillery punctuated the stutter of machine gun fire. Tracers from MK-47s lit up the night sky. Fiery reflections danced on the newly painted walls. Acrid smoke filtered into the flat, obliterating the spicy aroma of last night's pizza.

John and Mero lay on the carpet in the darkness, praying, shivering, cringing at gunfire, anguished screams, the *thwop thwop thwop* of the helicopters, and the growling rumble of the tanks until they faded into the dawn.

The arrival of a war zone to their balcony railing was not in their dreams for the flat they had so lovingly planned and painstakingly built.

The scene seemed to have been straight from a war movie one could not click off.

As the bullet fire faded into the distance, the newlyweds cautiously parted the blinds of their bedroom window, exposing the wreckage and aftermath. Corpses splayed across the courtyard amid pools of blood, shards of glass, spent shells, and rubble.

"That's the uniform of our guard!" John cried, pointing to one of the bloodied bodies.

On either side of the highway, rows of tanks edged forward. News feeds and messages flashing across John's phone screamed that ISIS had taken the area.

"God help us," John whispered, trying to hide the rising anxiety as he pulled Mero close.

The explosions died away, leaving a deathly stillness.

The lull won't last long.

From a crack between the shades, John scanned the streets. One lone woman hurried down the sidewalk. *No bullets cut her down. There must not be any snipers around.*

Leave now! his heart screamed.

"We've got to go! Grab your passport. The lull won't last."

Swiftly John scanned the cozy nest they had lovingly created with hearts full of hopes and dreams. The unpacked gift boxes of sheets, towels, and dishes . . .

He flipped the light switch. Quietly, he closed the door and turned the key.

We may never return.

The tranquil, innocent bliss of their honeymoon days and dreams vanished into the smoke of the battle. But nothing mattered except escaping the bullets and missiles that were sure to fly again, momentarily.

CLOSE CALL

"These things I have I have said these things to you, that in me you may have peace. In the world you will have tribulation. But take heart; I have overcome the world."

John 16:33

"Jesus calls us to dangerous places because He loves people who live in dangerous places. He loves the perpetrators of violence and the victims of violence. He loves the children and the old, the men and the women, the rich and the poor."

—Kate McCord

"Baba, I will risk my life for my wife," John said, impassioned. "But I will not risk hers unnecessarily. I am not willing to risk taking my wife through a war zone and checkpoints to get to the government offices to change her name to Samara so we can fly to the States. It's not worth it, Baba! Let's give it time, the war will soon be over, and life can go on as normal."

"John, the war will not soon be over. It's widely known you have lived in the West. You are a prime target for kidnapping. You've graduated from the university and don't carry a student exemption. You will be picked up by any of the factions and forced to fight. You need to leave." The building shook from the regime's shelling of the rebel suburbs a mile away.

John weighed his father's words. He had a point. The emotions of feeling like a refugee or exile those first traumatic months in the States twisted his stomach nauseatingly. *What would Mero do away from her family in a foreign land with a foreign language, unable to use her degree?*

But she'd be safe . . .

John studied the floor for a moment. *Dad's a man of God, what if he's right?*

He lifted his eyes to meet his father's. "We can't travel unless her last name is changed to Samara. I am not willing to risk the checkpoints . . ."

"You are in a dilemma, aren't you? It isn't safe to leave, and it isn't safe to stay. In God's will there is safety. Son, I will pray."

"If Dad is praying, that means, 'Pack your bags, God is going to work,'" John told Mero. "We don't have a home in Syria anymore, and we don't want to live in Baba and Mama's spare bedroom forever. But I don't see how we can go. . . ."

Across Syria, radical extremists targeted Christian villages, leaving ravished women, corpses, and traumatized children in their wake, sending streams of terrified, fractured family groups fleeing to the more secure areas around Damascus.

The Jesus of Nazareth Church networked with other congregations across the country in an organization called Ananias House and rallied their limited means to meet the needs of the refugees flooding to Damascus.

Like Jesus caring about the needs of the multitude, the church arranged clothing and relief package distribution, holding medical clinics at the church facilities. The desperate needs of refugees who had nothing overwhelmed the churches trying to be the hands and feet of Jesus.

Mero collected donated clothing from local businesses and supervised the 5:00 p.m. clothing distribution to the refugees three days a week.

As John and Mero prepared to head to the Jesus of Nazareth Church to oversee the clothing distribution, Mero's phone began to ring.

"Mero! Please come!" the frazzled voice of her assistant panted. "I can't handle them! Crowds of people pushing into the courtyard!"

And then moments later another call, "Mero! Come now! Please!"

A third call edged with frantic desperation: "Please, Mero! Refugees keep pushing in! Quick, before things get out of hand! People are desperate. Bring John to hold the crowds!"

John grabbed Mero's hand as they dashed to the bus stop. He pulled her up the steps as the bus began to move.

As the bus threaded through the traffic moments later, a bone-jarring explosion rocked the neighborhood behind them in a searing ball of fire, a cloud of smoke, dust, and debris.

John's phone rang.

"John! Are you okay?!"

"We're fine . . ."

"The bus stop just blew up!" the couple heard John's mother say.

Mero gripped her husband's hand. Exchanging John's awe-filled gaze, each knew without speaking what the other was thinking. *Only God!*

Only God knew the timing and destination of the missile before it was ever fired. Only God could have sent a crowd long before the distribution center opened. Only God caused the frazzled distribution assistant to phone them incessantly.

The crater where the bus stop once stood seemed like a hand-signed note from God reminding the newlyweds every time they passed the rubble: "War may have invaded your neighborhood, but I am here too, just like I've been from the time of Paul and the time of Abraham."

I am not willing to risk Mero's life driving through a war zone! One never knows where a checkpoint might pop up, who is manning them, or what they will take, a man, his wallet, his car, his wife, or all four. . . .

"WHEN WE OPEN OUR EYES WE WILL BE WITH JESUS"

(Damascus, Syria, circa 2012)

"Finally, be strong in the Lord and in the strength of his might. Put on the whole armor of God, that you may be able to stand against the schemes of the devil."

Ephesians 6:10,11

"Discipleship is not a free gift. Salvation is a free gift. Grace is a free gift. But for discipleship there is a cost we need to pay. In spite of suffering, Christians are counting the cost in the Middle East, in China, and in Korea. In those countries, the one who becomes a disciple pays a real price. Maybe his life."

—Rami Ibrahim

"Lord, how can I serve You during this time of war?" Nancy prayed, kneeling before the Father in an hour of intense intercession in the apartment in the outskirts of Damascus. From all across Syria, ISIS attacks and missiles sent refugees streaming to the more secure city of Damascus. The influx of refugees dropped countless needs and ministry opportunities to their doorsteps. Relief packages, classes, soup kitchens, Bible distribution . . .

While the missiles flew overhead, Nancy and Rami spearheaded the "Broken Heart for Syria" prayer gatherings drawing 800 Syrians, but there was so much more that could be done at the edge of the war zone.

Waiting breathlessly in the stillness, Nancy wondered, *Which outreach ministry will God lead me to invest into next?*

In the stillness she felt God whisper, "Will you give Me your life?"

Sitting in stunned silence, Nancy reflected on the request. *My life. . . . God, what are You asking? Are You asking if I am willing to die?*

She wrestled with surrendering. *I have a husband and two young daughters who need me.*

But how can I say no to You, who gave Your life for me?

Either God is worth trusting or He is not.

In her heart, Nancy determined, if the time came, she would give her life.

"Yes, Lord, if I need to die for You, I am willing."

Every day she wondered, *Will this be the day I die?*

Her heart pulsing with passionate love for God, Nancy prayed again, "Lord, how can I serve You?"

In the stillness, the answer came: "Will you give Me your husband?"

Lord, I gave You my life, but give You Rami?

How can I live without the love of my life? My protector, my soulmate?

But how can I refuse? You gave him to me.

Tearfully, Nancy shared God's request with Rami.

"Habibti, come." He took her hand and led her to kneel beside him.

Her face bathed in tears, Nancy prayed, "Lord, I offer my precious Rami's life to You. I don't know what this might mean, but my dear companion, my protector, my love . . ." She sobbed gently.

The taut lines of anguish on her uplifted, teary face melted into surrender as she lifted her hands. "Rami is Yours, to use how You wish. To take when You want."

As Nancy knelt before the Lord the third time, she rested her hands on her arms, her heart fluttering in trepidation. There was one more request the Lord could ask.

She wept and wrestled before Him, sensing He waited for her to ask once again.

"My Lord," she faltered haltingly. "How can I serve You?"

She knew what He would say.

"Will you give Me your children?"

Lord! My precious children! Oh, Lord. . . . Must I?

Lord, the radicals know we share our faith with the Muslims. They have us on their list. And they know where we live. Lord! Our daughters!

"It's Youanna and Priscilla, isn't it?" Rami knelt beside her when he found her crying. "Habibti, this is not something to be taken lightly. Let's pray and fast about it."

Rami and Nancy agonized in prayer, fasting without telling their daughters the reason.

"Rami, the girls are a gift from God; how can we refuse to give them back if He asks for them?"

"Nancy, is Jesus worth it? Is He worth surrendering everything? Even our girls?"

"He is, habibi, so worth it."

"This involves the girls; let's talk to them," Rami suggested.

When they gathered in the living room for the nightly 6:00 prayer time, Nancy put her arms around her daughters. "Girls, we've always told you that you are precious gifts from God. When I was praying this week, asking God how I could serve Him, I felt Him whisper in my heart, 'Will you give Me your children?'

"Baba and I have been praying and fasting about the answer, and we want to ask you what you think we should do."

"Of course, Mama!" the girls volunteered. "If God gave us to you, and He wants us back, you must give us to God."

Nancy and Rami held them close, their tears dampening the precious young heads. "We don't know what this will mean, but we will trust God.

"Let's kneel and give you back to God again."

Rami and Nancy placed their hands on the heads of their kneeling daughters. Nancy wiped the tears and bravely prayed, "Our Lord who gave us these precious gifts, we offer them back to You . . ."

"There is something we need to talk about," Rami said, drawing them close. "It is very important that you listen closely. It is very possible that men carrying swords could break through our door. Men who don't know Jesus. They may pressure us to convert to Islam. No matter what they say to you, do not answer them."

"Only tell them that Jesus loves them, and that we forgive them," Nancy added.

"There might be blood and pain, but only for a short time. If something like that happens, we will just close our eyes, and when we open them, we will be with Jesus."

Nancy dabbed at her eyes with a tissue. The scenario was entirely too plausible. She held the girls close and told them: "We don't need to fear because as long as God wants us to be safe, we will be safe. God is in charge. He is carrying our future."

"We must pray against evil," Rami explained. "But if evil comes, we need to focus on the Cross, not on the evil, because if we focus on the evil, we will feel frightened. But if we focus on the Cross, on Jesus waiting at the end of the journey and the joy before us, the fear will go away."

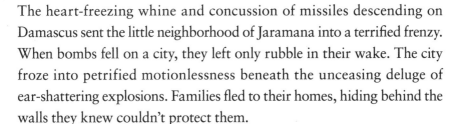

The heart-freezing whine and concussion of missiles descending on Damascus sent the little neighborhood of Jaramana into a terrified frenzy. When bombs fell on a city, they left only rubble in their wake. The city froze into petrified motionlessness beneath the unceasing deluge of ear-shattering explosions. Families fled to their homes, hiding behind the walls they knew couldn't protect them.

As bombs fell, the Ibrahim family ran down the stairs. Youanna and Priscilla giggled in anticipation as they scampered toward the wooden table they had claimed as their fort. Mama made the bomb raids a fun adventure. The comfort of eating popcorn in their fort while watching a video to distract from the crashing of the bombs wrapped the girls like a warm blanket while missiles flew overhead.

The house continued to shiver under the attacks. Like a rainstorm that had been building up for days, once bombs and missiles started falling, it seemed they left no block unscathed, and no atom of air uncontaminated.

"Why don't we worship and sing?" Rami suggested, sitting down at the piano, beginning to play. "Shine Jesus shine! Fill this land with the Father's glory."

The closer the missiles crashed, shaking the whole complex, the louder the family sang. As they lifted their voices with abandon, their hearts overflowed with joy as the fear vanished. Each of their lives had been surrendered at the foot of the Cross, leaving nothing to fear.

"Let's sing Psalm 91!" The girls clamored for the soothing lullaby their mother sang at bedtime. "Yes! Psalm 91!" They knew the entire Psalm by heart, and the words ministered deeply to their hearts.

"He who dwells in the shelter of the Most High will abide in the shadow of the Almighty. . . . My refuge, my fortress. . . . He will cover you with His pinions, and under His wings you will find refuge. . . ."

There was no worry. Just rest beneath the Cross and worship of a mighty Creator God who held them in His powerful hands.

"Praise the Lord in His sanctuary! Praise Him in His mighty heavens!"

Ambulances shrieked and wailed through the streets that trembled with horrific concussions of the barrel bombs blowing apart houses, hospitals, and schools in vast clouds of smoke and dust, burying screaming children and parents beneath the weight of the rubble. But the Ibrahim family sang all the louder.

"You are my hiding place! You fill my heart with songs of deliverance.

"Whenever I am afraid, I will trust in you! I will trust in you!"

The radiance of God showned on every face. It felt as though the angels had tiptoed into the room. The worship felt almost too joy-filled to stop.

Helicopters and planes vanished into the smoke and the darkness, leaving the shrieks of the grieving, the cries of those beneath the rubble, and the screams of the overloaded ambulances to wail into the night.

Rami and Nancy looked down on the beaming faces of their little girls, treasuring the sacred touch of heaven that surrender and worship carried to their hearts.

There was nothing to fear when everything of importance in their lives had been laid on the altar in surrender to God, however He chose to use them—through life or death. All belonged to God.

Surrender to a loving God didn't mean loss. It meant gain.

At the top of the stairs, the girls checked the motto on the wall. Other pictures rocked and fell, but the plaque on the Ibrahims' living room wall hung as secure as the vow engraved on it: "As for me and my house, we will praise the Lord."

How great is our God!

What will I do if the bombs start dropping at school where I am responsible for over 200 youngsters? Nancy wondered in the night.

BENEATH THE
BARREL BOMBS

"Do not be afraid or discouraged because of this vast army. For the battle is
not yours, but God's."

II Chronicles 20:15

"Just like the story of Joseph. We don't pray for God to *bring* evil, but we
pray for God to USE evil."

—Abraham Samara

The planes thundered out of the clouds, flying low toward the
Christian district ensconced in the walls of Old Damascus. A soccer
ball rolled to a corner in the courtyard of the Acts of God School near
Straight Street. Students gazed at the planes, their eyes wide with horror.
In the classrooms, the pupils hurled themselves beneath the desks, cow-
ering in terror.

Swooping over the apartments and souks, the planes and helicopters
disgorged barrel bombs encasing a deadly cocktail of a ton of bolts and
screws laced with explosives.

Massive explosions rocked the ancient city with flaming convulsions
of smoke and rubble.

The wails and terrified screams of school children tumbling down
the steps mingled with the rumbles and blasts in a soul-ripping cacophony.

Panicking youngsters threw themselves on their beloved headmistress,
wailing, "I want my mommy!" The little ones looked pleadingly up at
Nancy, dark eyes brimming with tears, clinging frantically to her skirt.
"We are going to die, Miss Nancy!"

Surrounded by frantic children clinging to her in the center of the
courtyard, Miss Nancy gazed at the plumes of smoke and contrails

overhead. *Jesus! What can I tell the dear children? They've memorized Psalm 91 and pray it every day. And now we are under mortar fire!*

"*Jehoshaphat!*" The answer flashed back.

Yes! Attacked by an overwhelming army, the biblical king of Judah sent singers before the soldiers. As they sang praises to Him, God defeated the enemy. Nancy knew exactly what God wanted her to do.

"Let's go to the chapel!" she shouted over the cries, screams, and explosions. The confidence of God surged into her heart as she led the way, singing above the chaos:

"How great is our God, sing with me. . . ."

For a few lines, Nancy's voice could hardly be heard above the roaring of the aircraft, the explosions, and the wails of the children who had seen what youngsters their age should never witness.

Nancy felt like a mother hen trying to direct a brood of terrified chicks who wanted only to scurry beneath their mother's wings. But she continued singing triumphantly, victoriously, as the children filed into the benches.

The students joined in feebly at first, rejoicing in God's splendor and majesty.

The staff and teens joined in. Gradually, the cowering, tearstained children disentangled themselves from each other's arms, and sat up, wiping their eyes, singing of darkness hiding and trembling at God wrapped in light.

"How great is our God!"

All across the chapel, children stopped shaking, lifting their hands toward the ceiling in praise. A miraculous peace swept across the faces.

"How great is our God!"

More youngsters chimed in with greater certitude, swelling words of praise in a grand crescendo with more confidence and power until the rumbles of the planes, explosions, and sirens seemed to fade along with the terror and tears.

The faces of angels! Nancy marveled, scanning the room full of radiant, tranquil countenances.

Bombs crashed beyond their shaking walls, smoke and sirens filled the air, but the sweet voices crescendoed, passionately carrying the notes with increasing volume and jubilance.

An electrifying energy mingled with joy surged through the chapel as if a host of angels descended to join the choir, to calm the hearts, and to protect.

Hands raised in jubilant praise throughout the chapel as the students swayed with the intensity and ecstasy of their praise.

"How great is our God, sing with me!"

Through the windows, Nancy observed clusters of parents gathering, joining in the praise, lifting hands toward the smoky skies.

The whole world seemed to sing, "How great is our God!"

The singing swelled with intensity and volume, ending in a surge of triumphant joy.

Nancy slipped out the door. "You are welcome to take your children," she called to the parents.

A Muslim judge tilted her hijabed head decisively, forcefully voicing the sentiment of all the mothers and fathers. "Why would we take our children from this place? God is here!"

Every student remained at school within the walls of the Old City. The youngsters marched triumphantly through the courtyard to their classes like Jehoshaphat's victorious, singing warriors.

God was here! What was there to fear!

As the students stood in line to exit the school doors, they shouted the quote Nancy taught them to say at the ending of a day: "God is good all the time! Even in war, God is always good!"

Whenever the missiles began to explode again over Damascus, the students knew the drill and marched to the chapel, singing praises to the Omnipotent God.

How great is our God!

ISIS MISSILES VERSUS GOD ALMIGHTY

"Little children, you are from God and have overcome them, for he who is in you is greater than he who is in the world."

I John 4:4

"We are safer under God's will, under the bombs than out from under God's will and out from under the bombs."

—Nancy Samara Ibrahim

"Miss Nancy! Miss Nancy!" Tearful, distraught students clamored about their beloved headmistress. "Miss Nancy! ISIS is planning an attack on our neighborhood this weekend!"

News outlets warned that 30,000 ISIS soldiers planned to attack the Christian community in Old Damascus that weekend.

"Miss Nancy! What can we do?" the children cried. They knew that when ISIS planned an attack, there was no way to prepare, no place to hide.

"Well, what is more powerful than ISIS? What is something that we can always do?"

"We can pray!" one student suggested. "The whole school can pray!"

"And we can fast!" another added hopefully.

"That's a splendid idea!" Miss Nancy agreed. "Who is stronger? ISIS bombs or God?"

"GOD!" they yelled.

"Let's gather in the courtyard and pray right now."

Nancy called together the staff and the students, explaining the attacks threatened this Saturday. Those dear little children began to cry out to God, pleading with him to protect the neighborhood from the ISIS missiles and bullets and praising Him for His power.

Oh, those children prayed as if shaking the very throne of God. Even the four-year-olds prayed with earnest passion, "Lord, God! Save our houses! Save our families! Protect our community! AMEN! Alleluia!"

Together they sang victorious songs of praise in that courtyard in Old Damascus, surrounded by thick stone walls with the open skies overhead.

"You are my hiding place! You always fill my heart with songs of deliverance. Whenever I am afraid, I will trust in you! I will trust in you!"

"Let's fast!" the students decided. "We will skip our sandwiches today. Oh, we want God to protect our friends and families. . . ."

"God is good . . ." Nancy led her students to chant as she did at the end of every class. "God is good all the time. Even in war His goodness does not expire. God is always good!"

As those children marched out of the school doors into the streets of Damascus that afternoon, confidence radiated from their faces and the bounce of their steps. Their God had heard their prayer! He was more powerful than ISIS! He would protect their neighborhood.

ISIS bombs particularly targeted the schools in Old Damascus, specifically after Friday prayers in Umayyad and the surrounding mosques. Out of fear of ISIS attacks, all the other schools in Damascus shifted their weekends to Friday and Saturday.

"If we fear ISIS enough to change our lives around in concern of attack, we surrender in fear to the enemy," Nancy told the staff. "God made it clear to my heart that ISIS is not the final decision maker. ISIS will not rule our schedule."

"ISIS can make all the threats they want, and they can even initiate attacks, but Acts of God School will run on our traditional schedule," she announced with a glimmer of confidence in her eyes. "God's word is always final. We will not be afraid and will continue to honor God's day of rest with weekends on Saturday and Sunday."

A massive explosion rocked Damascus at 7:30 Saturday morning.

Nancy and her daughters rushed to the windows of their home to see a ball of fire and billows of smoke exploding over the Christian enclave.

God! That's the neighborhood the students trusted you to protect from the ISIS bombs!

Tears of disappointment burned Nancy's eyes. Then anger surged through her.

Lord! You let us down! The students were so sure you would protect! Their faith will be shaken and collapse like the buildings around them.

God, why didn't you answer?! We trusted you!

And then, the stories began to pour in through news media and the students' accounts.

"Remarkably, no one was injured in the bombing of the apartment complex," news headlines announced. "The apartment building went up in flames, but every resident miraculously escaped."

"I was on the balcony before the blast. When the explosion died away, I found myself inside the house in the bathroom," a Christian woman shared. "I was carried by angels," she whispered in awe. "There is no other answer."

Another survivor told of finding herself in her bedroom after the explosion with no explanation as to how she arrived there. There was story after story of unexplained, miraculous deliverance.

Nancy told her girls, "God's angels must have hovered all over that building. He answered the prayers of the Acts of God students and protected His children."

God was looking down on Damascus, answering prayers Saturday morning. But he was also on guard the night before, preparing everything in his sovereign plan while his children slept, at ease, knowing their Father had heard them.

In the darkness of the midnight hour, a van had pulled away from a bar, weaving through the narrow alleys, careening around the corners over sidewalks, slowing, and drifting to a stop crosswise on the alley, blocking all traffic.

Hours later, as the minibuses drove through Damascus collecting the public school students, the drivers could not find a way around the haphazardly parked minivan.

The school bus drivers laid on their horns. Annoyed fathers pounded on the drunk's door yelling, "Hey, move your van! The buses need to get through!"

But the drunk slept on, undisturbed.

"If the buses had been able to navigate the blocked street, students would have been in the direct line of missile fire!" the parents realized. "The drunken parking job saved the lives of countless children."

Parents, who had been frustrated at the drunken neighbor, returned to knock on his door. "Thank you sir, for saving the lives of our children by blocking the road last night."

As Nancy walked down an alley in Damascus, she came up behind two ladies veiled in hijabs.

"Did you hear about the missile attack in a Christian neighborhood where no one was hurt?" one questioned.

"Isn't that remarkable? All the apartments burned except the ones with crosses where the Christians lived. Their God is the powerful God. . . ."

Nancy couldn't wait for Monday.

"So, did God answer our prayers?" she asked the assembly.

"YES!" the students shouted. "YES! GOD DID!"

Students fleeing ISIS atrocities from across Syria each had their own devastating story. "I will never forgive ISIS," many vowed.

"ISIS—UNFORGIVABLE"

"For I am sure that neither death nor life, nor angels nor rulers, nor things present nor things to come, nor powers, 39 nor height nor depth, nor anything else in all creation, will be able to separate us from the love of God in Christ Jesus our Lord."

Romans 8:38, 39

"Leave the broken, irreversible past in God's hands, and step out into the INVISIBLE future with Him."

—Oswald Chambers

"My students all bear the scars of the trauma of war," Nancy told Rami as the war progressed. "Whether Iraqi refugees or Syrian refugees, they all demonstrate evidence of the stress of being uprooted from home and community.

"And tragically, they carry wounds from seeing family members and neighbors murdered and abused."

"The scars affect their emotional and physical health, shaping the way these refugee children act, live, and make decisions, consciously or subconsciously," Rami agreed. "Especially without forgiveness for the perpetrators."

Chapel talks at Acts of God School began focusing on forgiveness and how to deal with the unspeakable trauma the youngsters endured.

These dear children had more to forgive than a whole country should have to forgive in a century. The girls abused by ISIS soldiers. . . . The brothers who had been forced to watch. . . . The children forced to watch the brutal murder of their fathers and brothers. The girls and boys who had seen explosives blow the limbs from a friend. . . .

"Forgiving does not mean we excuse the person who has hurt us," Nancy explained gently during a Bible session. "Forgiving means we leave revenge in God's hands. Jesus said if we don't forgive, God cannot forgive us.

"So, if we don't forgive the people who were mean to us, it is like burning the bridge to God. Being angry at those who hurt us is like swallowing poison, hoping to hurt those who wounded us. We are the ones suffering when we can't forgive."

Oh, these children had so much to forgive! Nancy could see the pain in their eyes as she spoke. She looked into the eyes of young girls and boys forced to work the nightclubs and brothels to support their families and saw their pain.

"The best way you can find healing for the terrible things that the enemies did to you is to forgive those who hurt you," Nancy compassionately explained. "When the German Nazis killed the Jewish people just because they were Jews, a Dutch woman named Corrie helped hide Jews."

The children identified with that. Their families had been targeted just for being the wrong sort of Muslim.

"Corrie built a special secret closet behind her bookcase to hide those Jews fleeing for their lives," Nancy continued. "But the soldiers discovered she was helping them. They never caught the Jews hiding in her house. But they punished her by sending her to a concentration camp, which is much worse than a refugee camp. Corrie and her sister Betsie were treated so terribly that Betsie died.

"After her rescue at the end of the war, Corrie shared her story at churches. After one of her talks, a former soldier from the camp came up to Corrie. He reached out to shake Corrie's hand. 'I am sorry for the mean things I did at the camp,' he told her.

"But Corrie felt no forgiveness in her heart for the man. He had done terrible things to her and Betsie. She probably would rather have slapped the guard. But she felt God telling her, 'Reach out your hand and forgive him anyway.'

"Corrie obeyed God and reached out her hand to show she forgave him. The moment she put out her hand to forgive the soldier, God filled Corrie's hurting heart with overflowing forgiveness.

"I know all of you have experienced terrible things that soldiers and wicked people have done to you," Nancy went on. "Forgiveness doesn't make the perpetrator right, it just makes us free. I will lead in a prayer, asking God to fill your hearts with forgiveness and to heal your hearts. Forgiving is the only way to find healing. Let me ask God to heal you.

"Our dear loving Father who loved us so much that You gave Your Son to come and be spit on and beaten, and mocked and even killed, You see the pain filling these hearts in these precious children in this chapel. And You feel the pain of the horrible, hateful acts done to these dear youth. I ask You to hear their prayers and give them the power to forgive the cruel people who don't deserve forgiveness.

"Forgiveness doesn't make them right. It just makes us free.

"Now if you wish, you can repeat after me,

"Loving Heavenly Father, please fill my heart with forgiveness for the cruel deeds others have done and said to me and my family."

A murmur of voices broke out across the chapel, repeating the prayer, accompanied by quiet sobs and sniffles.

"I release those who have hurt me to You to deal with and ask You to bring total healing to my heart. In Jesus's name, amen."

Across the auditorium, youth and children wept as God reached into the terrible scars deep in their hearts, pouring His healing balm and grace.

A hand went up. "Miss Nancy, can I say something?" a young girl asked timidly.

"Sure, come up front so we can all hear you better."

The girl cried quietly into the tissue Miss Nancy handed her. Nancy put her arm on her shoulder. The girl blew her nose and bravely began.

"Today is the first time I understand the meaning of forgiveness, Miss Nancy. I grew up going to the Orthodox Church, but I never understood forgiveness, and I was *never* going to forgive ISIS for what they did to my only brother," she sniffed.

"My family lived in Daraa. My brother's friend was an Alawite. He had done nothing wrong, but because he was Alawite, like President Assad, ISIS was searching for the friend to kill him. Of course, my family said the friend could hide in our house until ISIS went away.

"Soldiers with masks and swords on the end of their guns broke into every house, looking for my brother's friend. What could we do? If we sent him out, they would catch him, torture him, and kill him. Just because he was the wrong sort of Muslim!"

The girl paused, sniffling a moment, and then proceeded. "They broke through our door and tore our whole house apart. And they found him. They grabbed my brother's friend and beat him with their guns and kicked him and laughed at him. . . .

"And then they grabbed . . . They grabbed my only brother." The girl wiped the tears with the back of her hand, gathering the courage to continue.

"They shoved a gun against my brother's back and pushed him and his friend out the door. My brother looked back at us, and I saw the terror in his eyes. . . . But there was nothing we could do.

"My dad begged the ISIS soldiers, 'Please! Don't take my only son! Take my cow. Take this money. Take my truck! Take everything, but please don't take my son!'"

The girl wept softly, resting her head on Nancy's shoulder. With a sigh she continued quietly.

"But no matter how we pleaded, the ISIS soldiers took my brother along with his friend. They made them kneel on the ground in our yard. And then they . . . cut off their heads. Right there in front of our house, with their blood all over the grass . . . ." She choked, her eyes welling with tears.

She dashed away another tear before proceeding. "My mama fainted, and my Baba almost lost his mind. I said, 'I will never forgive ISIS for killing my brother!'

"But Miss Nancy, today I did!" The girl's eyes held a new light.

"Today, I proclaimed forgiveness for the murderers of my brother. And my heart feels so light! So relieved that I don't have to get revenge; that's God's job. I feel so healed!"

Thank you, Jesus! Nancy breathed. *This moment has repaid every ounce of effort, frustration, and sacrifice I've invested into these dear students.*

The girl's Orthodox pastor approached Nancy's father, asking, "Pastor Abraham, please come to Daraa and teach us about Jesus, the Lord of forgiveness."

Abraham took hope to Daraa, the location where Saul encountered the light, and the cradle of the revolution, the town resistant to the Gospel before the war, the village where ISIS beheaded Christians and hung them on trees. He taught them about the love and forgiveness of Jesus.

How great is our God!

"THE CROSS
YOU SPIT UPON"

"Do not be conquered by evil but conquer evil with good."

Romans 12:21 (NAB)

"There is no hope outside of the Cross of Jesus. At the nucleus of the Gospel
lies the Cross and the resurrection, the only hope for humankind."

—Abraham Samara

The eyes beneath the hijab blazed in anger as the woman spewed curse
words at the Christians distributing relief packages.

"Why are you upset?" Nancy asked, pausing to engage the woman
on the steps of the church compound.

A hasty glance showed her the furious woman clutched a bottle of
medicine from the clinic the church had opened in the school along with
the relief distribution center for refugees.

"Those nasty people won't give me any food!" the woman yelled, her
arms flinging her black abaya as she gestured wildly.

Nancy glanced at the pill bottle in her hands. "I see they gave you
medicine. That was very kind," Nancy spoke soothingly.

Refugees are most often denied a food packet due to lack of an ID,
Nancy knew.

"Did you bring an ID to show them?"

"No, of course not! I don't need to show any ID. I am a refugee and
need food and supplies!"

"I'm sorry you didn't get food. I am sure that's difficult. But if you
bring an ID, they will give you supplies. We have hundreds of people
coming here, and if there are no IDs, the same people can come in over
and over and get lots of packages, leaving none for others who need
them," Nancy explained patiently.

Without warning but with a practiced aim, the veiled Muslim woman spat a mouthful of saliva onto the Cross hanging from Nancy's neck. The saliva spattered across Nancy's neck and chin, and the frothy sputum slithered from the Cross down her chest.

Nancy could feel her cheeks reddening as her emotions rose within her. She wanted to grab the woman and shake her.

The very idea that here we are serving and giving free food and medicines, and all the thanks we get is a spray of spittle! She could feel an angry retort rise inside her. Weary and worn out, she wanted to lecture that woman, make her leave.

"She spat on *Me*," a soft voice whispered into her heart. "She didn't spit on you, she spat on Me."

Ah! The soft voice soothed Nancy's heart, and the revulsion drained away.

"Suffering is the best way to show the perfect love of Christ," she and Rami had taught their girls. "Suffering is the ideal opportunity to show the grace of God."

And then, Nancy saw beyond the hate-filled face venomously spitting on her. Deep beneath the black burka lay a bleeding heart scarred by hatred, wounds, cruel words, bombs, and killings. Even the woman's religious book did not teach love but survival.

The woman responded in the survival mode she knew best—hate. She had never experienced the love of Jesus and now was Nancy's opportunity to lovingly show this wounded woman a better way.

One does not overcome hate with hate, but with love.

Nancy's eyes softened in compassion. "Do you know it is because of this very Cross that we minister to you?" she asked gently. "You bombed our churches and were our enemy, and killed our people, but still we gave you medicine because through the Cross like the one you spit on, Jesus taught us to love people."

The woman wilted under her black scarf. Her gaze dropped to the floor as shame wiped the anger from her face.

"Friend," Nancy invited, "why don't you come to the meeting in the chapel and learn about Jesus who died on the Cross, and who showed us how to be kind to our enemies. And when you come back, be sure to bring your ID. We would love to give you a food packet."

The woman shrugged and sauntered away, clutching her pill bottle while Nancy wiped the spit from her neck.

She will be back.

"We have nothing," an Orthodox Christian family told the church relief workers tearfully. "We left everything and fled after radical extremists kidnapped and killed our son.

"After we recovered his body, we learned it was our Muslim neighbors who betrayed us to the radical soldiers."

For decades, Christians, Jews, Druze, Shiite, Sunni, and Alawites lived as one extended (mostly) happy family in Syrian neighborhoods. But now, most of Syria's Sunni Muslims would side with ISIS and other Sunni radicals rather than Christian neighbors who had been close, lifelong friends.

The Church of Jesus of Nazareth gave the grieving family comfort, food, blankets, clothing, and basic supplies. In the terrible loss, the devastated family truly found a deep relationship with the loving Savior and healing in His arms.

The family learned to know Jesus in an even more personal way, embracing Him into deep places in their hearts where the grief and displacement had cracked the complacency of a ritualistic religious life.

"Give us food packages, blankets, sleeping mats, diapers, and medicines," ISIS wives demanded, preparing for resistance. "Our husbands are fighters; if you don't give us what we ask for, they will deal with you!"

The church graciously shared the love of Jesus with these hearts trapped in the darkness of hateful beliefs.

"Why are you serving those ISIS wives?" other refugees demanded. "They killed my brother. They confiscated our homes and destroyed our lives! And you are sharing with them?"

"We share clothing, food, and relief packages with whoever is in need because of the love of Jesus," the staff assured the refugees. "Because of the love of Jesus, we reach out to everyone in need."

Because of the disillusionment brought by the hateful atrocities experienced at the hands of Muslim extremists, the hearts of many refugees softened toward the Gospel.

Searching Muslims flocked to the churches asking, "In the name of Allah, terrorists rape and kill. Who is God? We are living in hell!"

These war-shattered children of Islam had never heard about or experienced a God of love. Many were touched to tears to feel His love from the "People of the Book" reaching out to them. Deep within their hearts was a longing to be loved by a Creator God and to have a relationship with him, which they had never experienced from Allah. They became soft, impressionable clay in this tragic season of their lives.

While other relief organizations in the Middle East focused on the urgent physical needs alone, the Church of Jesus of Nazareth and the leaders of Ananias House knew God entrusted them with a rare opportunity, bringing to their doorsteps souls with needs far more urgent than physical survival. To qualify to receive food packets, refugees were required to attend a talk about Jesus in the chapel.

This Jesus who cared about the physical needs of people and fed the 5,000 was a God the Muslim war victims knew nothing about. They were intrigued to discover there was a God who loved them as they were, wanted to help them with the problems they faced, and to have a relationship with them.

Eventually, thousands of refugees heard the Gospel, often for the first time. Many knelt at the Cross at the close of Pastor Abraham's talk, finding joy and healing, taking the Good News to the countries where they relocated, and starting churches across the world.

Days after the spiteful, hijabed woman spit on her Cross, Nancy spotted the same black-clad woman slipping into the chapel, accompanied by a cluster of women and a young man.

"Hey!" she called, waving to Nancy across the courtyard.

"We didn't come for the food," she admitted with a sheepish half smile as Nancy welcomed her warmly. "We came to hear the talk."

People who gave food to their enemies and invited people who spit at them to return for more relief packages intrigued the woman.

As Nancy watched the woman lead her friends down the aisle, she marveled at God's work in the woman's heart. The hijabed woman, her friends, and son sat on the very front bench.

Abraham gave an altar call after every talk introducing the good news of the love of Jesus.

"Savior, I come. . . . Lead me to the Cross."

Nancy sang softly with the congregation. Her voice trailed off as she saw a young man walk up the aisle and kneel at the Cross, the Cross like the one his mother had spit upon. The very Cross she would one day kneel before as well.

Abraham prayed with the boy to receive Jesus, whose sacrifice the Cross represented. The teen's decision would cost him his friends, family, and perhaps his life, but he was not afraid. Love had vanquished hate.

How great is our God!

"I'LL WAIT FOR YOU!"

"Indeed, I count everything as loss because of the surpassing worth of knowing Christ Jesus my Lord. For his sake I have suffered the loss of all things and count them as rubbish, in order that I may gain Christ . . . that I may know him and the power of his resurrection, and may share his sufferings, becoming like him in his death, that by any means possible I may attain the resurrection from the dead . . . forgetting what lies behind and straining forward to what lies ahead, I press on toward the goal for the prize of the upward call of God in Christ Jesus."

Philippians 3:8, 10, 11, 14

"In spiritual warfare, remember that love and forgiveness are your most powerful weapons."

—Max Lucado

"My mother, my sister Maryam, my brother Lukose, and I were kidnapped by radicals, because we were Christians," Rahel Hassan, a student from a Christian home, shared with Nancy.

Like the mauling swipes of grizzly bears' claws across their bleeding hearts, Nancy's students bore the deep wounds of kidnappings, abuse, and witnessing the murders of family members. Horrific memories traumatized, haunted, and disabled.

Nancy listened to broken students sharing one tragic account after another. The abuses many girls endured were of the most heinous terror tactics of war, calculated to instill fear, humiliate, and dehumanize the communities.

"They chained our brother, forcing him to watch as the Islamic terrorists brutally tortured and violated my sister, my mother, and me. Lukose says our agonized screams still haunt him in his dreams. The horror of the memories of being helpless to protect his mother and sisters nearly drove him crazy. My father finally raised the money to pay the ransom for our release."

"If there is an omnipotent, loving God, why would He allow His children to go through such awful things?" Maryam demanded. "I want nothing to do with such a God."

"Why didn't He defend us? Why trust in a God who allows evil?"

So many questions tormented their fractured hearts.

"Jesus was there, in that terrible moment," Nancy consoled the girls as they wept in her arms. "You were not alone when those evil men tortured and abused you. Jesus was crying with you. He did not want it to happen. He experienced that horrible pain and shame right along with you."

Jesus, I trust your Holy Spirit's healing presence to minister to the fractured hearts, Nancy prayed, knowing words alone held little healing power.

"Your pain is very great. There's no way you can cope with the pain of your experience alone. But you don't need to carry it alone. Bring it back to His presence. Refuse to let the pain destroy you. Jesus knows what it feels like to be tortured unjustly, and He wants to heal you now. Lay the weight of it in his open hands and leave the healing to Him. You cannot carry it."

Love from the teachers, the church family, Bible study groups, and friends enveloped the girls, bringing healing. Praises sung in worship services in the midst of war and suffering encouraged their hearts. Stories of their God healing, delivering, and guiding brought hope.

"Man was evil," the Hassan girls realized. "Man was responsible for the pain we experienced, not God. God will avenge and wants to heal.

"If we can't trust Jesus, life is futile. Jesus is the only hope we have. We cannot let our hope be held ransom by the behavior of evil people in our past."

Nancy reminded her students experiencing pain and losses, "Jesus-followers suffer in this life because of evil. But as with the resurrection, God has a way of turning pain, horror, and loss into powerful, triumphant victory!

"Forgiveness is so powerful! It breaks the shackles that chain the victim's heart to the perpetrator. Forgiveness doesn't mean releasing the perpetrator from guilt and consequences, but it means turning those who hurt us over to God to deal with. He will deal with them so much better than you ever could. And forgiveness is the bridge to God's forgiveness of our own sins."

As Maryam and Rahel continued to pray, cry, release, and forgive, the healing grace of Jesus poured into their hearts and lives. And within the year they began to thrive, to serve, and even to lead.

Lukose faced his own journey of pain. Men were made to defend women. He was too traumatized to talk for months. The Holy Spirit kept pursuing him, healing him at every turn. Slowly, his wounds began to close. Rahel and Maryam saw their brother learn to look them in the eyes again without pain. They saw him breathe deeply and relax. He became a worship leader. And as he worshipped and led others in praising God, the healing power of God flowed over his life.

Nancy marveled at the healing, restorative power of Jesus. The Spirit held those precious hearts. Redemption shone from their lives.

Rahel's journey filled her with compassion for the countless other Syrian girls still carrying the pain and shame of the horrendous atrocities at the hands of militants. She identified deeply with their wounds and felt a call to facilitate healing among the devastated young Syrian war victims.

We must get our family out of Syria as soon as possible. Our children will never be safe or succeed in Syria, Rahel's parents decided. *We need to find healing in the security of knowing these horrific atrocities will never happen to our family again.*

Her father, Mr. Hassan, filled out form after form at the UN, applying for his family to emigrate to the United States. The father explained the painful story of why the family needed to leave Syria.

Meanwhile, Mathai Taleb, studying to be a pastor, was totally smitten with Rahel Hassan. The two connected deeply. Their life visions meshed perfectly in a desire to bring light and healing to the ashes of war. Mathai's pure, gentle, respectful love soothed the scars of her heart.

And Mathai knew of no one who could better support his ministry in Syria.

Except for the formality, the couple was basically engaged. They couldn't survive without the other.

When the envelope arrived with the official UN stamp and return address, Mr. Hassan ripped it open and snatched the letter, quickly scanning it.

"We've been accepted!" he shouted, as family gathered around him to investigate the cause of his excitement.

"We are emigrating to the US! Our application is accepted! We are going! Alleluia! Goodbye, war and missiles! Hello, peace and security!"

"Oh, thank you, Jesus!" Mrs. Hassan half sobbed, collapsing into a chair as if the weight of the horrific ordeal had fallen from her heart. "What an answer to our prayers!"

"Let's pack our bags!" Lukose shouted, dancing around the room with Maryam.

Only Rahel stood stoically in the hall, removed from the jovial celebrations, her face frozen into a mask of distraught terror. *I never thought the application would be approved. My heart is in Syria. I can't leave.*

"That's all fine for you, but just so you know, I'm not leaving," she disclosed quietly.

"Rahel dear," her mother said, holding her arms to the girl. "It will all work out," she soothed, sensing her daughter's turmoil and the cause. "Mathai can put in an application and come to America with us."

"No! You don't understand. Syria will never allow young men his age to leave." The words tumbled from her distraught heart. "They need every last male for the front lines. They don't let them emigrate.

"And he wouldn't leave if he could, you know that. His calling is here in Syria. And so is mine," she finished with a quiet decision.

The parents exchanged worried glances. *How can this be happening?*

"I am so happy for you and want you to go, but I can't go."

"But you *must!*" Mr. Hassan scanned the page again, his voice rising with frantic emotions mounting within him. "You *must* come with us! There is no option. We are accepted to emigrate under the conditions that the *entire* family goes to America together! None of us can go if you don't!"

The urgent intensity of the dilemma dropped a dark pall, extinguishing the celebrations of the moment before. How could they stay in Syria? But how could they force Rahel to leave and break her heart?

"If we can just get her to the US, she'll forget Mathai," Mrs. Hassan encouraged her husband that evening as they discussed the quandary privately. "You are right, we have to go. And we all must go."

Quietly, the family began selling their furnishings.

"Rahel, just come with us so the rest of us can emigrate," her father pleaded.

"And you will let me come back?" she asked, not daring to hope. "If I go with you temporarily so the rest of you can relocate to a safe place, then you will let me return?"

Mr. Hassan read the look in his wife's pained eyes. The two had discussed this option. "Yes, habibti, come with us, and when we are settled, you can return to your Syria and your love."

Rahel threw herself into her father's arms. "Then I will go—on that condition that you will let me come back and marry Mathai."

Had Damascus International Airport ever witnessed a more anguished separation? Through the tears of her convulsing sobs, Rahel could scarcely see the handsome form standing forlornly in the distance. She could barely make out the one waving hand and the other over his heart. But she remembered his words. "I'll wait for you, hayati, my rohi. I'll be waiting."

She will get over Mathai once she is in the comforts of America, her parents assured each other.

But Rahel did not get over her lover. She had been kidnapped and abused in Syria. Yes, she could peacefully live in the US, far from the bullets and missiles of war and beyond the reach of the radical terrorists. But her heart was in Syria. Her heart was with the young pastor. With her people. Her church. And her calling.

"Syrians are highly educated people of dignity who invested much into themselves; having their identity stripped away is not easy. Without identity, a man feels desperate," John encouraged Mr. Hassan.

"Find your identity in Christ first, not your nationality. Secure your identity in being a follower of Christ."

The Hassan family began to adjust and embrace their new home. Except for the love-smitten daughter, who continued to cry as she read the precious messages from the young pastor in Syria.

The family held many tearful discussions, but her parents refused to honor their promise to let Rahel return.

"Absolutely not. There is no way we will permit you to go back to Syria, to the war, to the rebels . . ."

"To my calling! My people! My love!"

"Never. Now forget him."

"God! How can I forget my soulmate? How can I forget Your calling?" she sobbed into her pillow night after night.

While her family healed, thrived, and became active in leading youth groups, Rahel pined and felt her soul shrivel. She fasted and prayed. And read and sent many endearing messages.

"I kept my part of the agreement," Rahel broached the subject once the family was comfortably settled. "Now I am ready to go back."

Mr. Hassan leaned forward in his chair, speaking gently but firmly.

"I am sorry, habibti, but Mama and I have talked, and we decided it is best you don't go back."

Rahel cried. She FaceTimed her beloved. She prayed and read her Bible. And fasted. And then she found her answer: "Whoever loves father or mother more than me is not worthy of me. . . ." Matthew 10:37.

And then she knew. She could not stay. Her parents could not block her from following God's will for her life. There was more to life than being safe! Safe was sterile. Safe was lifeless. Her heart beat with passion to serve God on the front lines where she was meant to be. With the man who loved her like no one else ever could.

"At least wait until you have your green card," friends urged her. "If you leave now, you will never be able to return."

But Rahel's heart could not wait. Maryam found the passport their parents had hidden. Friends purchased a ticket to Beirut from the airport in a neighboring state.

"I'm coming!" Rahel messaged her love, sending him her flight schedule.

Rahel caught a taxi to the airport, and when she was about to board the plane, she called her parents.

"I am flying back to Syria. My heart is in Syria. My love is in Syria. And my calling is in Syria. You cannot keep me from God's calling for my life. You promised."

The young pastor swept up his fiancée at the airport in a blissful, tearful, delighted embrace. "You've come home!"

Home to the Middle East with the sniper bullets, the rubble, the helicopters dropping barrel bombs, the radical terrorists, the empty grocery shelves, and propane shortages. Home to the people who loved and needed her.

Rahel walked the aisle to marry Mathai a week after her plane landed. Life was not about being safe or comfortable. It was about being where God called. On the front lines of the battle for Him. Even in a war zone.

Nancy wiped a tear as the glowing bride and the adoring, protective groom vowed to love in sickness and in health.

Only God could heal a crushed, traumatized victim of abuse and rape so entirely that she would risk leaving the security and comforts of the United States to return to the setting of her trauma, where the radical soldiers continued to rampage, and bombs and bullets still flew. To the country ranking last on the Global Peace Index, making it the most violent country in the world. . . . only God.

"CHRISTIANS
TO THE STAKE!"

"For we do not wrestle against flesh and blood, but against the rulers, against the authorities, against the cosmic powers over this present darkness, against the spiritual forces of evil in the heavenly places. Therefore take up the whole armor of God, that you may be able to withstand in the evil day, and having done all, to stand firm."

Ephesians 6:12

"No healthy Christian ever chooses suffering; he chooses God's will, as Jesus did, whether it means suffering or not."

—Oswald Chambers

"If you *must* travel to Aleppo during the war, absolutely do *not* take the bus," Pastor Abraham warned Silva.

"The radicals are stopping buses, pulling everyone off, checking IDs. And when they see you without a hijab and with a Christian name . . ."

How could Syria have changed so drastically?

"Daughter, you've been a missionary in Lebanon. You haven't heard how the black masked extremists in Syria yell, 'Alawites to the grave, Christians to the stake,' crucifying Christians in Aleppo and Raqqa.

"You don't understand their mentality. Not only do they say we are infidels, but they say Christians aren't fighting with them so they must be siding with the regime."

"But Baba, we prefer to contribute to society through humanitarian aid rather than fighting with any of the factions."

"So true. But you have to understand that fighting is such a part of ISIS's religious fabric. It's all they know. A prominent Syrian intellect has said it better than I could: 'Do not ask me about the number of Syrian Christians in the Syrian army, but rather ask me about their contribution towards the buildings of factories, hospitals, and schools; I can list many.'"

"You have to go, don't you?" Mama asked as Silva shouldered her backpack to head for the train station.

"God's work doesn't shut down in a war, Mama. It picks up the pace. I need to work out the arrangements for the youth conference. The difficulties of the war have shaken the youth. Their hearts are tender and ripe for God to work. Baba says, 'It's God's time.'"

Amalee nodded, "Then I will pack you some sfiha for your trip and a couple apricots I picked from our tree. All I can say is you certainly are 'that lion's cub!'" She smiled with proud trepidation, nodding significantly toward her husband.

Abraham placed his arm around his daughter. "Come Mama, let's pray for Silva." Abraham petitioned God to direct his daughter with wisdom, and to keep His hand over her as she courageously ventured out in the Father's work. "Your Kingdom come, Your will be done. . . . Deliver us from evil!" he finished powerfully.

As the train hurtled over the bridges toward Aleppo, Silva flinched at the random explosions followed by the billowing smoke.

From the train window, the traveler caught a glimpse of the lush green Anti-Lebanon mountain range straddling the border between Syria and Lebanon. On the southern tail of the range, the regal 9,000-foot peaks of Mount Hermon rose majestically over the borders of Syria, Lebanon, and Israel, inspiring a worshipful aura as it had for centuries. Some of David's Psalms praised its lofty majesty, Baba said.

Still arrayed in a layer of his regal wintery coat, Mount Hermon's outer layers had melted into the pristine rivulets flowing toward the Jordan or the Barada Rivers. Baba said according to Deuteronomy 3:8, the mountain range marked the northern border of the Promised Land conquered by Joshua.

The pristine mountain vistas uncorked refreshing memories for Silva. She fondly recalled accompanying Baba and the family to the delightful, cool mountain villages during school vacations each summer when Baba discipled the church too distant to include on his weekly circuit.

Baba gave God his all, teaching or administrating the school during the week and itinerant preaching across Syria on weekends. Dear Baba must have been exhausted, living as intensely as he did. No wonder he passed out one Sunday while preaching in the fifth church.

The refreshing mountain slopes sheltered resorts hosting wealthy guests from exotic places such as Saudi Arabia. While Baba taught and discipled the local believers, Silva's older sisters Nancy and Joanna courageously engaged the affluent, fully covered Saudi women, sharing the love of Jesus.

As the train wheels rumbled beneath her, Silva relaxed into the seat, savoring each spicy nibble of Mama's delightful sfiha with hints of tomato, onion, and rich spices tucked among the fried meat and the soft dough, knowing what it had cost to make. *A kilo of tomatoes that once cost 40 Syrian pounds now costs seven hundred.*

Mama is the most selfless, generous person I know, Silva thought.

Mama even invited Bedouin women dropping off market orders to sit on her couches after squatting among the market dust and critters all day and listened to their troubles.

If I ever have a daughter, I will name her Amalee.

As the train chugged north through the desert, the ancient fortress of the Aleppo Citadel rose in imposing command above the souks, mosques, and madrassas of the ancient walled city.

According to tradition, the patriarch, Abraham, pastured his sheep on the mountains of Aleppo on the way to Canaan, sharing the milk with the poor, which gave the city its name.

Silva left the meeting with a notebook packed with ideas for an exciting, inspiring youth rally. Grabbing her backpack, she popped into the train station to book her return ticket.

"Sold out. Try the bus line," the agent yawned as if she had repeated the line all afternoon.

"Impossible! There must be a mistake! I must get on that train!" A hand of fear seemed to clutch her heart.

"Sorry. Check about a bus ticket."

Buses are unsafe with their random checks by extremist militias, Baba had warned.

"Everyone's heading to Damascus tomorrow," the agent divulged. "The sick and the wounded going to hospitals, refugees fleeing. . . . Everyone's going. All 480 seats are filled. It's most unusual, I know. I'm sorry."

Unbelievable. What would Baba and Mama say if they knew? Silva felt weak, and her stomach twisted with nausea. *Why didn't I purchase the ticket sooner?* But she hadn't been concerned because the train to Damascus was never filled. As she stumbled into the bus station and purchased a ticket for the next departure, her legs felt like the yogurt Mama served for breakfast.

Baba's warning flashed ominously in her brain: "Absolutely do *not* take the buses. ISIS soldiers are stopping the buses and pulling everyone off. . . ."

Lord, I thought You were watching over me!

"I am watching over you, my child. I've got you covered," the Lord whispered to her heart. As she collapsed into a bus seat, her heart relaxed into a restful peace.

The entire trip back, Silva felt at rest. *Whatever happens, God's hand is over me. I am his daughter.* She leaned back in her seat and slept.

She stirred as the bus slowed, approaching Damascus. The ancient walls that embraced the city for nearly two millennia emanated the feeling of security that had drawn so many refugees to the city. Since 3,000 BC, people had settled in this "axis of the world," drawing caravans traveling the Silk Road and pilgrims journeying to Mecca.

The clear Barada River flowed along the highway, carrying melted snow from Mount Hermon to ancient Roman aqueducts, delivering drinking water to Damascus and watering the oasis of the Ghouta surrounding the Damascene plateau.

I can understand why leprous Naaman, general to Damascene King Haddad, stormed off when prophet Elisha told him to bathe seven times in the Jordan. " 'Are not . . . the rivers of Damascus, better than all the waters of Israel? Could I not wash in them and be clean?' So, he turned and went away in a rage." II Kings 5:12.

Like a lush green belt of olive, nut, apricot, and citrus groves, the Ghouta separated Damascus from the dry grasses bordering the Syrian Desert. The groves were glutted with olives hanging from crippled trees, blood-red pomegranates splitting their skins, swollen walnuts, mulberries, figs, mandarins, and dangling clusters of grapes.

"The gardens . . . embrace it (Damascus) like the chalice embraces its flower. . . . Those who said, If paradise is on earth, then without doubt Damascus is part of it. If it is in heaven, then it competes with it and shares the glory."

But now, rebels began holing up in the countryside, resulting in one of the most devastating sieges of the war, followed by the dropping of barrel bombs to flush them out.

Yet, today, Damascus felt sleepily serene as Silva stepped off the bus.

As she walked through the door of her parents' flat, Mama looked up at her with startled, tear-filled eyes.

"Silva! How did you get here! Oh, thank God! Thank God you are safe!" Baba's dark brows puckered in concern.

"Of course, I am safe, Baba! You prayed for God to deliver us from evil. What's upsetting you?"

"You haven't seen? There's been a terrible train accident! The passenger train was sabotaged! The radicals removed a connector between rails right at the curve before a bridge. They intentionally planned to ditch this passenger train into the water. The first car derailed and caught fire.

"The engineer was killed. Other cars derailed, throwing the passengers out and injuring dozens. And then the rebels shot at the train and the passengers! Mostly women and children coming to Damascus for medical care."

Silva sank into the well-used sofa. ISIS soldiers might scream, "Christians to the stake, Alawites to the coffin," but a mighty God in heaven had the last word. He really did have the reins in his hands, like the lines of Mama's favorite song: "Though storms surround, You will not forsake us. Through wisdom, You alone have the world in Your control. The reins are in Your hand."

How great is our God!

Early in the morning after his nightly prayer time with God, Abraham knocked briskly on John and Mero's bedroom door.

"Get ready. Mama and I are taking you and Mero to get her documents," Abraham announced. "Don't worry about the checkpoints. God will take care of them."

CHECKPOINT

"Stand therefore, having fastened on the belt of truth, and having put on the breastplate of righteousness, and, as shoes for your feet, having put on the readiness given by the gospel of peace. In all circumstances take up the shield of faith, with which you can extinguish all the flaming darts of the evil one; and take the helmet of salvation, and the sword of the Spirit, which is the word of God, praying at all times in the Spirit, with all prayer and supplication . . ."

Ephesians 6:14-17

"Jesus didn't die to keep us safe, He died to make us dangerous. Faithfulness is not holding the fort. It's storming the gates of hell. The will of God is not an insurance plan. It's a daring plan. The complete surrender of your life to the cause of Christ isn't radical. It's normal. It's time to quit living as if the purpose of life is to arrive safely at death. It's time to go all in and all out for the All in All. Pack your coffin!"

—Mark Batterson

John blinked sleepily at the silhouette of his father standing in the darkened doorway.

You have got to be kidding. Driving several hours through a war zone with more checkpoints than streetlights!

Dad, it's too dangerous—even for you! You are on the hit list! John wanted to say. But he knew his father must have heard from God. Besides, few could navigate the roads around Damascus with the combined speed and dexterity of Abraham. John didn't argue with his father.

As he opened the car door for Mero, John noted the bullet holes riddling the side of Baba's car, evidence of past divine protection. He couldn't forget his father's warning, "You've got to leave, John. You know what happened to Mikayel's son. If you get stopped at a checkpoint, you don't have the exemption of a university student since you are through school, so you will be forced to join the regime forces, the rebels, or the radicals. It isn't safe for you to live in Syria."

Scarcely a shred of color brightened the landscape for miles, except a brave leaf or two sprouting from a shredded vine. Putrid smoke of burning rubber and tanks smothered Damascus's jasmine-scented breezes.

"*'Behold, Damascus will cease to be a city and will become a heap of ruins . . .'*" Pastor Abraham murmured. "Isaiah 17:1 has never yet been fulfilled in history."

The car windows framed an apocalyptic view. The outskirts of an ancient city lay ravished and disgraced. Missile fire stripped her of her draping bougainvillea vines, toppling courtyard fountains, lying shattered and silent on her dusty mosaic tiles. Ancient aristocratic edifices, hospitals, and schools crouched as crumbling shells, flanked with rubble and debris.

The Syrian proverb once claimed: "A virgin may travel alone at midnight and be safe, and a purse of gold dropped in the road at midday will never be stolen." But not anymore. Not in the war in 2011.

Beyond the headlights of the small car, half a dozen gunmen loomed out of the smoke, shrouding the skeletal remains of bombed buildings on the outskirts of the ancient city of Damascus. Mounds of sandbags and manned tanks towering along the roadsides signaled the entrance to the war zone. A "flying" checkpoint—a temporary and unannounced makeshift checkpoint—one of the most dangerous spots in Syria. One never knew which militia group monitored this artery. One could never tell who they might be trolling for—the opposing militia, Christians, or men who had failed to enlist.

Pastor Abraham braked, easing the car to a rolling stop at the end of the line of vehicles. In the back seat, John read the apprehension in his bride's gentle eyes. He longed to reassure Mero. But in the crossfire of war, there was no promise of security. He prayed the mantle of darkness hid her loveliness from vile eyes.

CHECKPOINT 137

"This is the place they shot up my brother's car." Abraham gestured toward a bullet-riddled vehicle with every window blown out, abandoned among blackened, molten shells of battle casualties along the road. He eased the car forward as the vehicles in the line ahead began to move toward the gunmen flanked by massive tanks and sandbags.

John squeezed Mero's hand. "If we can just get through these checkpoints, we'll have your passport and be on a flight to Houston," he assured her with his endearing wink she so loved. "No missiles exploding in the night, no cries for help, no crumbling churches, no stench of bodies on the roadside, no ISIS checkpoints. . . . Just wide-open, peaceful, grassy prairies."

His rapid breathing betrayed the cover of bravado he put on for his young wife. The tapping foot betrayed the tension inside.

Don't let them figure out we are Christians! Please, God!

The crumbling skeletal remains of an ancient church building on the roadside, hatefully stripped of its crosses, screamed of the acidic animosity of ISIS toward Christ's followers.

John shoved the tales from his mind, those telling of the torture, crucifixions, forced conversions, and stolen daughters. . . .

Beyond the checkpoint, John spotted shadowy clusters of children and hijabed women burdened with bags, bundles, and babies, trekking toward somewhere far beyond the range of bullets.

A gunman thrust the barrel of his AK-47 into the driver's open window inches from Abraham's unflinching face as the car rolled to a stop. "IDs!" the soldier snapped. "And be fast!" Gunmen surrounded the little vehicle, barrels of AK-47s trained on its occupants. Rows of manned tanks towered above the road on either side.

John's glance took in the assortment of camouflage uniforms mixed with street clothes, combat boots, loaded taupe ammunition belts, black balaclavas covering the bearded faces, and machine guns. *Radicals.*

His heart pounded as the armed checkpoint triggered the unwelcome flashback of the Lebanon border encounter. He remembered the

Hezbollah soldier discovering John's Bible in his backpack . . . *the disbe-lief and doom as the cold handcuffs closed around his wrists . . . the nausea of the putrid, black, rat-infested cell.*

While the occupants extracted the IDs from their wallets, Abraham reached into a briefcase John had not noticed before.

"I would like to give you the most precious gift the world has ever known." Abraham smiled warmly, handing the soldier a *BIBLE!*

John felt the air being strangled in his lungs. *Baba! What are you doing?*

I would never have gotten into this car if I knew you brought a bag of Bibles!

The soldier snatched at the book, but Abraham kept it firmly grasped between his hands.

"If you promise me you will read this book, I will let you have this most precious gift the world has ever known," Abraham declared, locking his gaze with steely black eyes glaring out from behind the mask.

"Only if you promise to read it." While Abraham kept the gaze of the gunman, he gripped the book the soldier tried to yank from his grasp.

John knew, any second, the terrorist would lose patience.

The fearless pastor and fierce radical soldier each gripped a side of the Bible with mutual determination.

Dad, LET GO of the Bible! If he wants it, let him have it! Let's just get out of here before they decide to take more than we offered!

But Abraham would not release the Bible without the soldier's promise.

"I'll read it," the soldier snapped, snatching the gift from Abraham, yanking the car door open. "Get out!" the guard ordered.

"Have you heard about how God loves us . . . " Calm, gentle, coura-geous Baba began sharing the Gospel with the masked soldiers, unfazed by the AK-47s and munition belts. And that was Dad. He lived all out for Christ with no fear of death.

"Say a prayer to your God for us!" the soldier commanded.

Baba placed his arms around those radical soldiers. He prayed with the same passion, intimacy, and confidence John heard him pray in his living room at 2:00 in the morning. If one picture was imprinted on John's mind regarding his father, it was Baba on his knees. Praying.

But how vulnerable his father appeared, surrounded by radical soldiers. One wrong word would unleash a volley of bullets. First, the slugs would drop Baba, and then . . .

John wanted to pray for his father, but the terror squeezed the air from his lungs.

As Abraham shared the Gospel and prayed, the passengers witnessed a flicker of life and healing amid violence and war.

The line of vehicles continued to grow behind the Samaras at the checkpoint, but none of the impatient drivers dared honk.

With his arms around the soldiers, Abraham prayed confidently, loudly, to the God he knew so intimately, interceding for the salvation and welfare of these precious souls so blinded by the enemy. He prayed for their families, their leaders. . . .

"Now, Father, we ask You to show these precious men You are the God of love and relationship instead of hate and revenge. The God who loves these soldiers so much that You gave Your precious Son to be slaughtered for their sins so that they could get to heaven. So these precious soldiers can get to heaven without having to die a martyr's death because the Son of God has died the martyr's death in their place."

John and Mero could almost feel the glow of the transcendent love of God overpowering evil in that dark checkpoint surrounded by tanks and AK-47s. Amid the violence and hate, the healing of the Cross had reached down to spread the light of hope.

As Baba slid back into his seat, bringing the car to life, John released his breath in a muffled, relieved chuckle. He met his wife's eyes. *Unbelievable! Only Dad!*

No one spoke a word in the tension and awe of the moment.

Whenever John drove with Baba, there was little conversation as

Baba's fervent prayers always filled the vehicle. As the small car bounced around the rubble-strewn, missile-pitted road, Abraham prayed for the soldiers who received the Bible. And prayed over the soldiers at the next checkpoint.

The next checkpoint! John clenched the seat ahead of him in panic. Checkpoints could come and go overnight. Especially lying like the "Millionaire Checkpoint" manned by criminals charging hundreds of dollars in "tax" to those transporting merchandise. Occasionally, the radicals demanded vehicles at the Millionaire Checkpoints. Sometimes, they abducted boys and men, forcing them to serve their diminishing army.

The opposition forces, the regime, and the radicals all snared forced recruits at their checkpoints to join their forces. Syrian law mandated every male between the ages of eighteen and forty-two serve two years in the military unless they carried a signed exemption to study at a university. The university sent lists of graduates to the government. The regime soldiers screened for the new graduates at the regime checkpoints. John carried no exemption.

To avoid forced conscription into the army, Aleppo men dressed in burkas to slip through checkpoints. In response to the men hiding under burkas, the army set up a team of female soldiers to search suspicious burka-clad passengers at each checkpoint.

Syrians didn't fear the barrel bombs or dying, but if they were arrested, they would die a thousand deaths. Arrest inevitably meant brutal torture, and the terrifying risk of betraying family or friends on a different side of the conflict than the captors.

Another checkpoint!

"*God, close Baba's mouth.*" John prayed. "*Don't let him speak. We just want our documents so my bride and I can leave this war-torn country. I don't want Baba to get all of us killed trying to get through the checkpoints to get our documents!*"

"Baba, please! Don't try that again!"

"John, how can we neglect sharing the most precious gift with those who need the love of God the most?"

A truck loaded with putrid, swollen bodies passed from the other direction, punctuating Abraham's urgency.

Abraham slowed the car but not his prayer as the traffic stopped ahead. John peered around his father's head to see the AK-47-toting gunmen. He slunk lower in the seat.

Please, Jesus, save us. Don't let Baba speak!

Abraham did seem to have a special connection with God, but one could not expect the mercy of a second radical Islamic soldier if Dad tried to hand him a Bible! Mercy from multiple radical soldiers in one day was too much to expect!

As the line of cars eased ahead, starting and stopping as the militants scanned the occupants of each vehicle and inspected their IDs, John thought of how his father really seemed to live under the shadow of God's wings.

"I don't know anyone else with such a close relationship with God," John often told Mero. "He lives so close to the Lord, he's so in tune, that he constantly hears the guiding voice of God.

"I live in awe of Baba," John had admitted to his wife. "He is kind of a legend of a man who emanates the divine spirit of God with whom he spends so many hours."

How many times has God spared Baba? he wondered. *But he is not invincible. These radical militants can't be trusted. Doesn't the Syrian proverb say, "It is not every time the clay pot survives?"*

As the car inched to a stop, a soldier whipped open the door, not waiting for Abraham to open his window.

"Give me your papers!"

"I want to give you the best gift the world has ever . . ." Abraham's dynamic, confident voice rang with authority as he extended a Bible toward the soldier. "Because we love Jesus . . ."

Somehow, the soldier waved them through. And so it went through each checkpoint.

By the time Abraham pulled into the crowded parking lot in front of the government agency, John's nerves felt shredded.

"I will walk the documents through for you," Abraham offered, willing to use his diplomatic experience to navigate the labyrinth of Arab bureaucracy. Abraham took Mero's file on one hand, and the briefcase of Bibles in the other, striding confidently toward the agency staffed with Muslim and Marxist officials.

Not here! Please! John wanted to say. *You'll jeopardize our chances of leaving the country!*

But respectfully, he remained silent. He lagged far behind his father, pretending not to know him.

John had learned to act with caution in order to survive. One needed to maneuver with discretion in this Islamic nation with Marxist government officials and Mukhabarat interrogation dungeons. Memories of the Hezbollah prison cell were still too fresh for John.

Under the rule of the president's father, Syrians whispered, "One can mention the name of God, but not the president." Citizens used different nicknames for Hafez al-Assad to avoid being overheard by the Mukhabarat and tortured. The fear lit a paranoia in the hearts of the citizens, casting a shroud over even the ordinary tasks of applying for a passport or driver's license.

And the Mukhabarat were everywhere.

But Abraham was fearless. He felt the presence of God within him so powerfully that he was not intimidated. Nor was he about to miss this opportune moment to share "the best gift the world has ever known" with these government officials gripped in the crisis of war.

Abraham took a place in the line with his briefcase of Bibles. With the erect bearing, well-groomed hair, and dignified features, he could certainly be mistaken for a diplomat.

John stood aloof to the side of the wall with Mero, monitoring his father's progress from the corner of his eye.

Abraham handed the documents to the clerk at the desk. As she processed them, John noticed his father dialoguing with her. And then the pastor opened his briefcase and began offering her "the best gift the world has ever known."

A cold tremor ran through John's body. *Baba, you know how offensive it is to share the Christian faith, in a Muslim country, at a government office, especially when you have a long line behind you!*

Please, please God. Beads of sweat dripped from his forehead. Panic crushed the air from his lungs.

Moments passed with those in line behind the pastor growing restless.

Glancing at the clerk, John's breath caught in his throat. *Tears? Really?* The receptionist was actually crying!

John's muscles sagged in relief and he wiped his forehead with the back of his arm. *Only God. Only Baba . . .*

A gentle Voice seemed to whisper gently to John's heart: *This war-torn country is filled with people desperately searching for a ray of hope. And you have that hope. Can't you share it?*

The tormenting claws of fear and shame fell away. An overwhelming awe of the power of the Gospel, the power arming his dad with confident, fearless authority, wrapped his quaking heart like a woolen blanket.

It was God's time for Syria, and Abraham would not miss the opportunity, even inside a government agency.

You are right, Lord. Because of the uncertainty of wartime, Syrians are more desperate for hope than ever. And more open to the truths of the Bible.

John and Mero followed Abraham from office to office as he snipped through the red tape. But they followed at a distance, just in case.

A few hours later, with a broad smile and a flourish, Abraham handed Mero the documents—her key to leave Syria.

It would have taken anyone else weeks, John knew.

Maneuvering back through the war zone, the small car shot past the armed tanks, shells of burned vehicles, sandbags, rubble heaps, and collapsed buildings like a rabbit pursued by a fox.

Baba continued to share the world's most precious gift with the radical militants at the checkpoints, but John no longer cringed.

Baba had it right. Distributing "the best gift the world has ever known" is far more urgent than acquiring documents or flying out of this war zone. Baba operates with an eternal mentality, while I fretted about temporal, physical safety.

Thank you, God, for not answering my prayers.

Like Rami said, "Dad carries his Cross all the time, everywhere he goes. It's in every part of his life." For Abraham, sharing the Gospel was a way of life.

What a treasure we have in the Word. What power.

With what simplicity Baba shares the Gospel. "Because we love Jesus."

John refocused, slipping back under the Cross, running hard beside his beloved dad, his eyes on the goal and his ear to the heartbeat of God. *God, I am totally invested into fulfilling your mission for my life.*

"So, Dad, since I apparently am going to try to be a bridge between the churches in the West and the suffering churches in the MENA region, what shall we call this organization?"

"Why not go with Ananias House, connecting it with our Ananias House organization here in the Middle East?" Abraham suggested. "Ananias House after Ananias who prayed for Paul here in Damascus, helping the persecutor become the proclaimer."

As John and Mero buckled their seatbelts, the pilot welcomed the passengers, announcing, "You are very fortunate. This is the very last international flight out of Damascus. We won't be flying in and out of Syria any longer."

"If someone says 'Syria' three times, I will faint," John whispered to Mero, draining his Coke. For the first time in months, he began to relax from the immense strain of the continual adrenaline surges of sheltering from barrel bomb attacks, living in a war zone, and serving the desperate needs.

The airliner lifted over the smoke. John brushed away Mero's tears as they scanned the trampled vineyards, shredded orchards, crowded graveyards, and the majestic "bearded" mountains dusted in snow.

And they wept for the ravaged church buildings—empty and dark, stripped of their Crosses, littered with ripped songbooks, walls covered with graffiti and bullet holes and filled with rubble and dust. They cried for the suffering church family left behind to face the ISIS soldiers, the missiles, and the empty market stalls. And they wept for the hearts turning to Jesus when their world collapsed around them.

Far below, they could make out the Damascus-Airport Motorway heading north from the airport to the Jaramana neighborhood of their beloved apartment with the wedding gifts and their dreams. They saw the rows of tanks and the flattened buildings around their apartment. But in the light of the war, their love nest no longer mattered. Buildings, wedding gifts, and furnishings could be replaced, but limbs and lives could not.

As the plane entered the clouds, the smoke of war vanished beneath them, leaving behind the smells of putrefying bodies, burning tires, chlorine barrel bombs, and gunpowder. And among the Syrian ruins lay part of John's heart.

He would return to the Middle East, serving as a bridge between the suffering persecuted believers in the Middle East and the supporting, praying churches in the West. He would come to mentor young leaders who would be beaten, kidnapped, and shot at as they tried to reach his training conferences. He would become a "voice crying in the wilderness." And a price would be placed on his head. But he was "that lion's cub."

What lies ahead for Syria? For the Middle East? And for the precious churches? the couple wondered as the smoke of the conflict vanished behind them.

ISA—"ALLAHU AKBAR!"

(Aleppo, Syria, circa 2012)

"So we have the prophetic word made more certain . . . as to a lamp shining in a dark place, until the day dawns and the light breaks through the gloom and the morning star arises in your hearts."

II Peter 1:19

"The Cross is the greatest example of humility and devotion in the universe. Jesus put your needs ahead of His own. He considered you more valuable than Himself."

—Chip Ingram

With little warning, Aleppo, the second largest city in Syria, found itself in the maw of the civil war. Rebels holed up in the souks, tunnels, and ancient citadel.

And like a swarm of angry wasps, helicopters and planes followed the rebels to Aleppo, south of the Turkish border, dropping barrels of chemicals and cluster bombs.

Rumors claimed that only 10 percent of Aleppo's 70,000 factories continued to function. Roadblocks and ravished farms sent egg prices soaring, while rocketing meat prices stripped kebabs and kibbeh from the household tables, replacing them with lentil soups, when propane could be purchased, and plain pita bread. Electricity functioned for one hour and then was off for five. While the villagers nearly starved, it was said ISIS hoarded food surpluses.

"I can't figure it all out," one of Samira's youngsters ventured. "The war's too complicated for me. There's the Turks, Iranians, Russians, and Jihadists from all over the world, the Americans, and then the Syrian army."

With his military connections, Abdul had untangled the confusing snarl of the octopus's arms of the war.

"It's like this: everyone is serving their own interests, wanting to reach in for a piece of the lamb's leg. The Saudis and Turks want to replace our Shia Alawite president with a dependable Sunni patron. Iran and Hezbollah cling to their lone toehold in the Arab world. Russia has its own political goals while Obama dithers around, hoping the regime will collapse on itself. And, of course, the Jihadists see this as their opportunity to grab land for the caliphate.

"The president is like a man on two false legs—one is Russia, and one is Iran. He keeps hopping from one leg to the other because the ground he is standing on is scorching. And now, it's all boiling down to the people realizing the regime is the only barrier against a more toxic chaos. And it's been said the president is the only one that can protect us from his own devils."

And so, the nation was embroiled in a war few understood, and no one could stop bringing on the brutal siege of Aleppo, the battle known as the "mother of all wars."

With planes overhead and carriers from various nations flanking the coast, and the extremists holing up in the labyrinth of passageways of Souq al-Medina like rats in a sewer, the situation looked increasingly worrisome.

Samira embraced the ancient Syrian proverb, "The door that brings in the wind, close it and rest."

"Whatever disturbs you, shut it out," her mother had often said. "Keep away from trouble and sing to it."

But trouble would not be lulled to sleep, nor would war stay outside a closed door. When mortar supply ran low, the regime pounded Aleppo with barrel bombs loaded with metal shrapnel and occasional chemicals, while the Free Syrian Army (FSA) dropped hell's canons, improvised rockets equipped with a gas canister to intensify the explosion. The devastating, indiscriminately launched barrel bombs drove terror into the hearts of the Aleppines and motivated tens of thousands to flee their homes and country.

The rumble of the incoming bombers sent Abdul's family diving beneath their beds, hands covering their ears, bracing for the blasts.

With a spark that changed Aleppo forever, stripping her of centuries of history, a skirmish around the Souq al-Medina ignited an inferno blasting through the 500-year-old heart of the city and the crown jewel of Aleppo. Insatiable tongues of flames dove through the vaulted, medieval labyrinth of stone passageways like fire-breathing dragons pursuing the very soul of Aleppo. Rapacious flames devoured sacks of wool, silks, carpets, textiles, ceramics, pastries, mounds of spices, and priceless antiques, leaving behind thick ashes, heaps of rubble, and thick black smoke. And stripping the city of her beating heart.

Dark clouds of smoke draped over the city for days as if cloaking it in black robes of mourning.

"First they stole everything, and now they are burning the rest!" Abdul stormed.

Jihadis and rebels holed up in the well-fortified ancient fortresses and historic sites. A missile took out the historic iron gate. Snipers shot from slots in the twelfth-century fortification as if the Medieval Ages had never ended. Finally, an explosion in the tunnels beneath the citadel did what the crusaders and invaders had not done in eight centuries of history, leaving the regal monarch sprawled in ruined disgrace with only dusty memories of its grandeur.

After the children slept, Abdul and Samira sat up, discussing their options. *Should we flee to Lebanon, Jordan, or Türkiye for a few months until the fighting dies down?*

The savage foreign ISIS soldiers worried Abdul more than Syrian fighters on either side.

"I keep hearing ISIS is kidnapping boys Ali's age and forcing them to fight," Abdul divulged. "But that's nothing towards what I have been hearing about the fate of the girls . . ."

"Like the father's terrible dilemma." Samira shivered. She thought about the story of how ISIS extremists broke into a home, bursting into the room where the man's lovely daughter was hiding. The father tried to protect his daughter, but the terrorists forced him to his knees, holding a knife to his throat while they prepared to take his daughter to become a bride for the ISIS prince.

The father pled with the terrorists to take anything he owned but to leave his only daughter. When the father's eyes met the daughter's, he remembered the pact they had made if this time ever came.

"Well, if you must take her for your prince, let her prepare to go as a bride," the father conceded charmingly.

A bride prepared for their prince, why not? The ISIS terrorist agreed to return. When they came back at the appointed time, the girl's body lay in the graveyard.

The story of the father's terrible predicament kept Samira awake at night. *I am so thankful my oldest daughter is married and safely out of the country, but what of my six precious, fragile jasmine flowers!*

"Don't you think it's time to leave?" Samira asked Abdul. "All around us, families are heading out."

"And take the risk of our car being taken, our money stolen, and our daughters, too?" he bellowed. "That's what's been happening at the ISIS checkpoints. And if we made it through the checkpoints, then what? We'd live like animals in a tent with a dirt floor in a country where we'd have no work permit, and the children would have no education. And who knows what else goes on?"

"But wouldn't it be worth it to take the risk?"

"We are fairly secure here in the country. Samira, you worry too much. We are far more comfortable here in our own beds and with our own garden and cows. Let's not be in a hurry. The war could soon be over."

His confident tone soothed her troubled heart. Life would go on here in the shadow of the plateau where Abraham had grazed his sheep. All would soon be peaceful and normal again.

But in his heart, Abdul, the veteran soldier, knew it was a matter of time. He quietly began to sell the goats and cows to save money. Secretly, he asked his connections about the best destination for refugees, the safest route, and the most secure time to travel.

And then a truck of ISIS soldiers careened in the lane, dust flying, AK-47s and black flags waving, accompanied by the bone-chilling shouts of "Allahu Akbar!"

"Allahu Akbar?" *What kind of god was Allah to send his soldiers out to terrorize women and children in his name? And quoting his Qur'an as they beheaded their victims?*

The shrieks shot shivers through Samira's heart, cracking a fissure in the foundation of her religious beliefs.

The frenzied jihadi soldiers leaped from the bullet-riddled truck. Several masked terrorists ran across the meadow, snatching a pair of bleating goats, and others sprinted to the house, smashing through the doors, seizing phones, money, food, ripping open drawers, dumping their contents on the floor, slitting open mattresses to the shouts of "Allahu Akbar!"

Samira's heart froze when she saw the smirks on the masked faces spotting her daughters.

"A whole harem in one house!" one guffawed.

Not if I can help it! Samira's heart screamed.

Part III

In the Crucible of Conflict

(2008–2016)

"The LORD is my light and my salvation—whom shall I fear? The LORD is the stronghold of my life—of whom shall I be afraid?

Though an army camp against me my heart shall not fear."

Psalm 27:1, 3

"If our goal is reducing persecution, that task is easily achieved. First, just leave Jesus alone.

Second, if you do happen to find Him, just keep Him to yourself. Persecution stops immediately where there is no faith and where there is no witness."

—Nik Ripkin, *The Insanity of God*

BROKEN CROSSES

(Maaloula, Syria, 2013)

"Since Christ suffered in the flesh [and died for us], arm yourselves [like warriors] with the same purpose [being willing to suffer for doing what is right and pleasing God]. . . ."

I Peter 4:1 (AMP)

"Suffering is not the end of the road as most Christians think, but the starting point of our Christian life. The end is the joy set before us."

—Rami Ibrahim

Tucked into the sides of rose-colored cliffs, the ancient Christian city of Maaloula sat in the crosshairs of the radical Islamic terrorists slashing a swath across Syria.

"We will not fight," Maaloulan Christians determined early in the sectarian war. A quiet peace draped the remote village set among the apricot groves attracting songbirds fifty kilometers north of Damascus, in the foothills of the Anti-Lebanon Mountains.

For centuries, the Christians and their Muslim neighbors in the Christian enclave lived together as a happy family. But when Muslim men returned from working in Saudi Arabia and Qatar, Christians noticed they brought back frighteningly radical dogma. Their speech echoed the frightening shouts of Al Baghdadi, the black-clad, self-designated guerilla caliph.

Observing the fracturing of Syria, Baghdadi rallied ISIS and al-Nusra radicals to take advantage of the unrest to conquer Syrian towns to begin forming the legendary end-time caliphate. His extreme brutality and predatory strategy alienated him from his al-Qaeda roots while energizing his followers. "Terrorism is to worship Allah," he ranted. And extremist Islamic Maaloulans embraced his cries.

The radical Maaloulans mysteriously disappeared.

"They joined al-Qaeda's radical breakaway, Jabhat al-Nusra," the community whispered. The Christians cared for the wives and children left behind. Until families quietly left town at the end of August in 2013.

As the sun rose above the cliffs on September 4, 2013, Maaloulans spied an entourage of trucks snaking through the valley. Pickups mounted with DShK Soviet anti-aircraft machine guns stole toward the gate guarding Maaloula. Beneath black flags long bearded foreigners waved guns and swords.

Village men sent frantic texts to the government soldiers guarding the entrance. Desperate calls to the guards' cell phones, their radios, and their landlines received no response. Villagers fired warning shots. But all was still at the gate.

A Jordanian suicide bomber slammed his truck into the ancient arched stone gate guarding the entrance to the picturesque mountain enclave. A massive explosion hurled stone, mortar, metal, and body parts into the morning air.

For two thousand years, Christians found refuge in this secluded mountain gorge protected by steep cliffs and narrow passageways. The legends and legacy of the old town were as rich as the priceless pre-Byzantine artifacts and medieval paintings soon to be looted, smashed, and burned by the al-Qaeda branch of al-Nusra and its radical brothers.

According to the first century Apocryphal story, Thecla, daughter of a pagan prince and a disciple of Paul fleeing persecution, found refuge and refreshment in the cliff's caves and springs.

Searching for tranquility and healing, pilgrims of all religions from across the Middle East streamed to the picturesque village. They hiked through a narrow cliff passage to reach the natural amphitheater sheltering Mar Thecla convent, the cave and the stream legendary for its healing properties.

For generations, doctors sent patients to the peaceful valley carpeted with grapevines and groves of olive and apricot trees and grazing sheep to find healing in the refreshing air, curative waters, and tranquil scenery. President Assad and his wife indulged in occasional excursions to the serene healing oasis.

Silhouetted against the sky, a Cross marked the fourth-century clifftop Mar Sarkis monastery high above the village, named for a Christian Roman officer who was beheaded for refusing to pray to Jupiter.

For nearly two millennia, the resilient Maaloulans maintained their Christian beliefs and Aramaic language. They took pride in being one of the last villages on the planet speaking Aramaic, the language of Jesus, and the language they believed He would speak at his return.

With its ancient churches, its Crosses, and its reputation as one of the oldest Christian enclaves, Maaloula served as a Syrian mascot of Christianity, drawing it into the crosshairs of Islamic radicals.

With chilling shouts of "Allahu Akbar!" pickup trucks of Libyans, Afghans, Saudis, Chechens, Turkestanis, Algerians, and Tunisians raced into the peaceful town. In the villagers' words, eighteen hundred screaming, "long-haired, long-bearded men with cruel faces," grenades, machine guns, and knives overran the ancient, peaceful town.

Frenzied shouts and the stutter of AK-47s ripped through the tranquil, picturesque oasis of healing as the radical Islamists from across the globe hunted down the Christian homes.

Christian fathers peered over their balconies to see men in Pakistani-Afghan garb, armed with Kalashnikov rifles and swinging swords, storming the streets. Their Muslim neighbors led the frenzied intruders.

In their cliffside home, a Christian family woke to the feverish jihadi screams, "Allahu Akbar!" Shock waves of terror flashed through their hearts. A glance between the curtains revealed men with swords and guns climbing the steps toward their home in the old quarter.

The six family members dove into the cave at the back of their house used as a grain storage pantry. Huddled the dark cave, Antoinette, her brother Anton, their elderly, infirm father, an aunt, Uncle Mikhael, and nephew Serkis, a fourth-year university student, heard the crash of the splintering door. Hearts hammered against their chests as terrorists' boots pounded across the courtyard, heading directly for their hideout.

A neighbor guided the radicals to this Christian home and to their hideaway, they realized.

"Come out! We will give you safety!" voices promised.

Anton, Mikhael, and young Serkis ventured onto the balcony to dialogue with the intruders.

As one of the intruders pulled the pin on a grenade, they yelled, "Don't! Only two women and an elderly man are still in the cave!"

The jihadi hurled the grenade into the cave as his companions fired their guns at the curtained opening.

In a deafening explosion, the grenade blew out Antoinette's elbow. A ricocheting bullet slammed through her. She lay in a pool of blood, praying, "Virgin Mary, have mercy!"

The woman tensed as the militants ordered, "Say the Shahada! Convert to Islam!"

"I was born a Christian, and I will die a Christian," Anton's voice rang confidently.

The bleeding woman in the cave heard the stutter of the machine gun echoed by a thud.

Mikhael and Serkis knew the cost but refused to say the Shahada. More shots and thuds. The three bodies lay in the shadow of the Mar Sarkis commemorating Sergio, the Roman officer beheaded for refusing to sacrifice to Jupiter.

The intruders fired bullets into the gas canister in the kitchen, igniting it as they rushed out of the home.

Racing engines, gunshots, and the jihadi shouts of "Allahu Akbar" echoed through the enclave. "Come out you Christian pigs!" the radicals screamed.

A few Christians slipped out the back doors with their daughters just as the frenzied jihadists smashed through their front door. A number of Christians escaped Maaloula through a drainage pipe.

The militants ransacked the houses and booby-trapped the doors. When returning villagers opened their doors, the movement triggered an electrical charge detonating a gas canister.

The radicals brought looting gangs to the village. They marked the doors of Islamic houses as "Muslim Home." On doors of the Christians' houses, they scrawled, "We will slaughter you!"

The terrorists took perverse pleasure in desecrating the churches, breaking Crosses, and destroying priceless works of art. They used the religious symbols for target practice, burning the buildings to erase traces of Maaloula's Christian legacy.

Jihadis took over clifftop Mar Sarkis monastery. They toppled the rooftop Cross and smashed and defaced the icons. Snipers fired down at the villagers from their clifftop perch with Russian sniper rifles. They shot Syrian soldiers in the legs when they tried to assist the nuns.

"Our souls are fractured," villagers grieved. "Our neighbors gave guns to the rebels, led them to the village, and helped in the looting, desecrating, kidnapping, and murdering of the Christians. They don't care about defeating the Assad regime. They just want to kill Christians and chase us out of Syria."

Learning of the tragic assault on the healing oasis favored by the president, the regime sent exhausted, overworked soldiers to drive out the radical extremists terrorizing the village.

As they fled, Islamists stole priceless works of art and ancient icons, destroying or burning what they could not carry. By the time the village was recaptured, all the churches had been vandalized, ninety homes had been destroyed, and graves had been dug.

After Syrian soldiers regained the ravaged historic cliffside city, Maaloulan villagers traveled 35 miles south to Damascus and found Pastor Abraham. "Please come to our churches and teach us the Bible," they pled.

"You want me to teach you the Bible?" Pastor Abraham asked, raising his eyebrows in surprise at the invitation from the ancient Christian enclave.

"We were so proud to be one of the last communities to speak the language of Jesus," the Maaloulans admitted. "But since the ISIS attack, we realized speaking the language is not what matters. We know the authentic language but not the words of Jesus. Can you please come explain to us the teachings of Jesus?"

And so it went across Syria; the war awoke believers from their cold orthodoxy, propelling them to seek to learn the heart of the Gospel.

The Cross became more than a symbol on the church roof, casting its shadow on attendees once a week. It became, instead, a concept believers embraced as they began living in the shadow of the Cross, in surrender to Christ, seven days a week.

How great is our God!

"ALLAHU AKBAR!" IN CHURCH

(Damascus, Syria)

"Fight the good fight of the faith. Take hold of the eternal life to which you were called and about which you made the good confession in the presence of many witnesses."

I Timothy 6:12

"As long as we see any person as an enemy—whether Communist, Muslim, or terrorist—then the love of God cannot flow through us to reach them."

—Brother Andrew

"Amazing grace, how sweet the sound, that saved . . ." As the song faded, congregants near the front turned to see what caused the music to stall.

The long-bearded Muslim sheikh with the red and white checkered head gear and flapping kaftan strode up the middle aisle of the packed auditorium. Fear glistened in the eyes of the worshippers gripped in a chilling paralysis. The song faded until only a few oblivious worshippers near the front of church continued carrying the melody lustily. "I once was lost. . . ."

Was there a suicide vest hidden beneath his robe? A sword? A gun? What other purpose would have brought the Muslim sheikh to a Christian church service?

Damascenes seeking healing and hope from the wounds of war packed every church bench of the Jesus of Nazareth chapel. Seekers stood in the courtyard and crowded the stairwells.

War's missiles had accomplished what massive evangelistic crusades could never have done. The concussions of bomb blasts rattled the hearts of the Syrians from their complacency to a pursuit of truth and hope.

And while the Syrian conflict brought revival to the churches, the unrest created a vacuum drawing the boots of tens of thousands of jihadi soldiers and bearded ISIS extremists in black-bannered brigades to claim the regions of the Levant.

And now an Islamic extremist had invaded the heart of the Church of Jesus of Nazareth. Parishioners tensed, gripping the benches in front of them, poised to leap out of their seats.

Will fleeing make us a target? Will staying still provide greater safety? Several men rose cautiously to get a better view of the actions of the bearded, turbaned intruder. A few attendees tiptoed out of the chapel while they could.

"Through many dangers, toils and snares I have already come, 'Tis grace has brought me safe thus far . . ."

The worship hymn's minor notes died away like flames doused in water as the stranger reached the front of the auditorium.

Every eye watched as he pressed himself between the packed bodies seated on the front bench.

Pastor Abraham's alert eye caught a glimpse of the intruder the moment he walked through the door, taking in the beard and checkered shemagh of a sheikh with calm grace, silently calling out to God for wisdom.

Every eye was riveted to Pastor Abraham, watching for a cue. If Abraham showed fear or signaled exit, mayhem would break out.

Abraham observed no obvious sign of a weapon. But could that be a suicide vest beneath his kaftan?

Continue with the service, Abraham sensed in his spirit. The pastor rose calmly, standing behind the podium with confident dignity and authority. His calm smile reassured the apprehensive audience and graced his guest. He discreetly kept the unusual visitor in his peripheral vision.

It's futile to try rallying the crowd to sing another hymn, Abraham realized as the notes faded away.

With poise cloaking his pulsing heart, Pastor Abraham quoted Romans 8: "'For I consider that the sufferings of this present time are not worth comparing with the glory to be revealed to us. . . . Who shall separate us from the love of Christ?'"

As he recited the reassuring verses, he observed the sheikh from the corner of his eye. *Please Lord, give me wisdom. Protect the lambs. . . .*

"Shall tribulation, or distress, or persecution, or famine, or nakedness, or danger, or sword? As it is written, 'For your sake, we are being killed all the day long; we are regarded as sheep to be slaughtered.' No, in all these things, we are more than conquerors through him who loved us. For I am. . . .'"

"ALLAHU AKBAR!" The bearded stranger exploded. A visible tremor shot through the congregation, accompanied by gasps and muffled shrieks. The jihadi war cry sent icy fingers down every spine and several worshippers bolting for the door. Women clutched their babies. Men grabbed the edge of their benches, muscles tensed in readiness.

The pastor paused mid-sentence but scarcely flinched. *Please, Father, protect your lambs,* the pastor prayed silently, analyzing the bearded face of the man gazing intently at him. The unique visitor stayed seated and made no move to detonate a bomb.

I need wisdom!

The visitor's expression doesn't seem evil.

Abraham calmly continued, "For I am sure that neither death nor life, nor angels nor rulers, nor things present nor things to come, nor powers, nor height nor depth, nor anything else in all creation, will be able to separate us from the love of God in Christ Jesus our Lord."

"Allahu Akbar!" the guest erupted passionately.

Audible gasps and stifled cries swept across the congregation, and several more congregants fled out the rear door.

Was the suicide bomb malfunctioning? Was the sheikh working up his courage?

Scarcely missing a beat, Pastor Abraham continued, speaking more powerfully than before, "I Peter 4 teaches since Christ suffered physically, we are to expect suffering, and suffering will produce a glory. The Greek word for glory is the same word as for Shekinah—the glowing, majestic splendor and presence—that led the Israelites and the brilliant presence of God that threw Saul off his horse.

"When we suffer, there will be divine radiance about us. And suffering brings that powerful manifestation of God to those attacking us in the darkness of hate.

"So, do not be surprised and discouraged when there is suffering," the pastor encouraged. "But expect suffering. And expect the majestic presence of God to radiate from your life when that happens."

"ALLAHU AKBAR! ALLAHU AKBAR!"

Pastor Abraham's eyes swept the audience and announced a closing prayer. Several more shouts of "ALLAHU AKBAR!" punctuated the benediction, sending more parishioners rushing for the door.

The remaining congregants clutched their closed Bibles, hunched on the edges of their pews, silently urging the pastor to end the service.

"Dear friends, let us not forget that Jesus is coming soon." Despite the intensity of the moment, the beloved pastor would not shorten the service to end without the words with which he punctuated every gathering. "The hour has come for you to wake from sleep. For salvation is nearer to us now than when we first believed. The night is far gone; the day is at hand. So then let us cast off the works of darkness and put on the armor of light." Romans 13:11, 12.

I've never ended a sermon without an invitation, and I won't skip it today, Pastor Abraham decided, closing his Bible, calmly smiling as he scanned the faces of the congregants and the guest.

"The Creator God loved mankind so compassionately that He gave his Son as a sacrifice to pay the penalty for our sins. I invite anyone who wishes to accept His gift and receive God's son, Jesus, into their lives to kneel at the Cross."

The sheikh leaped to his feet and knelt at the altar. "Allahu Akbar! I have found God!" he cried. "How great is our God!"

The icy fear melted across the auditorium into understanding smiles and soft, relieved chuckles.

As he prayed with the sheikh, Abraham realized, *The message of the love of God resonated deep within the heart of the searching Muslim. He had never heard the words "Hallelujah" or "Amen." The only words he knew to express his profound emotions were "Allahu Akbar!" and "Our God is greater!"*

How great is our God!

THE COST

"An inheritance which is imperishable . . . and undefiled and unfading, reserved in heaven for you, who are being protected and shielded by the power of God. . . . In this you rejoice greatly, even though now for a little while . . .you have been distressed by various trials so that the genuineness of your faith, which is much more precious than gold which perishes . . . may be found to result in . . . praise and glory and honor at the revelation of Jesus Christ."

I Peter 1:4–6 (AMP)

"God's work is not dependent on economics. A calling is a calling, regardless of circumstances. God's call, His Kingdom, and His purposes must proceed irrespective of our economics, circumstances, and the sacrifice it may cost. His ministry and mission are never a deletable option."

—Pastor Abraham

The question whispered and echoed through the hearts of each believer assembled in the church in the Old City of Damascus as explosions rocked the outskirts of the city.

The brothers of the church placed their hands on the two black, curly heads of the swarthy young men kneeling in the front of the auditorium.

How is God going to provide the money for two airline tickets to send these two young newly commissioned missionaries to Sudan? each member wondered. *We have to decide, shall we buy groceries or kerosene this week? How can we pay for two airplane tickets?*

And even deeper in each soul, every attendee wrestled with the questions the missiles of war had blasted into each heart: *Should we stay in Syria, or should we flee the sniper bullets, the kidnappings, chlorine barrel bombs, and the rubble?*

Soon after the turn of the second millennium, the families of Fawzi and Idris fled from Sudan to escape the mass killings, kidnappings, forced slavery, famine, and disease during the genocide that claimed hundreds of thousands of lives in 2003–2005. While few welcoming arms reached out to the Sudanese refugees, the compassionate arms of Pastor Abraham and the church embraced them, mentoring and discipling them.

God gave two young men a call, and the Church of Jesus of Nazareth a vision, to plant a church in Sudan. Pastor Abraham mentored the Sudanese youth, preparing Fawzi and Idris to return to take the Gospel to their own people.

The audience looked expectantly at Pastor Abraham as he spoke: "War doesn't stop a vision God has given. Suffering, death, agony, pain, and lack of resources don't stop it. The more obstacles placed before God's vision, the more it advances. The unrealistic becomes realistic.

"We see the Kingdom of God beyond the struggle. And God beyond the obstacles. God's vision for the church remains the same, and the economy never impacts that vision," he encouraged.

"The first missionary, Paul, left from Damascus two thousand years ago," Pastor Abraham reminded his congregation. "How appropriate that missionaries should set out from the ancient city once again!"

The anticipation of the believers attending the commissioning service in Damascus that evening was tangible, electric with expectation, as the ushers passed the collection bags through the crowd.

God would provide, but how?

The occasional jingle of metal evidenced the sacrifice of another coin. A woman discreetly unclasped a necklace—a family heirloom. Another loosened a bracelet gifted by her husband.

Carefully, the treasurer poured out the contents of the offering bags. Flashes of gold mingled with the silver coins and bills as bracelets, rings, and gold jewelry spewed from the bags.

The congregation, facing the crises of war and on the verge of fleeing for their own lives, had given their best. To pay the price to release these two sharpened arrows into the front lines of the battle, they gave their gold with its unchanging value, their financial security in a changing world.

A quick tally revealed the value was more than enough to purchase two flight tickets to Sudan.

When Abraham traveled to Sudan to encourage the African churches, he heard hundreds of voices lifted in joyous worship. He listened to the Sudanese school children quoting the scriptures in the classrooms. The youngsters sat cross-legged on the floor, since there were no funds to purchase books or desks. But they were learning.

While taking the light of the Gospel to their devastated homeland, the two missionaries nearly died of malaria, they braved bullets from political turmoil, and they refused to give up.

When Fawzi married a bride from his flock, Pastor Abraham asked Idris, "Is there a young woman on your heart?"

"Pastor Abraham. I'm too busy preaching to earn money to buy cows!"

"Cows?"

"For the bride price, Pastor Abraham. Cows for the bride price cost $5,000 I can't afford to pay!

"The ladies in Damascus gave up their jewels for Jesus, and I can give up a wife for Him."

FIVE MISSILES,
FIVE CHURCHES

"I will build my church, and the gates of hell shall not prevail against it."

Matthew 16:18

"No enthusiasm will ever stand the strain that Jesus Christ will put upon His worker, only one thing will, and that is a personal relationship to Himself which has gone through the mill of His spring-cleaning until there is only one purpose left—I am here for God to send me where He will."

—Oswald Chambers

"Father, do we flee, or do we stay?" the Christians caught in the crosshairs of missiles and bullets prayed several times each day. "We've got to have an answer!"

Shall we leave our homes, our businesses, our relatives to try to find safety in a tent in a refugee camp in a foreign country? In a country where we are unwanted and have no future? Or does God want us to stay in Syria?

In a hidden lair, beyond the city walls, radical jihadists bent over a map, locating five Damascene churches.

Like a tightening noose, the brutality, risks, and destitution threatened to strangle the courage of believers. Across Syria, parents and church groups discussed the risks.

Throughout Christian districts across Syria, toppled buildings, kidnappings, electrical outages, fuel shortages, and sieges strangling supply lines challenged survival itself.

Across the Middle East, ISIS, al-Nusra, and their radical Muslim cousins fought to brutally obliterate Christianity from the Levant, leaving dismembered bodies, abused girls, crumbling church buildings, broken Crosses, shattered hearts, and pools of blood in their wake.

Yet each drop of blood spilled in the fertile furrows behind their frenzied ravages sprouted into the richest of harvests. Across the Middle East, the hateful, brutal atrocities turned Muslims from a god of hate and murder to the loving, nail-pierced hands of a Jesus who laid down his life for them.

"This is our harvest season!" Brother Abraham told the Church of Nazareth congregation as hundreds of seekers crowded into the auditorium, the courtyard, and stairwells.

"But what is the responsible course of action?" believers asked each other. "Will we regret staying? Will our children survive the barrel bombs, missiles, and sniper bullets? And if they survive, what scars will the memories leave on their souls? How long will the food and the fuel last?"

"Should we leave while we can?"

"Or do You want us to stay, Lord? To help the suffering? To guide the searching? To harvest the ripe fields? To suffer for Your glory?"

"Let's band together and spend this Saturday praying and fasting at the church," Pastor Abraham urged.

While the terrorists loaded the missiles that Saturday, the Damascene Christians gathered at the Jesus of Nazareth chapel to pray and seek the heart of God.

Rami often shared three points on effective prayer:

1. POWER: be connected to the Source.
2. UNITY: fight the enemy, not our brothers.
3. GLORY: pray for God to be glorified.

"ISIS is not our enemy. Al-Qaeda is not the enemy. Islam is not the enemy," Rami and Abraham taught. "We have only one enemy. We need to fight against the enemy in prayer and pray for our brothers. Then, we will be one in spirit.

"We waste time praying for things that will not glorify God. For five years, we prayed, 'Lord, stop the war! We need peace!' Instead of wasting time praying for peace, we should pray that God will be glorified. And sometimes, that means suffering. When we pray, it is not about us but Him.

"If God will be glorified by us leaving Syria, we want to leave. If He will be glorified through us staying, we will stay. We want what glorifies Him."

"Amen!"

"Yes, Lord!"

"Alleluia, now join with me, raise your right hand in prayer, and let's pray for the power, for God to fill us with His Spirit to strengthen us."

Across the auditorium, brothers and sisters lifted their hands, pleading to know the will of God.

"Abba Father! Show us Your heart."

"Make Your will so clear that there is no doubt!"

"We want Your will! We want You to be glorified!"

As the believers prayed on their knees before God, tears streaking their faces, planes roared out of the sky over Damascus.

Souk vendors hastily shuttered their stalls, and villagers hunkered in their homes.

But the believers in the Jesus of Nazareth Church prayed louder, with more passion and tears than ever. "Lord! Please show us Your will so clearly, we cannot doubt!"

"Help us know what will bring You the most glory—leaving or staying."

Rami's low, resonant voice rose above the petitions. "Pour out Your Spirit, Lord, the only Source that can empower and strengthen us. We know the enemy is strong, but we are not afraid of him. We know our God is great and awesome. You have everything in Your control as You sit on your Heavenly throne. Thank You, Father.

"We pray that Your name be glorified, and only Your name. We are not praying that the war be stopped, but we pray that You *use* the suffering that Your name be glorified.

"We know our war is with the powers of darkness, but we know,

Lord, we have the light because You are the light of this world. And that the light is more powerful than darkness.

"So now, with the great power You have in Your hand, show us very clearly what will bring the most glory to Your name. Not what is most comfortable and safe for us, but what brings Your name the most glory—for us to stay or to . . ."

The building convulsed as a massive explosion rocked it, shaken as if by a massive paw. Shards of glass showered the worshippers diving beneath the benches. The lights flickered out.

Acrid smoke and dust poured through broken panes. The reflecting glow of flames danced on the dark walls.

The men ran to the wooden church doors, opening them a crack, peering through the smoke to see a great belching crater just beyond the church.

We were the target! they realized, awe tingling through their bodies like an electric shock. *But God!*

After a moment of shocked silence, praises began to burst from their hearts.

"Alleluia!"

"Glory!"

"Thank you, Jesus!"

The ardent praises burst forth like the water rushing down the slopes of Mount Hermon.

As the beige haze settled over the chapel, someone began to sing, "To God be the glory, great things He hath done . . ."

The dark, shaken, debris-filled building echoed with jubilation.

"Praise the Lord! Praise the Lord! Let the people rejoice. Praise the Lord! Praise the Lord, let people rejoice! O come to the Father, through Jesus the Son, And give Him the glory, great things He has done!"

"So, has God spoken?" Pastor Abraham asked when the congregants had brushed the glass and debris from the benches and settled down.

"YES!" the believers chorused. "Amen!"

"Alleluia!"

"And what has He said?"

"STAY!" they shouted in unison.

"He said, '*Stay!* And I will take care of you!'"

ISIS fired missiles at five Damascene churches that Saturday. The missile targeting Jesus of Nazareth Church had fallen short of its mark, but its failed delivery carried a message from the Almighty God to His beloved children.

How great is our God!

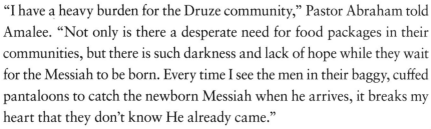

"I have a heavy burden for the Druze community," Pastor Abraham told Amalee. "Not only is there a desperate need for food packages in their communities, but there is such darkness and lack of hope while they wait for the Messiah to be born. Every time I see the men in their baggy, cuffed pantaloons to catch the newborn Messiah when he arrives, it breaks my heart that they don't know He already came."

"I will pray with you," Amalee committed, knowing the Druze would stop at nothing if they felt their religion was being threatened.

"WE WILL BLOW UP
THE CHURCH"

"The light shines in the darkness, and the darkness has not overcome it."

John 1:5

"The history of missions is the history of answered prayer."

—Samuel Zwemer

What have I done that Allah would curse me by giving me a deformed son? Leyla cried, rocking her infant. Life was cruel enough during a war, and then a son with a deformity was more than she could bear. *What future is ahead for my precious baby? It would have been better if he had never been born!*

The birth defect draped a black shroud of shame and judgment wherever she went, defining Leyla. But most painful, the deformity destined Zaki to life with no future. His diaper hid the deformity, but Leyla felt the judgmental stares. The whole town had heard she had birthed a malformed son who could never be a real man.

"Ahh! What great sins Leyla and Zahir must have committed for Allah to curse them with such a child!" the entire Druze community whispered. Everyone noticed Leyla's heavy sadness after her son's birth. Her repeated attempts at suicide were no secret.

"It's all your fault," Zahir growled. "Your body should have produced a healthier son."

"It's not my fault!" Leyla cried. "It was your sins who deformed your son!"

"It was *not* my sins!" Zahir shouted. "You birthed the child! And now we have this stack of medical bills we will never be able to pay, and they still haven't fixed the baby!" he yelled, slamming the door to punctuate his anger.

Leyla wept into her son's blanket. The mounting tension and continual accusations doused the last flickers of love she felt for her husband. None of the surgeons offered hope to resolve the defect. Her spirit withered and faded beneath the black cloud of despair. Life was too heavy. Too dark and too hopeless.

Even the leaders of their Druze religion had no answers. They looked very religious in their conical, white cloth-covered hats and long, thick mustaches. The baggy black pants cuffed at the ankle, designed to intercept the Messiah, allegedly to be born to a man, gave them an air of super spirituality. Perhaps if Zahir became initiated, he would understand the deep secret wisdom of God. But it would be several years until he turned thirty and was old enough for initiation. It was too long to wait.

There is nothing to live for. The pills didn't work last time. Maybe a knife. . . .

Her baby stirred in her arms. His bright eyes popped open, and his face broke into a sweet smile as he stretched his pudgy hands, cooing at her.

Oh God, what about Zaki? Who will care for him if I die? Leyla cried, cuddling the baby protectively against her and kissing his downy dark head of hair. *I will wait for another day,* she decided.

A solid meal will make Zahir happy again, but we used the last rice and lentils. He left me no money to buy more.

Ah! The Isa people from Damascus! Maria says they give away free food packs!

"It's so easy!" Maria had bragged. "All you have to do is to pretend to listen a couple minutes to a speech, and then they will give you a box of food for free! Spices, dried milk, rice, sugar, even coffee!"

Even coffee! And sugar.

What makes Isa people care to share with us? We Muslims have broken their Crosses and killed and tortured their people, Leyla wondered. *And what do they speak about that makes our leaders forbid us from attending their talks?*

"You stay away from those Isa people!" Zahir had groused. "We will be shunned if you are seen near them."

Leyla could only imagine what the elders would say or do if they discovered.

I don't want to live anyway, so what's the harm? Leyla decided, wrapping up the baby and heading for the door before she could change her mind.

"Never forget, God loves you," the "Man of the Book" said kindly. "Sin brings evil, war, and suffering to this world, not God. But God loves you so much He will turn the evil and use it for good."

Like a flower reaching for the sunshine, Leyla absorbed the soothing words. A light began to shine into her heart and to lift the cloud of darkness.

What if God really did not cause my son's deformity to punish me?

"Joseph's brothers sold him to be a slave in Egypt," the man of "the Book" continued. "Joseph was sold and then thrown into prison when he was innocent, but God used those terrible experiences for Joseph to save up grain and save Joseph's family from a famine," the man said kindly.

Could God use my son's birth defect for good, too?

"When we look to the Cross, we see what evil men have done to Jesus, whom your Qur'an calls Isa. But at the same time, we not only see evil but the full goodness of God to offer his Son to us. That is what Romans 8 says, 'God who loves and did not spare His own Son, how will He not give us everything?'

"That is the goodness of God. There is evil and suffering, but at the same time, God is good and turns the evil for good, using it all to his glory."

God turns evil for good! The light of the truth shoved back the oppressive darkness smothering her. The joy radiated from her face. She felt like a Persian lily sprouting from the cold, dark earth and bursting out in brilliance and color. Leyla had never heard of this Isa God before.

Her shriveled heart yearned to learn everything she could about a God who died for people and would turn evil for good.

After the talk, Leyla juggled the baby and the food box she had been awarded. She sauntered home like a woman who had won the lottery, promptly preparing a delightful meal for Zahir, complete with a weak cup of coffee with a pinch of sugar.

Zahir looked at her sharply when he walked through the door. He expected to see his wife sulking in a corner or even lifeless. Not that he cared. But to see her bustling around the kitchen, smiling and humming a song!

"Where have you been?" he demanded. "Did you go to one of those talks by the people of the Book?"

"I did and heard such joyful words!" she bubbled. "I heard that God does not cause disease and deformities! He loves us! God loves us! Have you ever heard anything so beautiful? Something happened to the darkness in my heart, and I feel such happiness!"

"I forbid you from ever going back again!" Zahir stormed, furious that she had disobeyed him. And fearful of the community's rejection and censure.

Yet her new glow of happiness piqued his curiosity.

"Zahir, please come with me and hear for yourself about this loving God," Leyla pleaded gently.

I'll go so I can know how to argue with her about how wrong these people are, he relented when her pleas wearied him.

Zahir stood in the shadows, listening skeptically. But the life-giving words drew him in. "And we know that all things work together for good to those who love God . . ."

And the singing! He had never heard such precious words and touching melodies sung with deep passion and longing.

"At the cross, at the cross, Where I first saw the light, And the burden of my heart rolled away, It was there by faith I received my sight, And now I am happy all the day!"

A sprout of hope emerged from the darkness, the rubble, the despair.

"I can breathe again!" Zahir admitted to Leyla as they walked home, carrying their son and one of Pastor Abraham's Bibles.

Zahir began to read about the life of Isa from the Bible. The couple couldn't wait for the next meeting to learn more about this loving Isa who turned terrible things into good, who said disabilities didn't happen as punishment from sin but so that the "works of God could be displayed" in them.

"We are ready to follow Isa," the young father confided to "the Man of the Book" after one of the talks.

"You understand what this could mean, Zahir," Pastor Abraham asked, looking deep into the young man's eyes. "I have personally met with the leaders of the Druze, and they have been quite hostile."

"We understand," Zahir replied. "We've talked about it and know it will mean our Druze community will cast us out and persecute us. We know it could mean kidnapping. Beating. Or death. But you have to understand the life we lived before, with no hope, was worse than death. To follow Isa, your Jesus, is to live—even if we die. So, we are ready."

The radiant joy and love transforming the home intrigued the entire community.

What happened to Leyla to make her so filled with happiness instead of darkness and despair and wanting to kill herself? neighbors asked each other. *And her baby is still deformed. It's like a candle has been lit in her blackness. And look how they love each other!*

Villagers stopped by their home to find out whatever could have replaced this family's despair with happiness. *Where could a person find hope in such dark times of war and fighting?*

The villagers had to know. And they wanted that happiness for their own hearts.

Leyla and Zahir told the neighbors, "We learned Isa loves us. He died for us. And God turns evil into good."

The Druze community, so desperate for a glimmer of hope in the darkness of missiles, abductions, terror, and death, packed into the apartment where the Jesus people told about this God of love and joy who cared intimately about them.

Aware of the desperation for hope in hearts all across Syria, the couple sensed God's call to take the light of the Gospel to other dark places beyond their community.

In their own village, people crowded into the apartment where they met to teach about the hope of Jesus, and to worship him. When the building could hold no more, people crowded in the doorways and hung in through the windows, straining to hear the life-giving word of God. And still, the church grew.

The believers rented an adjacent apartment to accommodate the swelling crowds. The words of God spoke such life to the dark, cold, hurting places of the hearts of the battle-ravaged community stemming from centuries of darkness.

"Let's meet every day!" the new believers decided. "We need to be encouraged and strengthened."

Zahir knew the Druze leaders would be furious. And they were. Neighbors reported these new gatherings to the leaders. Twenty armed men stormed into the building, yelling threats and brandishing swords and guns.

"If you meet tomorrow, we will blow up the church with you inside it."

Leyla and Zahir knew the fury, brashness, and intensity of the men passionately fighting for their traditions and the control of those they considered to be their followers. And they knew they would certainly carry out their threats.

The women cried, devastated, unable to bear the potential loss of encouragement of gathering together, hearing the word, and singing.

"Please, God, show us a new way," they prayed, "Show us a way forward."

"Why not meet in homes like in China?" someone suggested. "Why not have house churches?"

Why not?

As those small groups spread out across the town, the Gospel spread like hungry flames across a parched field fanned by the wind. As the Kingdom of God exploded across the community, the believers started youth groups and reached out to orphanages, sharing the love of God.

During this time of spiritual healing, the couple's son also began to heal.

"Remarkable!" the doctors marveled, observing the development of the deformity. "There is no rationale to explain his healing. It's unheard of."

The same God that had healed the Syrian general's leprosy when he dipped in the Jordan River almost 3,000 years ago was still healing the Syrians who sought Him.

But while the loving God brought healing and hope to the community, the leaders in their white cylindrical hats, kaftans, and baggy trousers met to plan to kidnap and kill the leaders of the church.

Despite threats, Zahir and the leaders boldly continued ministering, and God protected them. The church continued to grow to more than sixty families, in addition to the many believing families who had left the country.

The light of this church continued to spread through this eclectic offshoot of Islam, bringing light that the community had not seen for a thousand years. A kinship church came alongside this group and helped them purchase a van to transport families to the house churches and the training seminars in Damascus.

The Druze leaders would continue to threaten. They would kidnap and beat the Christian leaders in the future, but they could not snuff out the hope and faith in Jesus. The persecution only fanned the fire of the Gospel, spreading with fervor across the Middle East.

How great is our God!

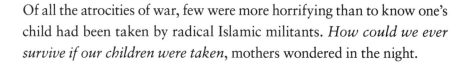

Of all the atrocities of war, few were more horrifying than to know one's child had been taken by radical Islamic militants. *How could we ever survive if our children were taken,* mothers wondered in the night.

TEEN HOSTAGE

"But if anyone suffers [ill treatment] as a Christian [because of his belief], he is not to be ashamed but is to glorify God [because he is worthy to suffer] in this name."

I Peter 4:16 (AMP)

"It's like God has a heavenly factory—He transforms the bad things that happen to us into something He will use for good."

—Abraham Samara

"Why are you taking me?" Amar screamed, kicking and struggling against the radical Islamic soldiers dragging him into a truck. His schoolbooks scattered along the roadside.

"I'm just a schoolboy; I haven't done anything wrong! Let me go!"

Doors slammed. A fist smashed into his face. The thirteen-year-old melted onto the pickup floor, licking the blood from his lip. He scrunched his eyes closed, sniffling softly as the icy fingers of terror threatened to choke him.

How will my family ever find me?

Tires spinning and peeling, the truck roared onto the highway, careening through the traffic.

"Don't tell us you haven't done anything!" a captor snarled, spitting into the boy's face. A boot crushed the teen's ribs. "We know exactly who you are. You are a good little Jesus boy. Your neighbor told us all about you. And now you will soon be a good little Muslim boy helping the radicals fight!" he finished with a hideous laugh.

The truck lurched to a stop. The doors flew open. A rough hand grabbed the boy's hair, yanking him from the truck.

"Ah! A new Jesus boy! A slave to break in!"

"Convert! Say the Shahada, and we will stop beating you. There is no god but . . ."

"No! I will never convert to Islam! That's a lie! Allah is not the true . . ."

Fists balled into powerful battering rams slammed his face and body until he swelled and bled.

The boy rocked back and forth, straining desperately at the ropes. The knots securing him to the tree were secure.

"Are you ready to say the Shahada?" the voice boomed. Huge hands slapped his wet cheeks. Cords and sticks whipped his defenseless body.

The child trembled. He wanted to answer, but he couldn't control his voice.

Day after day, the teen, and others much younger, served the radical soldiers fighting against the regime. The boys carried their machine guns. They loaded ammunition on the front lines of the battle amid flying bullets, falling bodies, and pooling blood.

In payment, Amar received brutal beatings for refusing to convert.

Boots slammed into his ribs, and sticks beat his back.

"Please stop! I will never convert!" he screamed, curling up in a fetal position.

Why would I wish to convert from following a loving God to a god of cruelty?

At home, a hand of fear clutched the heart of Amar's mother. The hours ticked by, but her son did not return from school.

"Have you seen Amar?" His family frantically checked with neighbors, the police, and the Mukhabarat. "He has gone missing!" But no one had seen the boy. All the clues indicated Amar must have been taken by the radicals. One of the neighbors seemed to think so.

The wailing mother threw herself onto the floor, her hands clenched in desperation and heart convulsing in anguish.

Oh, Jesus, what is my precious son enduring in the hands of the radicals? If he even lives. . . .

Sleep eluded her as she pled with God, day and night. "Bring him home! Bring him home!" she sobbed.

The mother flipped page after page on the wall calendar. Six calendar pages, and no word of her son. *It would be easier to know he had died. . . .*

Amar cowered beneath the blows and threats, straining against the ropes.

A huge face loomed over him, hissing, "Say the words, Jesus boy." The foul breath and body odor made his stomach churn with nausea.

"Just say the words: 'There is no god but Allah,' and we will stop beating you!"

A steely fist smashed his nose with a crack. He tasted blood. Blow after blow. His lips swelled. Steel-toed boots smashed his bruised body.

"Say the words, boy, and we'll let you go home!"

Jesus, I can't bear it!

Amar felt the pressure of gun barrels against his body. "Sixty seconds! Say the words or I will shoot! There is no god but. . . ."

"Thirty seconds and we will blow your brains out and send them to your mama." The voice cackled hideously. "Twenty. Ten seconds. . . ."

The cold metal pressed into his temple.

The abuse and endless psychological torture month after month broke his body and spirit until he could take it no longer.

"Stop! Stop! I will say it!" he screamed in desperate exhaustion. "There is no god . . ."

Oh Lord, forgive me! He sobbed. *I betrayed you! I didn't mean it! I didn't say the words with my heart!*

"Allahu Akbar!" the radicals shouted victoriously. "Our god is greater! Your God is weak!"

God, I'm so sorry! How can you ever forgive me? The grief of his betrayal tormented him more than the wounds from the physical blows. The anguish of his heart crashed over him like powerful waves. *Jesus, can you ever forgive me for what I've done?*

Amar's mother stared at the note in her trembling hands. "Your son has converted to Islam. We will release him—when you pay the ransom."

"Oh God! No! May it not be true. Surely, he didn't convert!"

The reported conversion doubled her desperation to get her son back. But she had no money. The hardships of the war had drained the finances.

Desperate to accumulate the demanded ransom, Amar's family sold their furniture at far below their value. They sold everything they owned of any worth to attempt to collect enough pounds to satisfy the radicals.

Amar must come home!

When negotiators arrived to collect the ransom money, Amar's mother climbed into the vehicle. "I'm going with you."

"Absolutely not! We can't take you along. They will take you captive, too!"

"I'm coming!" The woman slammed the door. "I *must* see my boy."

The mother's eyes flew across the camp, straining frantically to see her beloved son.

"AMAR!" She threw open the door and rushed toward her son. Her feet gave way beneath her before she reached the boy. Pent-up anguish of the days of uncertainty released in convulsing sobs and wails.

Spotting his wailing mother, Amar dashed to meet her. "Mama!" He hurled himself into his mother's arms, squeezing her as if he could never let go.

The captors counted the bills and sauntered away.

Amar's mother stroked her son's hair, holding him against her heart. Could she ever stop hugging that dear wounded boy who had experienced and seen more than any grown man should have to endure?

"The torture and beatings were too much. They were going to shoot me . . . so I said the words," the boy wailed as the negotiators drove the boy and his mother toward home.

"I couldn't stand the pain any longer. But I didn't mean them! Oh, I am so sorry for saying that! Will God ever forgive me?"

"Of course, you had to say the Shahada," his family consoled him when they heard of his horrific abuse. "No boy your age should be put through such torture. God understands."

The lacerations and bruises from his beatings healed, but the wounds of Amar's heart continued to bleed. The sight of every Muslim ripped the scabs from his heart, fueling fury for the trauma he endured at the hands of the radical Muslims.

Shame flung its dark mask over him, snuffing out any happiness at being home.

"I let down my Lord!" he cried at every recall of the memory, struggling with the guilt and the anger while processing the experience. "I let him down!"

"Amar, God has forgiven you the first time you said you were sorry for your words. You just need to forgive yourself," Pastor Abraham encouraged when the family came to Damascus. But forgiving himself would take months.

Amar and his family knelt at the altar of Jesus of Nazareth Church, surrendering and rededicating their lives to the Lord. God became more than an icon on the wall of their church. And their hearts began to heal.

"I know God loves and forgives me, but how can I forgive those awful men?" he wondered, his fists tightening every time the sight of a Muslim reminded him of the ISIS atrocities he endured.

We've got to leave the country, Amar's family decided. *The risks are too high to stay. Besides, there is nothing to keep us here. We've sold everything of value.*

Fleeing Syria, the family moved into a refugee camp surrounded by Muslim refugees. Rubbing shoulders every day with the followers of Islam triggered deep emotions in Amar.

The camp pastor, Yosef, helped Amar to process his pain and shame. "Peter betrayed Jesus three times. But the disciple repented and became a fearless leader for the Gospel," he encouraged gently.

"And you only betrayed Him once. Peter was much older than you and wasn't even being beaten. Jesus forgave Peter and used him powerfully. He wants to use you in a unique way, too, Amar."

I want to become a fearless leader like Peter, Amar decided, releasing the pain of his past, forgiving, and looking forward.

In the cavity of his heart carved by the cruelty of the radicals, God poured compassion for the Islamic refugees of the camp. Amar identified with the losses of the Islamic refugees, the abuses, injustices, and despondency. And he knew the Source of the hope they lacked.

"Amar, I could use your help to distribute relief goods and food packages," Pastor Yosef invited.

Eventually, Amar began ministering to as many as 700 Muslim refugees a week, bringing hope and healing to the people of those who tortured him.

How great is our God!

The Syrian war raged on. *Could the suffering church survive the horrors like a strangling siege? Or would the Christians all flee the country, leaving the church to die out as the radicals hoped?*

"WILL THIS BE
THE DAY I DIE?"

(The Siege of Aleppo, Syria)

"Be strong and courageous. Do not fear or be in dread of them, for it is the Lord your God who goes with you. He will not leave you or forsake you."

Deuteronomy 31:6

"In countries where Christians suffer severely, I've observed the accuracy of the words in Romans 8:35 that 'nothing can separate us from the love of God.' Love for God becomes stronger because suffering purifies us, helping us to focus on Him alone because the distracting loves of possessions have been taken away. Though the love of God doesn't change, it is felt more strongly during suffering because distractions have been removed."

—Rami Ibrahim

Beneath the black mantle of darkness, an elusive figure stole through the rubble-strewn alleys. The pale moonlight illuminated stacks of bombed bus shells fortified with mounds of sandbags barricading Aleppo. Bombed apartment complexes, hospitals, schools, and businesses slouched like collapsed houses of cards reeking of smoke, decaying corpses, and garbage.

A large bucket hung from each hand of the shadowy figure dodging the mounds of rubble, shuffling through a slurry of ash and rubbish. At each intersection, the figure paused, peering around the corner, as if listening for sniper fire.

Moments later, the same figure ducked from doorway to doorway, stealing back the way he had come, his movements slower and labored, attesting to the weight in the dripping buckets.

The figure paused at the gate of a spacious residence, glancing furtively in either direction before slipping inside as the gate swung open to receive him.

As the gate shut silently, a woman welcomed the man with open arms of delighted relief, lifting one of the heavy buckets. In the house, a lone candle fought against the darkness to illuminate the comfortable furnishings.

"The most precious treasure in all of Aleppo," the woman whispered, dipping a cup into the bucket, catching each precious drop, and offering it to the man. "Praise God, you made it safely, Mikayel!"

Water.

The regime's soldiers laid a crippling siege to Syria's commercial hub held by rebel forces, including hardline Islamists. They blocked supply routes to the city. Aleppo lay darkened without electricity, with ruptured water lines and severe shortages of food, medicines, and fuel.

Regime and Russian bombers swooped out of the clouds like falcons diving after their prey, skimming above the ancient city walls silhouetted against the night sky. The planes disgorged their payloads in a flash, vanishing as a deafening explosion rocked the countryside, spewing flames and smoke high over the ancient walls. As the white helmet rescue teams rushed to the scene, the planes flew around for a "double tap" bombing raid.

The couple cringed with each explosion, bracing for the inevitable as they lived life under constant threat from the air.

With every explosion, the businessman calculated the distance and direction. And then one night he knew. The location of the flames against the night sky confirmed the missile strikes had taken out their bus assembly plant and the toy factory, covering nearly a city block.

Flames leaped high into the night sky, spewing Mikayel and Hannah's lifework, dreams, and source of financing ministries into a torrent of sparks and thick twisting blood-colored plumes of smoke. All that remained of the massive factories were a few brave pieces of rebar with chunks of concrete clinging to them rising from the rubble. A flash of missile fire vaporized the efforts and dreams of a lifetime.

Hannah sobbed softly on Mikayel's shoulder. *Where is God?*

Mikayel held her close. *Life will never be the same. I have no resources to rebuild. . . .* He knew. But he held his wife, consoling her, "Don't cry, habibti. Where is God? He's taken care of the important things in our lives. Not so much as a bullet has punctured our home. You and I are safe. Our sons are safe. And God protected Javin when he was caught in sniper fire. So far, he's kept Davit safe on the battle front."

Mikayel and Hannah prayed constantly for their sons. Especially Davit, who'd been forced to join the regime forces. The last they heard, he was working for some of the country's top military officials.

Mikayel dreaded news updates. When he read, "Damascus blast kills top Assad officials," he forced himself to scan the article: "National Security headquarters in Damascus . . . Top military and security officials of the Syrian government killed. . . ."

Oh God. Not Davit. Please.

His eyes flew over the list of dead and injured. Davit was not listed. He dialed Davit's phone, but the call went straight to voicemail. "I hope you are okay, son. Call me at your soonest convenience. Be safe."

Mikayel accepted the call from an unknown number, startled to hear Davit's shaky voice on the line. "Baba, I'm fine, no worries. Thank God I'm fine. I have three minutes. The generals and top brass of the Syrian army met in the headquarters crisis room to strategize the next phase of the battle. They sent me out to pick up the lunch they ordered. While I was gone, a bomb blew up the building, killing almost everyone inside. The hour I was out. . . ."

"Oh son!" Mikayel hit the speakerphone button so his wife could hear.

"We kept hearing strange noises under the floor. We suspect the rebels dug beneath the building and placed explosives, detonating the charge remotely."

"Just in the few moments you were gone!" Mikayel sank into a chair. "It's a pure miracle!"

"But there's a bit of a problem," Davit's voice faded and cracked. "Because I was gone just when the explosives went off, they suspect I was out of the building because I was involved with the bomb . . . So . . . so, I'm in prison until they can investigate. . . ."

"Oh no, Davit! I'm so sorry. Mama and I will pray. I'll talk to a lawyer. We will get you out. God's up to something, son."

"My time's up, Baba . . ." And the line went dead.

"Come Hannah, let's pray. Our God gave us one miracle and He can give us another." Neither mentioned what they both were thinking. Their son faced torture, or worse . . .

When the buckets in the courtyard emptied and the battle explosions faded into the night, the businessman snuck out to the only well in the area to refill his buckets.

Each drop would be carefully rationed and recycled. The couple used the water sparingly for cooking and drinking. Then, they recycled surplus water for washing dishes and then bathing. They'd save the bath water for washing their clothes, and finally, the recycled water flushed the toilets.

After Mikayel's safe return in the night with more buckets of priceless water, the couple knelt, blessing God for safety again, for water, for a few food supplies. They prayed for the radical soldiers beyond the adjacent sandbags to find the love of Jesus. They prayed for the regime and the president. They prayed for their children, blessing God for Javin's safety when hit by sniper fire and for delivering Davit from the explosion, interceding for his vindication.

Like a grating alarm clock, the shouted commands of the ISIS general on the other side of the sandbags woke Mikayel and Hannah each morning.

Hannah shivered at the harsh tones, wondering how long the soldiers and the sandbags could hold back the radicals. In the changing war-ravaged world, one thing remained constant—the rallying cries of jihad, for a battle of holy war more than the defense of Syria.

"Those jihadi screams remind me too much of the spirit of Turkish soldiers driving my ancestors from Armenia on the death march," Mikayel reflected. "I can't imagine what our grandparents went through—hundreds of Armenian intellectuals executed . . . a million women, children, elderly, and infirm chased on death marches through the Syrian desert. A despotic effort to eliminate the Armenian Christians."

"But why, Mikayel, whatever motivated such horrific cruelty?"

"Our people were a threat to the Turkish Sultan. More intellectual, more successful. The Sultan feared Christians would side with Russia or the Allies against the Muslim government. The Sultan said he would box their ears to teach them a lesson."

The businessman/pastor sat silently, processing, before continuing.

"It's beyond imagination—they executed the men, forced the women and children from their homes into Turkish harems. Most were driven on the death marches into the blazing deserts, stripped of even under clothing by bandits. Deprived of food and water, violated, robbed, and massacred without a shred of protection. Our relatives were left to die at Dier ez-Zor. Their bone fragments in the sand still cry out for justice. Only 200,000 survived out of roughly a million sent on those death marches.

"Sadly, the same spirit of hate and death holds these radical soldiers captive."

He paused in deep thought. "But you know, habibti, the Turks were not the enemy. ISIS is not the enemy. The spirit behind it all is the enemy. The Turks and ISIS radicals needed the love of Jesus."

As each new dawn awakened Aleppo to unveil the devastation

wrought under the camouflage of darkness, Mikayel greeted his wife with the exact words every morning.

"Habibti, will this be the day?" he'd ask, gazing meaningfully into her dark eyes while the passionate jihadi screams echoed just beyond their bedroom window.

"Perhaps this will be the day we go home!" she replied with joyful anticipation as she answered the question each morning.

Together, they knelt, thanking God for the safety of the night. They ended the prayer by asking God, "How can we serve you today?"

Mikayel ventured to the market stalls, returning to report, "Not so much as a lone potato was to be seen. Wheat is selling for $100 a pound and powdered milk is going for $150 for a pound."

Through the cover of darkness, Mikayel carried sacks of lentils to the war widows and their children.

"Thank you, Pastor Mikayel!" One of the youngsters clapped his little hands. "I don't like eating grass soup with cat meat."

"The siege will soon be over and we will all be eating kibbeh and shawarmas again soon." Mikayel patted the child's head. "God sees."

"Have you heard from Davit?" Hannah questioned.

"The attorney says since he was gone precisely when the headquarters blew up, the Mukhabarat is sure he had inside connections with the rebels. That's why they jailed him. Don't worry, habibti, we've got the best attorney defending him. He'll be out in no time."

"It seems so wrong for him to be held when he's totally innocent. I just don't understand. Where is God in all of this?"

"At least he's safer behind bars than on the front lines . . ."

"We hope . . ."

"And in jail he isn't forced to shoot anyone . . ."

A Russian Frogfoot swooped out of the sky. The Russian jet dove like a falcon after a squirrel, disgorging its 1,000-pound bunker-buster in a horrific blast.

"I hope that wasn't the hospital again!" The couple huddled in the smoky, dusty gloom, tensing for the roar of another plane.

"Please, Lord, not the hospital!" Doctors worked around the clock, sewing up amputated limbs and removing shrapnel and perpetually repatching makeshift operating rooms and operating in the streets between bombings.

Whatever the Russian bunker-buster hit would not be rebuilt again. Hannah shivered, knowing beneath the rubble lay trapped children and mothers.

Together, they prayed for the injured, the grieving, the brave doctors and nurses, and the white helmet volunteers risking their lives to rescue.

"My brothers keep urging me to move to Lebanon or Canada," Mikayel revealed to Hannah. "They'll help set us up in business again."

"But do you want to?"

"Do you? Why are we on this earth, Hannah? What's God's purpose for us in this season of our lives?"

For decades, Mikayel and Hannah had used the bus assembly plant and the toy factory to sponsor widows and to support ministries. But the missiles eliminated that option.

"How can we best serve God now? As I see it, there are few places on this globe where people need more encouragement than right here in our own Syria. Certainly, I could go start another business in Canada and send money back to Syria. But Hannah, you know the war widows, the fatherless, the elderly need flesh and blood right here with them to encourage them. These are our people. Our culture. We are equipped to minister right here in Aleppo like no foreign humanitarian agency could."

"It seems it would be the right thing to stay," Hannah agreed. "For now. But when the time is right, I'd be ready to move back to our roots in Armenia. This war is taking its toll on me."

Mikayel nodded understandingly, taking her hand in his. "You've been a brave woman, Hannah. I would be open. However God leads."

"These brave widows will need a way to support themselves,"

Mikayel mused as they returned from a visit. "What if I start up a bakery to employ seventy of them and use the profit to help support those who can't work?"

Hannah patted his shoulder. That was her Mikayel. "I'm with you. After all the miracles we have seen, I know we are bulletproof."

"And missile-proof and sniper-proof!" he inserted.

"Until our time is up," she finished.

"It sure seems the boys are bulletproof. Javin told me more in detail the other day what happened when he was hit the other week. He and Yara were driving through the city when they were attacked by sniper fire. Yara took the bullet in the head, killing him instantly. The bullet hitting Javin went right through his neck. He threw open the car door and collapsed on the ground, pretending to be dead. With the blood gushing out of the bullet's entrance and exit holes and choking him, it's a miracle he pulled through.

"If God wants us here, He will take care of us until our work is done. And now, Hannah, since we don't have the businesses anymore, I'm committed to pouring my life into serving God the way I once served business."

Hannah expected big things to happen for God with this influential, gifted man of hers.

Mikayel served the Aleppo community with the keen attentiveness and organization that made him so successful with his factories. His servant heart tuned in to the needs, and his gift of administration figured out how to solve those problems. Under Mikayel's servant leadership, the suffering church spawned and grew exponentially. He was a man who followed hard after God with all his heart.

Every day, there were miracles. While all around them, buildings lay in rubble heaps, not one bullet hole scarred the walls of their home.

While Mikayel and Hannah checked in with war widows and believers when it was safe to venture beyond the courtyard, they also checked in on disillusioned neighbors who began questioning, "How can we follow a Qur'an whose suwar inspire the atrocities of ISIS?"

Throughout Aleppo, apartment doors hung open, exposing furnished homes, abandoned set tables, disemboweled drawers, silent reminders of those who left to the many who wished they could leave.

Every night, Mikayel and Hannah and all the members of their churches across Syria knelt for an hour of prayer. When there was internet and power, Mikayel led online prayer meetings, and together, they worshipped, thanking God for His provisions, and shared their burdens and fears.

Mikayel noted the prayers of the believers had shifted from "Lord! When is this war going to be over?" to "Father, your will be done! May You be glorified!"

When the siege ended, the church gathered in a deserted building and worshipped, growing in faith and in numbers.

Widows shared, "Life was so good before the war. We had everything we could want, and it was peaceful. But now we have Jesus! It's not so terrible because we have Him. And we aren't afraid to die, because we have Jesus."

While the war ripped away every shred of security, comfort, and identity, the body of believers in Aleppo became a close-knit family. What precious moments praying together in candlelight and sharing resources, food staples, soap, and medical bills.

I could never have envisioned how a war could bring people together! The pastor marveled, surveying the Armenians, Iraqis, Turks, Kurds, and varied Syrian background singing with uplifted hands, eyes closed in earnest worship, cheeks bathed in tears.

From the depths of their souls poured the heartfelt Arabic Blessing Song with passion and vibrant joy:

"The Lord bless you, And keep you. The Lord make His face to shine upon you, And be gracious to you…. May His presence go before you. And behind you, and beside you. All around you, and within you. He is with you; He is with you. In the morning, in the evening. In your coming, in your going. In your weeping and rejoicing, He is for you; He is for you. He is for you; He is for you. He is for you; He is for you."

In addition to discipling and ministering to the needs of the Syrian populace of Aleppo, Mikayel mentored and assisted Turkish Kurds seeking Jesus. He walked alongside them in their walk with Jesus and assisted them with their needs for food and relief goods.

Turks . . . of the same people who had declared jihad on his Christian Armenian ancestors and sent them on their death marches through the Syrian desert. Turks who should have been his mortal enemies.

But Turks whom Mikayel loved, graciously served, and discipled because of the love of Jesus in his heart. The unvanquishable power of love was victorious over the power of hate once again.

"I've been checking into a larger building for us to meet in," Mikayel told his wife. "The church is multiplying faster than a dozen rabbits. God is giving us an amazing opportunity. This is God's season. The fields are so ripe, the harvest basically drops into our hands."

In his free time, Mikayel studied to complete a theological degree. Perhaps someday, when Davit was released, they'd all move to Armenia, but for now, Aleppo needed them.

And then a call came from Davit. "Dad, I've been exonerated and released. And you will never believe it. While I was fretting and miserable in jail, my entire regiment was killed in an attack. Every single one. God put me in prison to keep me safe. But now I'm out."

How great is our God!

Muslim men and women wept in terror in the Great Mosque of Aleppo. "How can you be so happy and peaceful?" Islamic neighbors asked Mikayel. ISIS pickups not only targeted Christian homes, but also rumbled into the farms of Muslim families.

ISA—THE ESCAPE

(Circa 2012)

"You are a hiding place for me; you preserve me from trouble; you surround me with shouts of deliverance."

Psalm 32:7

"When I survey the wondrous cross on which the Prince of glory died, my richest gain I count but loss, and pour contempt on all my pride.

See, from His head, His hands, His feet, sorrow and love flow mingled down. Did e'er such love and sorrow meet, or thorns compose so rich crown?"

—Isaac Watts

Samira's heart froze when she saw the smirks on the masked faces eyeing her daughters.

"A whole harem in one house!" one guffawed.

Not if I can help it! Samira's heart screamed.

A mother bear, she stood resolutely staring down the terrorists with an air of fearless spunk she did not feel, clutching young Isa to her chest. Meeting her eyes, the ISIS militants grabbed their sacks of loot. They left only their muddy boot prints among the remnants of ransacked belongings.

Samira slammed the door behind them, bolted it, and collapsed onto the floor in tears. The vile creatures had seen her greatest treasures, her daughters. And they would be back. Soon. They would not forget a whole house of girls. "A *harem*. . . ."

Icy fingers gripped her spine.

"Pack your backpacks," Abdul instructed his children in clipped tones when Samira told him about the visit. "And girls, your burkas." If they would take nothing else, they would wear those black burkas to cover their sweet, gentle faces.

He did not mention that he wanted backpacks in case the need arose to walk if the car was taken.

The stories he'd heard threatened to crush the courage in his heart like a desert lizard beneath a camel's hoof. But Abdul didn't let Samira know how terrified he was as he studied the map one last time before packing his documents.

"The neighbors said if we ever want to sell Shada, they will buy her, so I am taking her and the calf over. Along with a spare house key," Abdul decided. He had saved the beloved pet for last.

"Oh, not Shada!" the children cried unanimously. "Can't we take her with us?" the girls begged.

"She will be much happier in her own Aleppine meadows, and besides, how would we get a cow and a calf into the car and still have room for all of us? But come, I will let you say goodbye before I take her."

Abdul's children crowded around their beloved pet, pouring tears into her soft hide and promising they would return before her calf had grown.

"Look, she's crying!" one of the girls noticed.

"Naw, animals don't cry," Abdul chuckled. But leaning forward he could see the cow really was crying. Great drops of liquid pooled at the sides of the cow's large, mournful brown eyes.

Not knowing when the soldiers could return, Samira kept an ear tuned to the rumble of a truck as she resourcefully packed blankets, food, clothing, utensils, and water bottles into the vehicle.

Samira stashed anything of value out of sight, drew the shades, and finally turned off the lights and the gas.

Who will enter these doors next? Would squatters move into the temporarily abandoned home? Looters? Would a troop of radical soldiers leave their filthy tracks over the floors? Radical soldiers? But it didn't matter. Everything that really counted was in the car—their family.

The sound of the key in the door as Abdul locked the house behind them clicked with devastating permanence.

Wrapping the blanket tightly around sleeping baby Isa, Samira risked a backward glance at the darkened farm, representing their life earnings, their memories and dreams.

Will our next home be a tent? she wondered. *But Abdul has connections he thinks will share their room with our family. . . .*

Stars hid behind the black billows of smoke as Abdul cautiously maneuvered around piles of rubble, past ancient landmarks decimated beyond recognition illuminated in the faint moon rays braving the smoky haze.

Traveling at night and early morning was safest, Abdul knew; few skirmishes clashed in the night. He planned a circuitous route to avoid the battle fronts and most dangerous checkpoints.

"Expect to travel 24–48 hours," Abdul alerted his family. "The 222-mile trip used to take 6 hours, but we have to go to southern Syria before heading back up to Lebanon and take roundabout routes to bypass as many checkpoints as possible. And then, in the daylight, we may have to park and wait till dark again."

Spotting an occasional bullet-riddled body along the road and burned shells of cars and trucks, Samira blessed Abdul for traveling this section at night, sparing the children the gruesome scenes.

As they drove, Abdul drew from his military experience to train the children for what they could face.

He slowed the car as they passed the burnt shell of a vehicle. "We are staying on the roads as much as possible," he told them. "Militants planted landmines in the fields along the road so if cars try to miss the checkpoints, they will hit a mine, explode, and burn like that car did.

"There is always a chance a vehicle ahead of us could hit a landmine," he explained. "If a car ahead explodes, we cannot turn around and go back because in turning around, we could hit a mine. So, what we will have to do if that happens is to park the car, climb out of the windows onto the roof, slide down off the back of the vehicle into the car tracks, and walk back the way we came, staying right in the car tracks because where the car tracks went, there was no explosive."

The family traveled in silence as the children's faces pressed against the windows whispering. "Goodbye Shada. Goodbye Grandma. Goodbye farm. Goodbye friends. Goodbye Syria. . . ."

Abdul scanned the countryside, reviewing every possible scenario again. "At the first crack of a gunshot, all of you drop to the floor. And brace yourselves because I am going to drive this car like it's never been driven before."

And Samira believed every word. That was her warrior husband, for sure.

Approaching the first checkpoint, a quick glance in the rearview mirror assured Abdul his daughters had fallen asleep, their precious faces hidden in pillows and burkas.

Abdul sat tall and stern like a general leading his troop. The soldier approached the window, shining his light over the sleeping forms. "Give me your IDs."

Abdul handed them to the guard with money tucked among the documents.

Samira couldn't relax to sleep. She worried about the outcome of each checkpoint. She felt the roll of money stashed into her sock. It was still there.

She watched families trudging along the roadside, burdened with babies and duffel bags.

Don't let ISIS confiscate our vehicle. . . .

Something is wrong with Abdul's health. Stress has taken its toll. I should have urged him to get checked out, but when was their time for a doctor's visit?

She worried about the girls. Always, the girls.

"If the radicals tell you to get out of the car and try to abduct you," she warned her yawning girls, "It is better to run or try to get back in the car and get shot than to be alive and be their slaves."

As the car approached a checkpoint, Samira noted the black flag flapping overhead like a ravenous hawk about to pounce on a hapless mouse. IN THE CAUSE OF ALLAH! The white letters above the crossed swords seemed to hiss with each flap of the flag.

What kind of a god is Allah if he orders his soldiers to kill, steal, and rape in his name? Samira asked herself the questions that had begun to haunt her. *What god is that?*

The sleepy soldier waved them through with his flashlight, scarcely glancing at the slumbering black mounds in the back. Some Divine Being seemed to be watching over her family on this trip.

"Everybody out! The car stays here!" The masked guard at the next checkpoint waved his AK-47. "Out! Be fast! I will let you go, but you go on foot."

Samira couldn't cry. Let the jihadists take the car if they had to, but not her girls.

Thanks to taxis whose drivers grew rich from shuttling refugees, Abdul found intermittent rides in the direction of Lebanon.

"There's the border!" Abdul called cheerily, pointing to a white flag with a green cedar in the middle and a red stripe above and below it. Crowds of dusty, weary moms, dads, and children plodded toward the border, their eyes listless and sad, traumatized by the brutal scenes branded on their brains. Everyone was desperate to get out of Syria and into Lebanon. If two million Syrian refugees already huddled in tents in refugee camps across the country, how long would Lebanon continue to accept Syria's displaced citizens?

An occasional car and columns of bedraggled stragglers coming in the opposite direction indicated not all who tried to enter were successful.

What if they don't let us in? Samira wanted to ask, knowing the options were few. *Return home and face bombings and ISIS. Try Jordan, but Jordan is overwhelmed with refugees too. Try to get to Greece on the tippy, overloaded rafts and then on to Germany. . . . But smugglers charge $1,000 a person and crowd so many people into the rafts that they often capsize. Some tried overland illegal border crossings and were shot.*

Oh please, please let us get into Lebanon, her heart prayed. To whom she did not know. Not to Allah. He would not care.

The hope in their hearts seemed as fragile as bubbles from a child's bubble wand as the exhausted family faced the border guard.

"IDs. Purpose of your trip and destination."

Abdul handed the stack of documents to the guard. "Our lives are in danger, and we plan to wait in Lebanon with a friend until we get asylum in another country or until the fighting calms down."

"Sunni refugees," the frazzled guard muttered. "We've already got more of you people than we can handle. Do you know how many others I've turned away today? Sorry. Try Jordan, Türkiye, or Greece."

"Sir," Abdul pled with all his honeyed charm. "Do you have a family? What would you do if your children's lives were in danger? Your daughters?"

The guard flipped through the documents as he handed them back to Abdul. He paused as the name on the last document caught his attention. "Hmm. Isa. That's a Christian name." His eyes scanned the black burka-covered women. "Which one is Isa?"

"This one," Abdul pointed to the sleeping toddler in his mother's arms.

As the hopes of the future hung in the balance in those fragile seconds, Samira wondered, *Was the dream a* blessing *or curse? Will the name Isa given by the Man in White keep us out of Lebanon? Or will it be our passport to enter?*

Part IV

I Am a Poor Wayfaring Stranger

(Circa 2010–2023)

"Indeed, I count everything as loss because of the surpassing worth of knowing Christ Jesus my Lord . . ."

Philippians 3:8

I'm just a poor wayfaring stranger
while journeying through this Land of woe
But there's no sickness toil or danger
In that bright world to which I go.
I know dark clouds will gather o'er me,
I know my way lies rough and steep
But Beauteous Fields lie out before me
Where God's redeemed their vigils keep.

—Folk song

ISIS WIVES

"Fear not, for I am with you; be not dismayed, for I am your God; I will strengthen you, I will help you, I will uphold you with my righteous right hand."

Isaiah 41:10

"The whole message of the Gospel is to take your cross and follow me. To be under the cross is to focus on the whole message of the Gospel: to follow Jesus, and teach all of what He teaches, to teach the cross."

—Rami Ibrahim

"Nabil! They're coming!" Yasmine cried, glancing over her shoulder as she darted through the door and into his arms. She didn't have to say who. He read the answer in the terror glistening in her eyes.

The young pastor held his wife tightly. Her entire body seemed to vibrate with the thump of her heart.

The screams and gunshots drew closer.

To flee is suicide. To hide is impossible.

Yasmine's credentials as a professor at the university would give her no free pass with the radicals. Nor would his position in the local hospital grant him mercy.

Being the well-known Christian leader in this village earned Nabil a spot at the top of the ISIS hit list.

In a flash Nabil saw the fingertips of the pastor's young son falling away beneath the ISIS sword. . . . The son and his father hanging from crosses. . . . Courageous. . . . Uncompromising. . . . Knowing the victor's crown would soon be theirs.

His mind's eye saw the woman kneeling beneath the flash of the ISIS sword. He envisioned the brightening of her eyes and the sudden glow on her face as she gazed into clouds. He heard the joyful cry, "Jesus!"

"Yasmine, habibti, focus on the face of Jesus. He will give us strength to persevere."

Chilling screams of "Allahu Akbar!" and the sound of splintering doors filtered into the house. Reverberating explosion of machine gun fire punctuated shouts of "Lead us to the Christian leaders!"

How could life in Syria have changed so fast and so drastically? Nabil wondered. Despite occasional barrel bombs, life had been relatively normal in this Christian village.

Until the ISIS wives and families forced themselves into the village homes a year ago.

"Give us rooms in your houses for us and our children!" the black burka-covered wives of the ISIS fighters demanded, eyes flashing ominously beneath their burkas.

"Our husbands are fighters. If you don't give us a room and food, we will call them. They will torture you and kill you horribly. And then we will have all of your houses to ourselves, all your food, and all your animals. You can choose."

Various villagers tried to make life as miserable as possible for the ISIS families, hoping the unwanted guests would choose to leave.

Nabil, Yasmine, and the church discussed the dilemma. "What if God allowed these needy women and traumatized children to come to our village so we can show them the love of Jesus? Let's welcome them into our homes and show them love, no matter how difficult that seems," they decided bravely.

Nabil and Yasmine graciously welcomed Fatima and her brood of unkempt youngsters into a room they carefully prepared in their home, knowing the move would revolutionize their lives.

Hordes of screaming, scrapping wildcats tramped muddy shoes through the orderly homes of the Christian families. The sons and daughters of ISIS fighters swung pets by the tails, snatched toys from their babies, terrorized village children with stick guns, and broke dishes. The uninvited guests thanklessly gobbled down the villagers' meager food supplies, spilling half of it on the floors.

Patiently, Nabil and Yasmine showed the love of Jesus to these hurting, scarred savages who had never experienced affection. Tenderly, they reflected the love of Jesus to the demanding, angry mothers who had known so much abuse at the hands of their ISIS "fighter men."

Nabil kicked a soccer ball with the youngsters. Yasmine hugged the children and read stories when she came home from teaching at the university. She quietly swept up the crumbs and broken shards of glass. Uncomplainingly, she mopped up the muddy footprints and cleaned around the toilet.

Yasmine spoke sweetly to the surly, burka-clad mother, sharing her food and kitchen with the ISIS wife.

The cold, pain-filled eyes behind the mesh of Fatima's burka began to soften, and the heart beneath the long tentlike abaya started to open and share her stories.

"As young teens, the idealistic ISIS philosophy of the brave fighters conquering the world captivated some of our naïve hearts," she revealed. "We traveled to join the ISIS fighters. But Yasmine, we had no clue what we were getting into.

"The fighters compelled some of us to watch while they decapitated our fathers and brothers, and then they forced us to be their wives. Then forced us to bear their babies, serve them night and day, and cook their meals in their crude camps.

"They treated us with the same hateful, brutal spite they used on their victims. I'm telling you, Yasmine, it didn't take long till we got disillusioned by the cruel hatefulness instead of the glamorous promises." The young mother's voice died away, Her eyes pools of sadness.

"But Yasmine, we are trapped.

"There is no way out. Except death. And because of our children, we choose to live and serve the fighters."

Yasmine dabbed the tears from the corner of her eyes. *What pain! Such heartache!*

These precious ISIS wives, like hibiscus flowers transplanted to the parched desert, thirstily absorbed refreshing dew drops of kindness on their hearts so hardened by cruelty.

Over the year that Nabil's self-invited guests lived with his family, the ISIS women warmed beneath the kindness, slowly returning the love of their hosts.

When their masked, machine gun-wielding husbands rumbled into town unannounced in their Toyota pickup trucks with the black flags and anti-aircraft guns mounted on the back, the ISIS wives knew the drill.

"Mr. Nabil, our men are coming for you! They are just up the road!" Fatima screamed, bursting into the house, her face ashen beneath her burka. Several other ISIS wives tumbled into the house behind her, panting, arms laden with black bundles.

"Our husbands will break into every house until they find the leaders of the Christians," Fatima had warned. "And then, they will secure you to their mobile execution cross and slaughter you."

After living with Nabil and Yasmine for a year, the women knew these kind, caring people did not deserve to die. And these Jesus people had a powerful God watching over them.

"They will kill you, Mr. Nabil! If you want to survive, you and Yasmine must do exactly as we say!" Panic pitched her voice almost to a shriek.

A cold sweat filmed the young pastor's body. Spine-chilling shouts of "Allahu Akbar!" grew closer, punctuated by the fire of AK-47s and screams of the villagers.

"Quick, Mr. Nabil! Put this burka over your clothes!" A woman thrust a bundle of coarse black clothing into Nabil's shaking hands and another into his wife's. "And you too!"

"Quickly!"

The women tugged the burkas in place. "And now the abaya!"

"This is the front, like this. No one will recognize you," a woman assured them, adjusting the burkas on the couple with a nervous giggle. "And don't forget gloves; you have to hide those big hands."

"Our men won't detect who you are. But you must listen to us. If you act nervous, or if you talk and they hear a man's voice, you are a goner!

"So, Mr. Nabil, you cannot speak. We will talk to you. You have to walk slowly and like a woman without letting your big feet peek out. And you can't be nervous!"

I can't be nervous! How can I not be? he panted, stashing his passport, phone, and wallet in his pocket beneath his scratchy, voluminous costume.

The sweat began to drip down his back beneath the layers, reeking of the body odor of those who wore the garments before him. He desperately fought the claustrophobia trying to strangle him as the rumble of the trucks and gunshots drew nearer.

I've got to slow down my breathing. Breathe and hold. One, two, three, four. Release and hold. One, two, three, four. . . .

"Let's go. Follow us. Let us do the talking, and you will be fine," Fatima reassured the couple after quickly circling them for a final inspection and grabbing her grocery bag with shaking hands.

Nabil and Yasmine joined the troop of women heading for the market, trying not to stumble over the long fabric twisting about their feet. Yasmine had no large shoes or male voice to worry about. Nabil tried to walk as gracefully as if he had worn a burka all his life. But it was such a challenge. And the netting over his eyes obscured his vision.

Slow and easy. Jesus help us. . . .

"We are going to go out and watch the men and cheer for them. They like that. But Mr. Nabil, don't forget, don't talk, and don't act nervous. Just go slow."

The troupe of burka-clad women trudged down the street, their abayas dragging in the dust, hiding the large shoes beneath one of them. A gaggle of children scampered alongside.

"Slowly, habibi," Yasmine whispered as several Toyotas roared up the road. "Walk like a woman. Don't stumble. You're doing great."

A truck braked, and the black-hooded men jumped off, greeting the women as they sauntered over to the group. "Cook us up some kebabs! We're starved!" the terrorists snapped gruffly.

"We're headed to market now," Fatima responded charmingly. "We'll grill you the best kebabs you ever had."

"Stop shaking, Mr. Nabil," the woman behind him hissed from beneath her burka. "The men will know you are not one of us if you don't stop trembling."

After a few exchanges, the ISIS soldiers headed for the nearest house, smashing through the door yelling, "Allahu Akbar!" as they clambered over the splintered wood. "Where are the Jesus people?"

The women calmly picked up their empty grocery bags. Like a flock of black goats, the troop meandered toward the market. And to find a taxi.

Nabil stepped gingerly into the back of the cab, tugging the abaya over his large shoes. Yasmine handed the money to the taxi driver. "Take us to Damascus, she instructed, squeezing the hand beneath the abaya beside her.

Waving their gratitude to the gloved hands extending from the black cloud of women, the couple wondered, *What is the future for those precious souls?*

Nabil and Yasmine had plenty of resettlement options, but before long, the entire world would despise the ISIS families, leaving hundreds of ISIS wives, widows, and children to languish in squalid refugee camps, unwanted, and with no future.

As the yellow cab rolled out of the village, Nabil and his wife glanced back to see the gloves of the burka-covered women waving goodbye. And Nabil knew there were smiles beneath those burkas. And seeds of the love of Jesus planted and sprouting in the hearts.

Jesus take care of those needy lambs . . .

"WOULD YOU RISK IT?"

"For everyone who has been born of God overcomes the world. And this is the victory that has overcome the world—our faith."

I John 5:4

"A call is the assignment of the Lord—the urging of the Holy Spirit that won't go away. We will know God's will by the peace of God ruling in our hearts, according to Colossians 3:15. The word rule indicates peace acts as an umpire calling the verdict, settling the dispute. If the urgings are consistent, we gently move. Jurisdiction is so key—it is the conviction to confirm God's calling. God will bring together the people, the circumstances, and the place. There is the danger of being so busy that we miss the nudging. But the true servant of the Lord will know. God never disappoints. However, a calling sometimes comes with a price."

—Ervin

I must know! The seminary student paced restlessly. *I won't waste time getting to know her if the answer to one question is negative. That single answer will tell me all I need to know.*

Approaching graduation, the call on Marc's life was clearer than ever. The desperate needs of the persecuted Christians on the front lines of the Middle East and North Africa drew his heart. But would a girl put her life at risk to join him?

Mustering all the courage inherited from his fearless Middle Eastern ancestry, Marc searched Sarah's vibrant eyes, sparkling with joy and promise.

"So, would you ever consider going abroad to live in a *dangerous* country?"

The heaviness of the ramifications lying in her response crushed the breath from his lungs.

God called me to serve in the Middle East boiling with conflict and radical extremists. If she won't consider living there, there's no use teasing her heart. Or mine.

When Marc first met Sarah the previous semester in the seminary New Testament class, he was drawn to her gentle, sweet, gracious vivaciousness. He had never quite forgotten this pure ray of light, though their paths hadn't crossed again.

Until yesterday, when he passed her in the student center. Their eyes met and held momentarily. Her sweet smile did strange things to his heart in those brief seconds.

I have to know!

The immensity of the question swelled and morphed until little space remained in his tortured brain for focus on cramming for finals.

"God, if you want me to pursue the feelings I have for Sarah, please arrange for her to study at the same location tomorrow," his tortured heart pled as he strolled back to the dorm after the encounter.

When Marc entered the student center the following day, his heart lurched in his chest. Sarah sat at the table, her long blond hair falling across her books as she studied—alone.

God what are you saying?

"Mind if I join you?" Marc took a chair across from Sarah as her smile welcomed him. He engaged her in a conversation, the importance of which swiftly overtook the urgency to prepare for their finals.

"Cramming for your finals?"

"I am. I never study on campus, but the study group wanted to meet here yesterday and today. And the rest never showed."

Thank you, Jesus!

What an intriguing woman, Marc thought, listening to Sarah's musical voice describe the call to overseas missions.

"I went on short-term mission trips and pursued a degree in education, believing it would help me on the mission field someday. After the tsunami, I taught school for two years for missionary children in Indonesia.

"My parents hoped the mission stint would get overseas missions out of my heart." Her eyes glimmered with life and laughter. "But nothing could change God's call to lifelong international missions. Nor my commitment to embrace the calling. I came home from Asia and enrolled here at the seminary to further equip for my calling."

What a woman. Not only is she delightful, lovely, gracious, and brilliant, but she is also prepared and equipped to serve. Her tools are sharpened.

God had called Marc to return to share the Gospel in the dangers of the Middle East and he could not look at a girl who would be fearful of a life on the edge. Marc had to know.

"Sarah," he asked, his heart pulsing as if his entire life hinged on her answer. "Would you ever consider taking the risk to live abroad in a *dangerous* country?"

"Absolutely!" She didn't even hesitate. The glow in her eyes punctuated her response.

"Would you mind if we exchanged contact information?" Marc asked, rising to end one of the most engaging conversations he ever had.

Seven months later, Sarah walked down the aisle toward her enraptured groom. She graduated from seminary the next year. One week after graduation, Marc and Sarah's baby daughter was born.

Marc and Sarah talked of working in Africa. And then the war erupted in Syria.

"The harvest is so ripe here in the Middle East," Abraham Samara told Marc. "We have several thousand people a week coming to our services. Muslims are responding in droves. They are so disillusioned with the brutality and atrocities among their own people.

"But the harvest is probably ripest in the Syrian refugee camps where the people have lost everything. They are disenchanted with a religion where people kill each other in the name of their god. And Marc, they are open. I have never seen such responsiveness among the Muslims, or even the Orthodox for that matter."

"I can't forget the Japanese missionary who spoke at seminary," Marc told his wife as they prayed about their future.

"The one that grieved because the fields were so ripe, and the response was so feeble?"

"His words still haunt me. I can hear his shaky old voice saying, 'After the war in Japan, the fields were so ripe for harvest. I kept begging for workers to join me. But the response was so meager that, tragically, a wonderful opportunity to harvest ripened souls has been missed.'"

"The season for ripe harvest lasts only so long . . ."

"I'm hearing hundreds of thousands of Syrian refugees have fled to camps in neighboring countries. The needs are desperate."

"It's your culture."

"And my native language."

Two days before their flight left for the Middle East, the couple discovered God was giving them another baby.

"When I told you I'd be willing to serve God overseas in a dangerous country, I hadn't thought about taking baby girls to a country with bombs, ISIS radicals, and war," Sarah laughingly told her husband. "But I am going. God prepared us. He called. And He opened doors."

"Sarah dear." He took both her soft hands in his strong ones. "You don't know how happy it makes me to hear you say you support my call, and you trust God no matter what. . . ."

"Well Marc, we are safer *in* God's will, *in* the war zone, than *out* of His will and *out* of the war zone."

How great is our God!

Yet, in the darkened cabin, as the airliner cruised high over the ocean, Sarah couldn't help but think, *Babies add a whole new facet to the risk. I'm not afraid to die for God, but what if I am separated from my children through bombing, fighting. . . . How could I bear it?*

"DO ANGELS
WEAR HIJABS?"

"For the eyes of the Lord run to and fro throughout the whole earth, to give strong support to those whose heart is blameless toward him."

II Chronicles 16:9

"Our Lord did not die to provide selfish men with eternal life while they remained serving themselves. But as he struggled bleeding and beaten up Calvary's hill, bearing the cross on his shredded back, He intended that those for whom He was dying would redirect their self-obsession, into losing themselves in Him—thus in denying self would find the joy of fullness in God."

—Walter Chantry

As Marc prepared to drive to the camps to show the Jesus film one Saturday, he read loneliness in Sarah's eyes as he kissed her goodbye. Pregnant and caring for a toddler, Sarah struggled to adjust to the new culture, foreign country, and strange language while trying to find her niche in ministry.

"Why don't you and Lyla come along?"

"I'd love to!" Quickly Sarah filled a couple of bottles, scooped up several diapers and wipes, and they were off with the baby settled in her seat with a big bottle of milk.

What a treat to spend the day as a family and see more of Marc's ministry among the refugees.

Passing fields of potatoes, with women and children hunched over the plants, Sarah's face furrowed in compassionate concern. "Such brutal work for women. Where are the men?"

"The refugees are desperate to earn a little money, and there isn't much else available."

"But the men?"

"Some of them are Bedouins, lounging in their tents while the women work. Many are dead. Some work. A few are off looking for jobs in Europe."

"Such hard lives."

"It's hell, they tell me. Some say they wish they had stayed in Syria and died instead of coming here. 'This isn't a life worth living. We have no dignity,' they say. But what else was there to do, stay and let ISIS kill or kidnap their children? Risk the flimsy dinghies on the ocean waves?

"They lost not only their homes but businesses, equipment, vehicles, fleeing on foot.

"'I'd die a thousand deaths for my children,' a mom told me. Some have been forced to sell their daughters or arrange child marriages because they can't afford to feed them."

"There have got to be other ways!"

"That's why we are here—to discover the needs, to see how we can resolve them. Distribute food packages. Listen and to pray. Show the Jesus film to bring hope.

"'ISIS kidnapped and killed our neighbors,' they tell me. 'They violated our daughters. . . . Why would we want to serve a god who commands people to kill and torture? Who is God?' they ask.

"It's unprecedented, Sarah. John Samara from Ananias House says more Muslims are turning to Christ during this season than in any other time in history, and I believe it. Growing up in a Muslim majority country, I've never seen such openness.

"Muslims are turning away from Allah with whom they could have no relationship and from whom they could have no assurance of reaching heaven, turning from an Allah of darkness, hate, and killing, to a God of love, light, relationship, and hope."

The serpentine curves, rutted roads, and detours along the route played havoc, curdling the milk in the baby's belly, which erupted all over Lyla.

Marc calmly pulled to the side of the road. Sarah extracted the baby from her seat and peeled off the smelly, soaked clothing.

Standing at the roadside of this Middle Eastern village, the young couple swabbed the sour milk from the baby's body as best they could with the wipes. Lyla began to shiver in the breeze.

"We left so fast I forgot to grab an extra set of clothing for her."

Sarah looked up to see a hijab-covered woman emerging from her house.

"Do you have a plastic bag?" Sarah tried to ask in her halting Arabic. *Surely, it would not be too much to ask for a bag for the soiled garments.*

The villager raised her eyebrow, rattling off in Arabic and gesticulating.

Marc approached the women, asking what they were trying to say.

"I was hoping for a bag for the smelly clothes," Sarah explained with a smile.

Marc, in his native Arabic, communicated the request for his wife, gesturing toward the shivering baby.

"Ah!" The woman nodded and disappeared into her house, returning with a bag and two sets of clothing. The outfits were mismatched and the wrong sizes, but to the young mother, the clothing looked divine.

"Oh, thank you! That's thoughtful, but the baby only needs one set of clothes."

"Take two sets," the village woman insisted. "She will need two."

"You are an angel!" Sarah marveled, fitting her baby into a set of gifted clothing.

Sarah settled Lyla into her seat, and they resumed their journey. A few miles down the road, the baby spewed the rest of the milk over the fresh set of clothing.

Marc's eyes met Sarah's and they burst into laughter.

The couple cleaned up the baby for the second time, placed the dirty clothes in the bag, and dressed the baby in the second set of donated clothing.

"How did that woman know we would need *two* sets of clothing? She really was an angel. Do angels wear hijabs?

"How amazing was that? God knew we would need two sets and provided them."

I am watching over you so closely that I provided the two sets of clothing I knew you would need, God seemed to whisper to Sarah. *And I will watch over you and provide for the rest of your needs when you are on the front lines for Me.*

Sarah surveyed the clusters of white tents, streaked with dust and weighted down with old tires and concrete blocks hunkered in rows along gravel pathways. Flimsy plastic chairs and old cushions adorned modest patios. Rusty satellite dishes and pipe chimneys protruded from each roof.

A hijabed mother scooped water from a five-gallon bucket, pouring it over her son seated in a plastic tub. Young girls with eyes too old for their small faces balanced babies on their hips or lugged five-gallon jugs of water.

Sarah helped Marc set up the screen for the Jesus film near the endless rows of tents, absorbing the scent of sizzling garlics and onions overpowering the stench of sewer and mildew.

She shivered, thinking of the winter temperatures falling below zero, and the snowstorms and floods wreaking havoc on these fragile tents.

After the video, Marc and Sarah listened to the brutal journeys of the refugees in hijabs and burkas. They handed out relief packages, prayed with the ill and grieving, and showed the love of God to the hearts so broken, so stripped of all that was familiar and safe, so disillusioned with the religion they grew up with, and so open to the love of the true God.

Where did the child get the chocolate? Sara wondered, seeing the brown goo oozing from the fingers in the boy's mouth. A closer look revealed that he was sucking on a rock.

"There's a family you might want to check on," a refugee told Marc on one of his visits. "They've got the clothes on their backs and shoes on their feet and that's it. The landowner was exploiting them and not paying them. I rescued them and found them a room to live in. But they have absolutely nothing. Do you have anything you can give them? Blankets? Food packages?"

"I'll take food boxes over and bring blankets too," Marc promised.

The Kurdish family with six children met Marc with delighted smiles and claps of joy.

"I prayed, 'If you are real, if there really is a God, save us!'" The father's face shone as he spoke. "'I looked up in the sky and there in the clouds was a cross made of clouds. Mr. Marc, can you tell me about the true God? And the cross?"

Marc shared about Jesus's sacrifice on the cross to reconcile human relationship with the Creator God. The parents and their six children knelt in their tiny, bare room and asked Jesus to come live in their hearts.

Weary but with the rewarding gratification of a day well spent, the couple began the journey home. While the baby slept, the couple talked about the women in the camp and the opportunities to reach out to them.

"Everywhere I looked, I saw pregnant moms and young moms toting toddlers and babies," Sarah noted. "The cycle of life doesn't stop and continues even here among these tent villages.

"You know, Marc, we could start a class for moms and teach them about nutrition and appropriate exercise, give them vitamins, and tell them a Bible story, and you could be my translator."

"Sweetheart, that's brilliant. There's a huge need for exactly what you are describing. Let's do it!"

The outreach opportunities seemed as endless as the rows of tents across the fields behind them.

The green disks of the minaret lights glowed against the distant, black silhouetted mountains as if highlighting the need for the Light of the world in the dark valley.

Marc's phone buzzed. He accepted the call, enabling speakerphone so he could drive without distraction.

"Mr. Marc, are you busy? My friend's brother George is a taxi driver. He had this passenger who was a sheikh from Saudi Arabia, a professor. The passenger goes to the taxi driver, 'George, that's a Christian name.'

"The taxi driver was like, 'Well, yeah,' Then this Saudi Arabian sheikh asks, 'Do you know of anyone who could tell me about Jesus or give me a Bible?' Imagine that. Well, the driver asked his brother, and he asked me, and I thought of you. I'll give you the Saudi sheikh's number if you feel comfortable meeting with him. Salem is the name.

"I don't blame you if you don't want to risk it," the caller added. "You have a family. One never knows these days if it's legit or a trap, but he seemed to be really searching."

Lord, what would you have me to do? Marc breathed. *If it's a trap, I'm dead. But if this sheikh is really searching. . . .?*

CLANDESTINE RENDEZVOUS

"Whoever has seen me has seen the Father."

John 14:9

"'What do I do with all my doubts and fears?' he asked. 'Take them honestly to God,' I said. 'That's what people are doing throughout Scripture. I have doubts too sometimes. That's normal. But if in spite of all your doubts and fears, you are willing to give your allegiance to Jesus, that's enough. Faith isn't the absence of doubt, it's loyalty to a trustworthy King in spite of unanswered questions.'"

—R. Wenger

What if it's a trap set up for me by ISIS radicals? An icy chill slithered down Marc's spine. His mind's eye flashed scenes of mutilated bodies. One close escape from the jaws of a trap was enough.

It's not just me, I have Sarah and Lyla to consider. How can I put them at risk?

But what if the sheikh is sincere?

It's a risk, but I'll hazard it for Jesus, Marc decided after he and Sarah prayed about the potential encounter.

"My schedule is full until Tuesday, but if that works for you, I will meet you Tuesday morning at the basement coffee shop downtown." Marc tensed to pick up any cues from the man's words and tone on the phone.

"I am scheduled to fly back to Saudi Arabia that morning, but sir, I really want to meet with you. I am so desperate to know about your holy book and your Jesus. I will postpone my flight."

He sounds sincere.

223

Marc prayed as he drove. *Lord, help me. This has all the markings of a trap. I can still cancel. Not show up. . . .*

But if this Saudi is sincere, it could make a difference for eternity.

A snarl of traffic and detours stretched the drive from an hour and a half to three torturous hours. Three hours filled with prayer. And agonizing.

It would be safer to just connect online, Marc fretted. But he had learned these Middle Eastern people were much more responsive to flesh and blood than a screen. And giving the sheikh a link for an online site with a Bible wasn't possible in Saudi Arabia, as such sites were blocked there.

And searching Muslims have a respect for holy books. They want to handle a paper copy of our Bible, not see a digital form, he knew.

Marc scarcely smelled the roasting Arabica coffee beans or the sweet spicy cardamom as his eyes swept the remote basement coffee shop he had selected as an ideal clandestine rendezvous location.

A dignified, bearded, olive-skinned man sat across the room, dressed in white from his headgear to his flowing robe. The man sat erect, wide-eyed and leaning forward in anticipation.

The sheikh was alone.

Marc's eyes scanned the room as he approached the table with a smile. A few young students sipped on coffee as they typed on their computers.

"You must be Mr. Salem. I am Marc. I apologize, the traffic delayed me, but I am glad to see you waited."

"Of course! I was so excited I actually came an hour and a half early so I wouldn't miss you!"

Marc arranged his chair so he could watch the door. Just in case. *Please, Lord, guide my conversation. Is there a back door?*

I will ask a few questions and see if what he says lines up with what I have heard, Marc decided.

"Tell me about yourself. What is your occupation?"

"I am a professor and an Imam from a very conservative and deeply connected family."

That's what the taxi driver indicated.

"Saudi Arabia, as you know, is called the home of Islam, the birthplace of Muhammad." Salem's story poured out over cups of sweet, thick cardamom coffee.

"My family has connections with the oil business, bringing me to this country on occasion.

"I had connections supporting Islamic radicals. I became concerned about the radicals I supported being so focused on killing for Allah. Their spirit contrasted sharply with the love and kindness of Christians.

"Mr. Marc, I have been intrigued to observe those converting from Islam to Christianity go from wanting to kill people for Allah, to becoming people who lay down their own lives to please God.

"I asked myself, what does the Christians' holy book teach that is so different from the Qur'an, which teaches to kill those who disagree with us?

"I have been on a quest to find one of your holy books, a Bible. I often travel for my business, and whenever I come to this country where there are supposedly more Christians, I watch and listen to see if I can discover a Christian. When I find one, I ask them for a Bible. But Mr. Marc, all of them I ask, even the orthodox priest told me, 'I might have a Bible of my own, but I have none to share.'

"And that is why I want to talk to you, I want to know what your holy book has to say, and where I can find one. I want to know how to get to heaven for certain.

"Our Qur'an teaches Allah will tally our good deeds and bad deeds to see if we get to Paradise or not. We can't know what our deeds will add up to. Is there a way of being sure one can get to heaven, Mr. Marc? Can you tell me what your holy Book says?"

Marc swirled the thick coffee in his cup. He scanned the room again.

Some of the customers had left. Looking into the dark eyes riveted on him, Marc leaned forward.

"Our holy book tells how God created a perfect world. He wanted someone he could have a relationship with, so He created man. He created him to be perfect. In His own image, without sickness, trouble, or pain.

"But then man disobeyed, and sinned. . . ."

"Ah yes, he ate the fruit."

"True. And God is a holy God. Sin cannot come into His presence. So, there was a problem. God wanted to dwell with man, but man had sin in his heart. God gave the law and sent prophets to teach how sinful man is. Sacrifices covered the sin, but they could not *remove* the sin."

"Ahhh! We all disobey, and sin. So how can we remove the sin? How can we live with God?"

"Our Bible has four books, which the Qur'an calls the Injil, the revelation of Allah. We call them the Gospels. The fourth book of the Injil, or of the Gospels, is called the book of John. Here, let's read John 3:16–18 together." Marc surveyed the room once more before pulling a Bible from his satchel and laying it on the table between them.

"'For God so loved the world, that He gave his only Son, that whoever believes in him should not perish but have eternal life. For God did not send his Son into the world to condemn the world, but in order that the world might be saved through Him. Whoever believes in Him is not condemned, but whoever does not believe is condemned already, because he has not believed in the name of the only Son of God.'

"Mr. Salem, God not only wants us to go to Heaven, and tells us how to get to Heaven, but He sent His Son so we can go to Heaven."

"Ah, Mr. Marc. Such good words. But how do you answer those who say the Christians have corrupted the Injil? Your Gospels?"

"Well, according to the Qur'an, Surah 3:3, 2:136, 5:46 teaches the Gospels (Injil) are a divine revelation from Allah. You know Surah 5:68, 4:136, 29:46 say the Gospels (Injil) are authoritative—they should be believed and obeyed.

"If we compare the Gospels we have to the originals before the Qur'an was written, you will find no changes, which mean they are the same as at the time the Qur'an was written and need to be believed according to the Qur'an."

Salem looked thoughtful for a moment. "So then, the difference between the teaching about Isa, Jesus, in the Qur'an and the Bible would be . . . ?"

"That He is God's son. And second, that He died on the cross. And if every word Jesus says is to be trusted according to the Qur'an, then you must believe Jesus's words that He was God's Son," Marc explained, taking him to John 10:36–38. "'I am the Son of God. . . .'

"Salem, is Islam concerned with telling people how to get right with God, or is it focused on telling them how to behave before God?"

"How to behave, Mr. Marc."

"The Bible teaches God created in order to share himself with His creation, not to test them. He wanted to *dwell* with them. When they disobeyed and put a barrier between them, only a sinless sacrifice would *remove* the sin and redeem the relationship with a holy God. The sinless Son of God offered himself as a sacrifice to redeem the relationship between God and man, removing the sin, so God can live with man and man can dwell with God in Heaven. But man needs to accept Jesus's sacrifice."

"I would like to accept Jesus; how can I do that?"

"There will be a price if you leave Islam and return to your country. . . ."

"I want to live with Jesus in heaven. That's most important. What they do to my body here doesn't matter."

"If you want to accept Jesus as your Savior, tell Him you believe He is the son of God, you want Him to forgive your bad deeds. And then invite Him to live in your heart."

"I want to pray right now." And there in the basement coffee shop, the Saudi sheikh got down on the tile floor and prayed, inviting Jesus to remove his sins and to reign in his heart.

Dusting off his white robe, Salem grabbed Marc in an embrace as if he never wanted to let go. As they rose to part, Salem unclasped his expensive gold watch and handed it to Marc. "Please don't forget me. I want you to have this to remind you to talk to God about me, to pray for me. I need to go back and tell my wife and my children that I have become a follower of Jesus, and I don't know what will happen to me. I might not survive, but I must tell them."

Marc blinked away the tears as he accepted the heavy golden watch.

"And I have something for you. This is a secure copy of the Bible you can carry into your country without detection. Read the Gospels. Especially John."

"Can we do online video calls, Mr. Marc? I know I will have many questions."

"Let's do it, Salem. And I absolutely will be praying for you. God go with you, my friend!"

Marc watched the white swaying robes until the crowds swallowed them.

Marc and Salem kept in close communication, meeting each time the Saudi had opportunity to travel.

"I would like to be baptized," Salem ventured.

Marc searched for a church to connect Salem with for discipleship and mentoring, but every church he tried was apprehensive of the ramifications to their group for taking a former Muslim into their fellowship, and of the risks if he was not genuine.

"Let's meet at the beach the next time you come, and I will baptize you," Marc offered.

"I don't know what will happen to me," Salem shared as water droplets dripped from his dark beard. "But promise me one thing, Marc. If they kill me, bury me in a Christian graveyard. I want the world to know I was a follower of Jesus."

JESUS IN THE CAMP

"For here we have no lasting city, but we seek the city that is to come."

Hebrews 13:14

"They might take our building, they might take our life, but they cannot take Jesus from us."

—Pakistani pastor with Ananias House after the hateful burning of twenty-four church buildings

Who is the veiled older lady with the sweeping black robe attending our class for pregnant and nursing moms each Saturday? Sarah wondered. *She's far past childbearing age. Perhaps she comes for the free vitamins. Maybe she's bored.*

Saturdays, Marc and Sarah and baby Lyla (with plenty of sets of clothing) traveled to the tent camps. The women in burkas and hijabs gathered to hear Sarah, with Marc translating, teach about health, exercise, and diet for pregnant and nursing moms. The couple distributed packets of vitamins, finishing with a story from the Bible.

Every Saturday, the grandmother listened attentively. One morning, she brought a younger woman with her. After the class, the elderly woman approached Marc and Sarah. "My daughter-in-law has not been able to have a baby in six years of being married. We want you to pray to your God to heal her and give her a baby."

The dark, shadowed eyes beneath the younger woman's black hijab shimmered with pain. Her faced flushed in the shame that accompanied barrenness in this culture.

"We will be glad to pray for you for healing," Marc told the young woman, his eyes and voice soft with compassion. "But first, another healing needs to take place. A spiritual healing."

The women seemed open and intrigued, so the four sat down, and

Marc shared the Gospel with them. Both women prayed to accept the Lord.

And then, Marc and Sarah prayed for the barren womb and asked God to make the young woman and her husband fruitful and to give them a child.

Six weeks later, on a return visit to that camp, the young woman spotted Sarah. She broke into a run as she flew up the dusty path between the tents, her abaya flapping behind and her face aglow.

"Miss Sarah! God healed me! He is giving me a baby! I called all my family and friends in Syria and told them, 'God healed me! He is giving me a baby!'"

The sad, dark eyes beneath the hijab drew Sarah's heart to the young mother with the two little sons clinging to her black abaya.

"It was dark when the war front approached our Syrian village," the hijabed mother shared while her sons played in the dirt nearby. "We knew I had to flee immediately with the children. My husband had to stay behind to sell what he could and to settle business, so I had to leave alone with the three children. Pregnant. And by foot.

"I grabbed a few pieces of clothing, a couple blankets, a little food in a bundle I felt I could manage. I dressed the children for the trip, said goodbye to my husband, and headed into the night. I took one last look at our home, my garden, and my tall husband waving in the doorway.

"Somehow, I found my way to this refugee camp. I tried to make the small tent into a home for my three-year-old daughter and two young sons and for my husband, who would soon join me.

"One night soon after our arrival, Miss Sarah, I woke to find my daughter's body cold and still. I could not wake her. My daughter was totally healthy, but she just died like that in the night."

A tear fell on Sarah's cheek. *Did the child die of hypothermia?* she wondered, thinking of the small gas canisters that never had enough fuel to ward off the chill. And those who tore the clothes off their backs to keep the fires going.

"You dear woman. Life is hard enough in a refugee tent, alone without your husband and family—and then to unexpectedly lose your dear daughter! I'm so sorry.

"But Ameera, do you know there is hope to see your daughter again? Your daughter is in heaven with Jesus, with Isa. If you believe in Jesus, you can go to heaven to meet her again when you die."

"Oh, Miss Sarah, could I really? It's too good to be true! Please teach me the words to say so I can tell Jesus I want Him in my life."

When the husband arrived at the camp, he was surprised to find Ameera bubbling with hope instead of burdened with despair. Even the new baby daughter could not have made such a difference in the grieving woman.

"We ask God to bless the little bit of food we have," he shared with Marc. "And then even if it doesn't seem like much, somehow, we feel satisfied when we are finished. I, too, am ready to accept the Isa God."

After inviting Jesus into his heart, the bereaved father asked, "Mr. Marc, can you teach me how to pray? I want to learn how to thank God."

"Teach you how to thank God?" Marc glanced at the few blankets and cookstove in the small tent and the empty corner where the daughter had slept, and the floor beds.

This man who lost everything, including his daughter, has one concern, and that is how to thank God?

"Yes, I want to thank Him for my salvation."

Marc and Sarah mentored this family, who became leaders in their community.

Doors opened for the family to emigrate to another country.

"Ameera's family leaves such a hole behind," Sarah shared wistfully. "They led so well. Sometimes it feels like we are building on leaves that soon blow away. But I know they will take the hope of the Gospel and plant churches on the other side of the world."

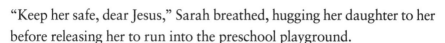

"Keep her safe, dear Jesus," Sarah breathed, hugging her daughter to her before releasing her to run into the preschool playground.

One couldn't live in a country with armed clashes between sectarian militias, suicide bombers, violent protests, machine gun fire, and rocket grenades without wondering, *Will I come home tonight? What will happen to my children if war breaks out between us when we are separated?*

Lord, I give my fears to you, Sarah prayed as Marc drove across the mountains to visit refugee camps. *I give my children to you.*

Twenty minutes after passing through a checkpoint, a suicide bomber blew up the same checkpoint they had just passed through.

"Suicide bombers are flooding the city," Marc heard. "The explosion closed down the road back to the city. No one can get through."

Marc read the terror in his wife's eyes. Her worst nightmare. *Lyla. Is she safe? How will we get back to her?*

"I've got this," God seemed to be whispering into their hearts.

After ministering at the camp, Marc learned of another roundabout route he could try taking back to the city. Sarah called a friend who picked up Lyla at the preschool.

Late that night, the couple picked up their daughter who was unfazed and had been having the best time with her favorite friend.

"When you give your worst fears to God, He takes care of them for you," Sarah whispered to Marc over their daughter's sleeping head.

Sunday mornings, Marc and Sarah gathered with the new believers and the searching refugees. They all sat on the floor, listening intently as Marc taught with his Bible lying open in his lap.

"The Lord has been stripping away our comforts and protective walls we built around us, teaching us to rely on him.

"Trees need to go through storms to develop deep roots. Studies show trees in greenhouses, or with protective stakes around them, never grow deep roots.

"When our securities are stripped away, our roots are forced to go deep into the Lord. When political crises, economic hardships, safety issues, or health difficulties arise, what else are we going to rely on if we don't have Jesus?"

"Lord," Marc prayed silently, "May our Muslim background believers be deeply rooted and strong spiritually, because they are the next generation of the Middle Eastern church. Make the DNA be so biblically and theologically strong that they would interpret Scriptures accurately and reproduce flawlessly."

Sarah glanced at her daughters and husband seated comfortably on the floor with the refugee families. A chicken and her brood scurried through the tent.

Sarah smiled, recalling Lyla's response to the churches they visited in the US during furlough. "This isn't a church! We aren't sitting on the floor! And there aren't any chickens!"

Her sentiments reflected what the refugee women often felt—*This isn't home. . . .*

Sarah joined the group with her sweet, pure voice as they sang from the longing deep within their scarred hearts about a home beyond the skies.

Marc caught his wife's eyes. Those eyes still did strange things to his heart. *What a very rare woman.*

Lord, you couldn't have given me a more supportive, delightful, capable wife to come alongside me in the calling you placed on my life. I'll always be so grateful. I couldn't do this without Sarah. Thank you, Lord.

MULTIPLIED CRUMBS

"Jesus looked at them and said, "With man this is impossible, but not with God; all things are possible with God."

Mark 10:27

"He wrestled with fear, second-guessing himself, wondering if in the end he'd be condemned to hell for worshipping Jesus. And yet—he couldn't banish the niggling hope that God really is that good: that the Almighty Creator and Judge actually loved us enough to sacrifice himself for us."

—R. Wenger

"A whole generation of children whose childhoods were robbed by war. Now without education, their futures are stolen as well." Sarah's teacher heart grieved, eying the youngsters slouched listlessly in the alleys. "Over half of the camp is under eighteen. There are fourteen-year-olds who can't write their names. Fourteen-year-olds married off because that is their destiny to survive in a refugee camp. Youngsters with no way of accomplishing their dreams of making a difference. Becoming a doctor or a teacher."

"If we don't reach the refugee children, they will grow up trained for jihad," Marc agreed.

"Children are an open door. We will make a difference, with God's help," Marc promised his wife. Together they spearheaded opening schools, eventually reaching 1,500 refugee children, showing the love of Jesus, staffed by Christian instructors teaching godly values and Bible stories as well as academics. An occasional disgruntled Muslim parent removed their children because of the Bible teachings. But because of the high quality of education the children received and the love of Jesus, the parents soon re-enrolled their children in the Christian schools. Many

Muslim parents didn't care if their children did convert to Christianity as they weren't convinced of their own religion.

"Everyone can see students from the loving Ananias House-sponsored schools score far higher than students in schools with Qur'an-based educations," village officials observed.

Dignitaries all clamored to have their children enrolled in the schools with the loving teachers with teaching based on the fear of the Lord being the beginning of wisdom, rather than the Qur'an-based schools where teachers intimidated and slapped the students.

Are the children really learning the Bible stories? Sarah wondered. *Do their parents train them to tune out Bible teachings?*

But when US youth teams came to hold vacation Bible school, these Muslim students amazed the teachers. They already knew all the Bible stories the team wanted to teach them.

"I couldn't understand how food could be left over!" a primary student told John Samara on one of his visits to the refugee camps. "There was so little food to start with, and so many students fed!"

"There are eleven of us students, plus the teacher," the refugee lad continued. "Everyone was supposed to bring a bit of food and we would all share it, but some had no food to bring. Others, including our teacher, forgot to bring food to share. My friend and I brought a loaf and a half of bread and a small bowl of food my mother cooked.

"So, we had enough food for two people, or maybe four, but everyone was hungry. The teacher said, 'Let's pray and asked God to bless the food and then share it.'

"And Mr. John, we all ate from that bread and the little bowl, all twelve of us, until we were filled. And there was still food left over. We decided to share the bread and food with the next classroom, because everyone is always hungry.

"Those fifteen students and their teacher ate until they were full, and still there was food left over for me to take home!

"All night I lay awake wondering, *How could a loaf and a half and a little bowl of food feed twenty-eight people and still have some left over?*

"I couldn't wait to get to school the next day. I ran to my teacher and asked her how it was possible.

"'Jesus,' the teacher said. 'Jesus heard our prayer and blessed the bread and the bowl of food just like He blessed the loaves and fishes. Never forget, He cares very much about hungry girls and boys.'

"And Pastor John, I will never forget. I saw that miracle God did with my own eyes. God cares about us, and He is very strong," the child finished, beaming up at him.

Tears shimmered in the eyes of the fourteen-year old student. "My parents gave me two options. I can marry my cousin who is an ISIS fighter in Syria." The girl wiped her tears on her hijab, and continued softly, "Or I can marry a seventy-seven-year-old man in another country."

The parents are desperate and need to marry off their daughter, so they don't have to support her anymore, the teachers realized.

"Let's talk to Jesus about this," a teacher suggested as the other instructors gathered around the distraught teen and prayed over the teary girl.

The girl skipped into the classroom the next day with a big smile lighting her face. "My parents decided sending to Syria to marry the ISIS cousin is too complicated. And they said there was something not right with me marrying a seventy-seven-year-old man!"

The teachers cheered with excitement, exclaiming, 'You know why your parents suddenly changed their minds, don't you?"

The girl's face glowed as she nodded. "It's because of Jesus."

"I have job for you to do in Syria," the father of one of the refugee students informed his son. Without telling the boy, he had sold his son to active ISIS fighters. The teachers never saw the student again. But they knew the seeds of the Word of God were planted in His heart. They prayed those seeds would bear fruit on the front lines of the ISIS battles.

"Jesus has really taught me how to love people like Jesus loves them," another teacher from an Ananias House-sponsored school told John as they walked through the refugee camps. "To see Jesus in every student. To see past what is on the outside, to see them as a deeply loved soul. That Jesus died for every one of them.

"There was this little girl I've actually been praying for since summer school. God put her on my heart to pray for her a lot. This year, very randomly, we were outside, and she came up to me and she asked for my phone. She wanted Google Translate.

"I'm like, uh, okay. Okay, what do you want to tell me?"

"She typed 'I had a dream about Jesus. He told me in the dream that He is the way, the truth, and the life.'"

"I am like 'Wow.' There are people around us, so I translated back, 'Okay, so how did this change your life?' She said, and I will never forget reading this, she said, 'I have made Jesus king of my entire life.' She said, 'entire life.'

"And just even telling the story touches me so much. I've always known there is something special about her, and to see her grow since then and the changes happening in her life have been amazing.

"There are numerous students here. Some have been in the open and some are secret that have decided to follow Jesus. They denounced everything they had believed previously, and they said, 'I want to follow Jesus in my life because I believe in Him.'

"And even if one student is added to the Kingdom, it is worth it. But here it is multiplied. There are so many. Some never expressed it to us teachers, but they wrote it in their final essay. I had one student who said she decided to follow Jesus because of all the teachers in the school—how we love them, the words that we speak. Even those who haven't necessarily said it, I believe many of them are so close."

"THANK GOD
FOR A WAR!"

"For this light momentary affliction is preparing for us an eternal weight
of glory beyond all comparison."

2 Corinthians 4:17

"Let us not ask of the Lord deceitful riches, nor the good things of this
world, nor transitory honors; but let us ask for light."

—*Assorted Authors*

"Mr. Marc, you might wish to stop by Mahir's tent. His daughter
is deathly ill," a camp volunteer suggested.

Marc answered many calls to visit the sick. The camps did not have
addresses and did not appear on maps, so it was pointless to call an
ambulance for someone who was dying. The driver wouldn't be able to
find them, and few people could afford the hospital bill.

There was nothing about the crude tent Marc approached to alert
him that Mahir and his wife came from a powerful, wealthy family with
close ties in the upper ranks of al-Qaeda. Luxury resorts in Saudi Arabia
had held no appeal to the family, because Mahir's parent owned similar
luxurious properties of their own. But the atrocities of war had driven
them in desperation from their comfortable home to the flimsy tent in the
crowded refugee camp.

The humble furnishings did not reveal that Mahir's wife, Duniya,
was a very devout student of Shariya Islamic law, who had taught the
Qur'an in the mosques to the female attendees.

Duniya met Marc at the door of their tent when he knocked. Her
black burka concealed all but her fiery eyes glaring suspiciously behind
the slits of her veil at the man of "the Book."

"Yes?" The frigid tone held not even a hint of the polite Syrian warmth as she recognized the "Jesus man."

"I'm so sorry to hear your daughter is sick," Marc's gentle eyes and soft tone conveyed compassion. "I would be glad to pray to God to ask Him to heal her if you would. . . ."

"Absolutely not!" The dark eyes flashed behind the netting of the burka as Duniya slammed the tent door in Marc's face. "Of all the nerve! I have as close connections to god as anyone!"

Her husband's well-heeled family sponsored the terrorist groups who killed these people of the book.

The pride ran deep. "That Jesus man certainly will not pray for our child. It would be better for her to die!"

The daughter became sicker, fading away.

Mahir and Duniya grew desperate.

"What will it hurt? She is dying anyway. . . ."

"All right, let 'the man of the Book' pray if he wants to," the devout teacher of Islamic law relented. "We've tried every other option."

Marc glanced around at the concrete floor softened with a simple, clean carpet surrounded with worn cushions, the drab camp blankets and the heating canister. The blades of a fan tried to push back the oppressive heat near where a flushed child lay on the floor.

In his gentle, caring manner, Marc read a story from his "Holy Book" about Jesus healing a girl who had died.

Laying his hands on the girl's forehead, Marc prayed with conviction and power, "Abba Father, we ask You to look on this precious child with compassion, to heal her, and to raise her up—to show the power of the living God through her restoration. For Your glory. In the powerful name of Jesus."

The girl stirred; her eyelids fluttered. Was the color returning to the pale cheeks?

A few days later, Marc noticed Mahir running toward him, flashing a wide smile as he rushed to exclaim, "Mr. Marc! Your God has power!

Your God is alive! He cares! My daughter is up running around, eating, and playing! Mr. Marc, she would have died. . . ."

Marc stared at Mahir for a moment and then broke into a smile. "Mahir! Jesus cares about your family! He showed His love to you through healing your daughter! I will give you His holy Book to read stories of Isa healing other people and telling more about the living God," Marc offered, reaching into his backpack for a New Testament.

Mahir looked at the Holy Book with fascinated intrigue. His eyes narrowed in fear and then widened in fascination. After a moment, his eyes flashed in each direction, and he snatched the book, hiding it beneath his kaftan.

Who is this Jesus who heals little girls? Duniya, the student of Qur'an wondered, growing curious about the holy Book her husband often read.

When the tent was empty, she opened the forbidden book and began reading. The student of Islam found the Bible intriguing, reading stories of healing, teachings to be merciful and good. And then the descriptions of heaven all drew her in.

I can't argue with the power I saw evidenced through my daughter's healing.

"Mr. Marc, we are ready to receive this Jesus," Mahir and Duniya said when he stopped to visit their tent sometime later.

Duniya graciously served a cup of precious coffee with sugar from their carefully rationed supply while they waited for his response.

"Mahir, you told me your family supports al-Qaeda. What will happen if you become a follower of Jesus?"

"We know the risks but are ready to face them." Duniya smiled calmly.

She thought of how miserable she had been for so long. *Where was God before?*

"Lord? Where have you been all my life?" the former teacher of Islamic law wept. "Why didn't the Christians share this good news with me sooner?"

While clinging to her commitment to the living God, Duniya kept asking, "Lord, where were you? Where have you been? Why didn't you come to me before?

"I suffered for years obeying, serving, and worshipping a god who did not exist, and you didn't stop me? Where have you been?"

As Duniya slept, the Lord spoke gently and lovingly to her. "My daughter, I have been hovering over you all your life, loving you, waiting for you to love Me. But it took a war for you to see Me."

"Thank you, Jesus, for war," she cried when she awoke. "I have never been so thankful for war before. Because of the war, I found Jesus!"

Back in the comforts of our own home, with our own friends, mosque, tight family ties to al-Qaeda, and good doctor for our daughter, Mahir and I would never have been open to reading the Bible or having a Christian pray for our daughter, she realized.

But the war had cracked their comfortable shell. And the atrocities of al-Qaeda, al-Nusra, ISIS, and extremists left the couple utterly disillusioned.

Somehow, the word of their conversion leaked back to the relatives. Mahir's father was one of Syria's wealthiest businessmen, with riches beyond millions.

"My son," the father messaged. "Come back to Islam, and everything I own is yours."

Come back to Islam and everything I own is yours. Mahir mulled over the words for a brief moment. His eyes met his wife's. *We can't even leave the refugee camp right now. We fled Syria because it was too dangerous . . . But even if we could . . .*

"Father, that's most generous of you," Mahir and Duniya responded. "But we won't be coming back. We would rather live in a tent *with* Jesus than in mansions *without* Him."

Not even the death threats could draw them away from their loving Lord.

Mahir sat down and wrote up an inventory of all the equipment he owned and sent the list to his family, who sought his life, finishing with, "Here is what we own; you can have it all; we aren't coming back."

Seeing the couple was not to be moved, their relatives plotted to kill Mahir and Duniya's family to restore their honor.

The matriarch of this proud family showed up at Mahir's tent to try to talk sense into the couple in person before the honor killing took place. While visiting Mahir's family, the grandmother had a dream.

"I dreamt a Man in shining white was standing in the mosque, and the green lights of the mosques were replaced with white lights," she told them. "God was speaking to me through the dream. It's okay for you to keep following the Jesus God."

Marc wrestled over the dream's significance of the green lights going out in the mosques, and white lights coming on.

Mosques are being turned into churches across the Middle East, he realized. *The green bulbs in the mosques are being replaced with a soft golden glow as the light of the truth spreads across the country.*

Marc and Sarah discipled Duniya and Mahir, discovering gifts for leadership. Mahir, the son of wealthy sponsors of al-Qaeda, and his wife, a former teacher of Shariya, became vibrant, fearless Christian leaders pastoring a church in the refugee community.

They attended the Ananias House leadership conferences and thrived under John and Abraham's teachings and the precious fellowship with other leaders across the MENA region.

The long-awaited and prayed-for letter came announcing that the UN had accepted their application for placement in a country in the West. South America welcomed Mahir, Duniya, and their children.

Mahir and Duniya's family found security, a house, a job, and schooling in the South American country. But it was not home. After six months in a foreign country, Duniya and Mahir realized their hearts and calling stayed behind them in the Middle Eastern refugee camp, with their people.

"Please help us return to the refugee camp," they messaged Marc after several months. "We must return, even if we have to live in a tent."

"You will never be able to return to the West again once you leave," the UN told the couple. "And besides, you can't legally return to the country you left. You will be jailed."

"We don't mind," Mahir responded. "We want to return no matter what."

Mahir, Duniya, and their family returned to the Middle East. At the airport, they were met with arrest warrants and spent several days incarcerated, but they didn't mind.

They came back to the tents that collapsed with winter's snows and flooded with muddy water in the spring. They came back to the church family, and to the niche God had for them to minister. And that was home.

ISA—THE MAN
IN THE DREAM

"In this the love of God was made manifest among us, that God sent his only Son into the world, so that we might live through him."

I John 4:9

"If we want proof of God's love for us, then we must first look at the Cross where God offered up His Son as a sacrifice for us. Calvary is the one objective, irrefutable proof of God's love for us."

—Walter J. Chantry

The border guard glanced from the document in his hand to the travel-worn daughters in their wrinkled black burkas and the bright-eyed toddler waking in the weary mother's arms.

The guard hesitated, pondering the millions of refugees that already overwhelmed his country, leaving no room for another Muslim family. He stared thoughtfully at the waking toddler.

"Isa," he repeated. "The baby's name is Isa. Jesus. That is a Christian name."

He thrust the stack of documents to Abdul. "Welcome to Lebanon."

With a smile, the guard motioned them to proceed.

"Ya Allah!" the children shouted. "We are in Lebanon, thanks to Isa!"

"No more ISIS bullets and missiles!"

"Thank you, Isa!"

Abdul flagged down a taxi. "Beirut," he ordered in a clipped tone.

"Where are we going, Daddy?"

"When will we be there?"

"I'm thirsty for some of Shada's milk. . . ."

As the taxi wove through terrain reminding them of their home country with fields edged by mountains, one of the girls asked, "So who did you name Isa after, and what kind of a person was He?"

"I read in the Qur'an that Isa was a pure boy born with no sin," Ali said. "He made doves of clay when He was a child and breathed breath into them, and they flew away. Al-Imran says Isa healed a blind man and a leper and raised a dead man. And then He was taken to heaven."

"Isa was a very good man," his sisters observed. "No wonder the Man in White told you our brother should be named Isa. But how did the Man in White know we would have a brother?"

No one answered.

The vision of the Man in luminescent white telling Ali that his mother would have a son and his name would be called Isa continued to intrigue the family. It was all a fascinating mystery they could not unravel.

Everyone knew Lebanon did not welcome refugees. Refugees found settlements where Lebanese landowners would rent them a small space, paid in money or in exchange for labor in the produce fields. The refugees would build their own tent from tarps and plastic.

But Abdul had connections. A friend's family invited them to share their tiny flat. The members of the two families might have to take turns lying down to sleep in the minuscule flat, but that was far better than a tent with a mud floor.

"Hopefully, I can soon find a job and rent a room or apartment of our own. . . ."

"If your health holds out," Samira sighed.

Being one of more than two million displaced persons in Lebanon without resident papers, jobs were as impossible to find as a camel swimming in the Mediterranean Sea. The rare exceptions required menial labor or laborious field work such as harvesting potatoes.

But even if there had been a job for Abdul, he was not feeling well enough to work.

As the stash of Syrian pounds diminished, Abdul's health deteriorated, and Samira's desperation increased.

"People of the Book give out food packages," her new neighbors whispered. "Ask for Pastor Yosef."

Growing up in the lap of wealth in Saudi Arabia, begging for food was something Samira never expected to do. *But I will muster the courage to do what I must for my family,* she decided.

After a long wait, Samira reached the front of the line. She stood erect and dignified beneath her burka, swallowed her pride, and, with a smile, requested, "I need a package of food to feed my family of ten, please."

"I am sorry," the man behind the table kindly apologized. "We have no extra packages. All of them are already assigned. But please come to our meeting, and we will pray for you."

"No, thank you!" Samira retorted, flipping her burka and pivoting on her worn heels. "I don't need or want your prayers," she snapped over her shoulder. *The very idea.*

She could hear Abdul rumbling, "We would rather die than attend the service of the Isa people!"

Back at the crowded flat shared with their friends, Samira had more than food to worry about. Her strong husband lay pale and weak on the mat on the floor, covered in blankets.

"The people of the Book have a free medical clinic on the other side of the camp," the neighbors informed her.

"The people of the Book again! They will probably have no slot for Abdul and want to say a prayer over him," she muttered. But finally, in desperation, she helped her husband walk to the clinic and waited in line with him.

The doctor ordered blood work. When the lab tests returned, the technician gently explained, "Sir, you appear to suffer from a rare blood disorder. We don't have a lot of experience with treating the suspected disorder. You need to see a specialist immediately. I will arrange an appointment for you and have the office call you," he stated, handing Abdul the name and address of a hematologist in Beirut.

"We only have enough rice for another day," Samira's daughters informed her when they returned.

There is only one option, she realized with disgust. *I will have to go back and ask again about a food package.*

"I'm so sorry," Pastor Yosef responded once again. "All the food packages are already designated. But please come to our meeting; it might encourage your heart; you must be going through a difficult time."

Something about the caring tone and look in the pastor's eyes softened Samira's heart, and she found herself drawn inexplicably to investigate. It couldn't hurt and would be a diversion.

Warm smiles and hugs soothed her hurting heart as she timidly entered the tent. Notes of sweet music bathed her tired soul. Samira found her tense muscles relaxing into the chair as she soaked in the warmth and love she felt.

"Jesus, who the Qur'an calls Isa, cares very deeply about the heavy burdens and griefs your hearts are carrying. . . ."

What? Isa cares? Isa? Samira's eyes popped open wide, and she leaned forward breathlessly. *Isa cares.*

"Isa, Jesus, says in His Book that He is like a gentle shepherd and wants to carry you, and to heal your pain. . . ."

The man began to pray for the pain and the burdens in each of the hearts and asked the kind Shepherd to carry these precious, wounded lambs.

A tear stung the corner of Samira's eye before she could help it. Quickly, she dashed to the door.

"Let me pray for you," a woman kindly offered, grabbing Samira's arm.

"No, thank you!" Samira tore away from the woman. Once out of sight of the tent, she walked slowly to quiet her rapidly beating heart. *I will not tell Abdul I went to a meeting by the people of the Book! Never. But I will have to tell him there was no food package.*

"You desperately need blood transfusions," the specialist told Abdul.

"But with so many needy displaced people, there is so little blood. We will see what can be done, because your case is quite urgent. You will have to try to find donors with your blood type who will come and donate blood for you."

On the way back to camp, the couple stopped at a market and bought a bag of rice, carefully counting out the pounds. *Something will have to change soon.*

The desperation of her heart, along with the love of the people of the Book, drew Samira back to their tent again for another meeting. The warm love was soothing oil on her heart, scarred from the stresses of war and displacement. It was a bright shaft of light in the black tunnel of her life. This Jesus tent was the one place where her perpetually stressed muscles relaxed, and the love wrapped around her like a blanket. The gentle music soothed her tight nerves. A haven. Like an oasis of refreshment to a desert traveler.

As the pastor began to pray, the lady grabbed Samira, hugging her tightly before she could escape, and said, "Let me pray for you." Before Samira could struggle free, the woman was saying, "Lord, I ask you to come down and touch this weary, tired woman. Heal her heart, lift her burdens, and carry her loads."

The heavy load Samira carried slid from her shoulders. Something stirred in her heart. The oppressive darkness and despair lifted. A smile played at her lips behind her burka. Her eyes relaxed, and her step quickened as she rushed back to the crowded little room before her family could discover where she had gone.

Samira continued to slip away to the services, listening intently as the pastor talked about Isa, the One Christians called Jesus. Pastor Yosef explained how He cared so much that He became the supreme sacrifice and let the Romans nail Him to an execution stake so that His blood could pay the price for her sins.

Samira thought of the ISIS soldiers fastening Christians to crosses.. . .

"And then Isa—Jesus—came out of the grave," Pastor Yosef

explained. "Jesus was taken to heaven where He sits beside His father God. He cares so much about what His precious children experience, and He wants to heal their hurts."

So this is what Isa is like, the prophet our son was named after. . . .

"Isa—Jesus—is alive today and is answering prayers and healing people," Pastor Yosef elaborated, telling stories of people God had healed in the camp when they prayed to Him.

At the end of the service, the pastor prayed for Samira, and she received Isa, the One Pastor Yosef called Jesus, into her heart.

Rushing back to the tent, Samira pulled Abdul out of bed.

"Abdul, come with me. You must let the man of the Book pray to Isa for you. The Isa of the Book heals people; He can make you better! Our Isa's Isa!" she insisted, tugging a shirt over his head.

Abdul had not seen his wife so excited for months.

Samira has got a head on her. She won't fall for anything stupid. . . . Besides, I am too exhausted to argue with her. Driven by desperation, Abdul relented. *It won't do any harm to get out of bed and see for myself.*

Pastor Yosef looked up with delighted surprise as he saw the couple enter the tent.

"You said Isa can heal," Samira bubbled like her overfilled coffee pot percolating on the little gas burner. "My husband is very sick with a rare blood condition, and we have eight children depending on him. We need Abdul to live and get better. Can you pray to Isa for him?"

The pastor sat down next to Abdul, looking compassionately into his weary, sunken eyes. "I am so sorry to hear about your condition. I know Jesus cares very much about you. He can heal you if He wishes. Would you like me to ask Him if He would heal you?"

Abdul nodded, not trusting to speak. The pastor called a friend, and together, they placed their hands on Abdul's head and asked Jesus, the Great Healer and the loving Shepherd who gave His life for Abdul, to touch Abdul's body and cure his rare disorder.

A warm, tingling sensation washed over Abdul as the gentle voice of the pastor spoke to Isa like a friend. And a strength pulsed through Abdul's exhausted being.

Abdul could not keep the tears back. *Something is happening and I don't know what.*

Samira and Abdul traveled to the hospital the next day for the scheduled blood transfusion. Before the procedure, a lab technician drew blood for a final preprocedural test.

The hematologist walked into the room where Abdul and Samira waited. Samira's hands grew clammy as she eyed the doctor's reddened neck and furrowed brows.

"I went to all this effort to work you in to have this procedure to save your life, and now you don't need it anymore," his words erupted in a torrent of volcanic lava. "Why did you see another doctor when I pulled so many strings for you? This is very unprofessional of you to treat me like this!"

Abdul and Samira looked at each other in puzzled shock.

"I don't understand; I didn't have money to go to any other doctor and to have a blood transfusion; there must be a misunderstanding. . . ."

It was the doctor's turn to look baffled. "You saw no other doctor, had no procedures? But your blood results are normal!" The doctor carefully scanned the report once more. "Absolutely normal. This condition never self-corrects, and you had no transfusion. I don't understand. . . ."

A smile spread across Abdul's bearded face. "Ah, you have to understand, doctor, we did not see any other specialist or any other doctor! We only had a pastor of the People of the Book pray for Isa to heal me, and Isa must have heard his prayer! No doctor and no human blood could give me life, but the blood of Jesus has healed me!"

The couple rushed home to tell their family what Isa had done for them.

"Father!" one of the girls burst out. "Do you think Isa was the Man in glowing white who came to Ali in a dream? The One who told us to name the baby Isa?"

"I think you are right," Abdul agreed. "Isa was watching over us way back in Aleppo and loved us so much that He came to Ali in a dream. And then He used the name Isa to soften the border guard's heart to let us into Lebanon!"

"What would have happened if we had not obeyed the vision and not named our baby brother Isa?" one of the girls questioned.

They agreed the family would not have been allowed into Lebanon if they had not named the baby Isa.

The pastor had said, "Isa, Jesus, says, 'I am the door. If anyone enters by me, he will be saved.'"

And Isa had not only been the door to salvation, but the name Isa had also been the door to deliverance from Syria.

Ali's heart smoldered. *My parents and sisters are so weak, rejecting everything they have ever known because of one miracle. They have become infidels. And that means someone must restore the honor. . . .*

They've shamed the family name. It is my job to restore the family honor. But how can I overpower them all at once?

Pastor Yosef and his wife dropped by to check in on the family. The pastor observed the scowl on Ali's face.

"Tell me about your dream, Ali."

When the lad recounted the vision, the pastor said, "Ali, the Man in White loved you so much to give you the message. I believe that Man was Jesus himself, the One you call Isa. He loved you so much He laid down His life for a sacrifice so you can have the assurance you can enter Paradise."

"The Son of God laying down His life for a sacrifice? How honorable is that?" Ali spat. "Defending one's life is far more honorable than lying down and dying!"

"Ali, would you rather be part of a religion where a loving God laid down His life for His people to secure their place in Paradise? Or to be associated with a religion where the god promotes hatred and killing? With a god who doesn't care to have a relationship with his people? A religion that teaches the only way to be certain you'll get into Paradise is to die killing others?"

In a flash, Ali saw in his mind's eye the tall, radiant Being with the gentle, loving face contrasting so sharply with the savage rage of the masked radicals screaming "Allahu Akbar" as they stormed through his home. There was no comparison.

Ali knelt, surrendering his heart to the Isa in his dream.

How great is our God!

"John, we have overflowing churches and very few leaders." John heard the exhaustion edged with desperation in Abraham's voice. "Even Imams, Druze, and Kurds are converting. There are lots of men with leadership potential, but they need to be taught. John. . . ."

The leadership conferences Baba used to talk about when I was young. . . .

"I would absolutely love to have Ananias House facilitate training conferences, Baba, but you know I can't return to Syria, or I will be conscripted into the army. And with the need for soldiers to replenish the bodies on the battlefront, the regime won't let any healthy men out of the country to attend any classes."

"If you can find an accessible location, we will get the men there."

That means smuggling, John knew. *And smuggling means risking bullets. . . .*

Part V
Frontline Warriors

(2012–2019)

"But thanks be to God, who gives us the victory through our Lord Jesus Christ."

I Corinthians 15:57

"The remarkable thing about God is that when you fear God, you fear nothing else, whereas if you do not fear God, you fear everything else."

—Oswald Chambers

THE IMAM

"See what kind of love the Father has given to us, that we should be called children of God; and so we are. The reason why the world does not know us is that it did not know him."

I John 3:1

"As Christ struggled up Calvary's hill and bled upon it, His aim was to eradicate self-love and implant the love of God in the hearts of men. One can only increase as the other decreases."

—Walter J. Chantry

Pastor Abraham studied the man seated across his desk from him, the clean-shaven face and graying hair. He noted a hint of Iraqi facial features, and the simple garb indicated he could be a refugee. *Who is this person? I have a thousand people coming to church; I don't remember this man, much less know anything about him.*

"I would like you to baptize me," the visitor announced.

"I am delighted to hear that. You are making one of the best decisions you could make. I want to hear your story. Are you aware that those who follow Christ, especially in the Middle East, may need to suffer?"

"I know that well and am willing."

"As a matter of protocol, could I see your ID?"

Abraham scanned the card. *Abdullah Mustafa. The name matches the one the visitor gave, but that is all that matches.*

With rising bewilderment, Abraham glanced up at the clean-shaven man in front of him, and back to the picture on the ID showing a sheikh wearing a head turban and sporting a long beard.

This is not the same man. Why is he using a false identity?

Abraham studied the man in front of him, thinking of the two secret members of the Mukhabarat that had tried to rip his church apart.

A shepherd had to protect his flock. He had to carefully screen prospective members.

"Abdullah, I need to see your personal ID."

"This is my personal ID," the man insisted.

"You don't understand; in Syria, we need to have our personal picture on our ID."

Abdullah smiled, nodding. "I understand your confusion. This picture really is me. It was taken when I was a sheikh with a big beard and turban."

Abraham leaned forward, crossing his arms on his desk, listening intently as the story poured out.

"I was a sheikh, an Imam. An evangelist for Islam in Iraq, a leader in my mosque.

"The men from my mosque, my sect of Islam, kidnapped ten innocent men from another sect of Islam . . . and killed them. Because they were the wrong branch of Islam.

"'Allahu Akbar!' the men from my mosque screamed, 'Our god is greater!'

"I heard the cries of the innocent men. I saw the writhing bodies covered in blood. I watched the blood flow into the streets while the men from my mosque shouted, 'Allahu Akbar! Our god is great! Our god is greater!'

"I cried, 'Who are you, God?! What have these men done to deserve being killed in your name? What kind of a god are you to cause ten innocent men to be slaughtered while others of the same religion shout, 'Our god is great!?'

"I was a sheikh, the Imam, the religious leader over these killers, but I was afraid to try to stop them.

"In retaliation, the Muslims from the other sect kidnapped innocent men from our mosque and beheaded them.

"'Allahu Akbar! Our god is great!' the killers screamed.

"Who are you, God? What kind of a god are you? We slaughter and say, 'God is great.' They kill and say, 'God is great!' Both groups believe in you, yet they kill each other, screaming, 'God is great!'

"The question haunted me in the mosques, in my bed, and as I walked down the streets. 'Who are you, God?'

"I wanted nothing to do with a god of such hate and cruel slaughter of innocent men who believed in him.

"And then, as I passed the open doors of your church, I heard the words: 'For God loved the world so much He gave his only Son for a sacrifice, that we would not need to die but can live forever.'

"My heart shouts, 'Yes! This God is greater! This God is the true God!'

"So, I got the courage to walk into the back of your church and sit in the last seat. You were preaching, 'God is a God of love. God gave His only son because He loved the world.'

"I hear you teaching God wants us to love those who curse us. To pray for them. And bless them.

"My heart shouted, 'Yes! This God is greater! A God who died instead of killing! This is the God I have been searching for! I will worship Him!'

"I went home and shaved off my long beard I had been so proud of and took off my turban, a sign of wisdom and position in the Islamic faith. I will serve the God of love, I decided.

"And Pastor Abraham, God opened my eyes to see the truth, and He saved me."

"How great is our God!" Abraham exploded in delighted worship. "How great is our God!"

CRISIS

"Give us aid against the enemy, for human help is worthless. With God we
will gain the victory, and he will trample down our enemies."

Psalm 60:11, 12 NIV

"When Christ calls a man, He bids him come and die."

—Dietrich Bonhoeffer, *The Cost of Discipleship*

When the former Imam first removed his turban and robe and drew
out his razor to shave off his beard, Abdullah realized, *I am
removing the symbols that brought me respect wherever I go. I will no
longer be looked upon as the respected Imam of the community.*

He held the razor a long moment, shocked by the new look on the
shaven side of his face. Staring into the mirror, he weighed the consequences, not the least of which would be the wrath of his vain wife. *Farida
was so proud to be known as the wife of a prestigious Imam. She will
yell, spit, and hit. But I am stronger than she is. . . .*

"What are you doing? Have you lost your mind?" Sparks of fury shot
from Farida's eyes as she watched the strands of hair drop from the razor.
"You left the mosque, and now you are shaming your family. And looking
like a woman!"

"I'll do what I want to do!" the former Imam roared, slapping her
face with the back of his free hand.

"I'll turn everyone against you, you shriveled wimp of a man!" She
whirled away, sobbing loudly.

Furious at losing her identity as the wife of a prestigious Imam, Farida
degraded, humiliated, and taunted Abdullah. She turned his family
against him. And she betrayed him to the Mukhabarat.

And Abdullah tried to subdue her with well-placed blows.

"Pastor Abraham, there's no going back. I've found the true God,"

Abdullah's eyes shone with confident determination. "My wife humiliates and shames me, but I won't turn back."

As an afterthought, he added, "But don't worry, I slap her hard across the mouth, and that shuts her up for a while."

Sadness clouded Abraham's eyes. "I've never slapped my wife. The God of love teaches us to love our wives like Christ loves the church. Even if they don't respect us."

"That's what your son John told me, too, when he was mentoring me. But Pastor, she will think I am not a real man if I let her talk sassy like and don't hit her. She will never stop abusing me if I don't show her I am the boss."

"Abdullah, when people spit on Jesus and beat him, He did not fight back. He didn't hit them back to show He was God. He taught us to bless people who speak meanly to us. When your wife mocks you, try telling her sweetly, 'I love you, Farida.' Perhaps you can love her and lead her to Jesus."

"Those words are very hard to learn," Abdullah pondered the concept so foreign to what his former religion taught. "It will be very hard, but I will try to show love like Jesus, Pastor."

"Let's pray for God to give you the power to speak lovingly when your hand feels like smacking her and for God to soften Farida's heart toward you," Pastor Abraham suggested as the two knelt.

Watching the former Imam shut the office door, Abraham thought, *Abdullah's got exceptional leadership potential, but first, he needs a lot of teaching and discipling to help him unlearn the misguided habits he grew up with.*

But when, Lord? The church, the courtyards, and stairwells overflow with searching, disillusioned people who even stand outside the windows, seeking truth. We arranged fourteen services a week to accommodate the 2,000 people searching for hope in the oppressive dark despair of loss and pain.

Lord, You see we travel around a circuit of the churches throughout

Syria to disciple the masses of people pressing into the churches. Then when we come back to the first church, the building is overflowing with the friends and family of those who attended the previous service. When do we have time to train leaders?

"Son," Abraham said to John, exhaustion edged with desperation in his voice. "We have overflowing churches and very few leaders. The war machine left behind broken, fertile hearts. We make a circuit around the churches of Syria, discipling the churches, and when we come back to the first church, it is filled with the friends and relatives of those who were at the first service. It's our season of harvest—but we have so few to reap."

"Baba, at Ananias House, we are observing more Muslims are coming to Christ in the last seventeen years than have come to Christ since the beginning of Islam 1,400 years ago."

"Exactly, John. You know that before the war, the church rejoiced when one Muslim background person came to know the true God. Now the churches are filled with searching Muslims. Imams, Kurds, the Druze—they are all coming to the true God in droves."

"The Druze?"

"Yes, they are so excited to learn the Messiah has already come. The men don't need to wear those awkward baggy pantaloons to catch Messiah when he is born to a man because the Messiah has already come.

"I suppose the leaders are irate."

"They are, son. They interrupt meetings, threaten to kidnap and kill. . . . They are so desperate to keep their youth that they started teaching the secrets of their religion at a younger age instead of waiting until they turn thirty.

"I visited the leaders to offer to explain to them more about the living God."

"You didn't! They wouldn't think twice about killing you."

"I've been told I am at the top of their hit list. But you know I'm bulletproof until God's done with me."

John waited, sensing his father needed to talk.

"The church is growing exponentially in width—but in depth, John? There are lots of men, like Abdullah, the Imam, who just came to the Lord. They have leadership potential, they are starved for truth, but they need so much instruction to help them sort through the aberrant and eclectic teachings of their past.

"I've been working with Abdullah, who told me you had mentored him. It's so hard for these Muslim background men to change the mindset from beating to loving their wives. Mama is praying every day for someone to come teach the women to love their husbands, to deal with the cultural baggage they grew up with, and to really know the love of Jesus to find healing for the traumas they experienced."

A thrill of excitement stirred in John's heart as his mind began to race with the possibilities—until the ideas crashed against a wall. *I am willing to risk my own life, but how can I risk the lives of the future Christian Middle Eastern leaders to smuggle them across the border?*

VALIANT SOLDIERS

"Be on guard; stand firm in your faith [in God, respecting His precepts and keeping your doctrine sound]. Act like [mature] men *and* be courageous; be strong."

I Corinthians 16:13 (AMP)

". . . Hast thou no wound? No scar? . . . Yet as the Master shall the servant be. And pierced the feet that followed me. . . . Can he have followed far who has no wound or scar?"

—Amy Carmichael

"Suffering and glory are like two sides of the same coin."

—Rami Ibrahim

A dozen shadowy forms hunkered on the rim of the twenty-foot ditch marking the border dividing the two Middle Eastern countries. Every muscle tensed for the tread of a boot, or the silhouette of the ISIS soldiers rumored to guard this strip of the border.

"This is the last place for hours around you will have a chance to get through," Andros warned, looking intently into the apprehensive eyes of each of the men clustered around him. "We've tried the other two options.

"This is a weak spot between the two countries. They move ISIS soldiers through here all the time. But listen to me, if we are seen, they shoot to kill. At the deep ditch, we wait until you are certain it's clear. And then, run like you've never run before."

Hidden beneath the mantle of darkness, Karam and his comrades tensed for the signal. Karam's breath came in gasps as he scanned the dark horizon, straining to hear the sound of a boot fall or the crack of a branch.

The countryside slumbered beneath the starless sky. A quivery wail sent icy fingers up his spine. *It's not a bad omen or the spirit of a dead warrior. I know it's just a Pharaoh eagle-owl. . . .*

"There!"

"Empty oil barrels," Andros, the group leader, murmured reassuringly, surveying the barren landscape.

Each of the previous border crossing attempts shaved more of the courage from their hearts.

One of these times, we'll get a bullet in the back, they knew.

Andros surveyed his dozen men, armed only with Bible-laden backpacks.

"Endure hardness as a good soldier of Jesus Christ," Andros whispered, thumping Karam on the shoulder, hearing the young teen's rapid breathing.

"Let's do it!" the leader whispered. "It's not going to get any darker or more desolate than this."

The group slid the twenty precipitous feet down the muddy sides of the moat-like ditch. They clambered up the slippery slope. A quick scan revealed a slumbering terrain cloaked in the blanket of night. Only the barrels. . . .

At the signal, Karam took off at a run to keep himself from turning back and heading to the safety of his bed. *The church is depending on me.*

Like detonated missiles, soldiers shot out of every oil barrel in an explosion of gunshots and shouts.

"Halt!"

Bullets whizzed just above their heads. The men dashed toward the safety of the dark chasm, flinging aside their backpacks.

Gun barrels struck them in the legs, hurling the men to the ground.

"On your knees!"

Karam hit the ground as a boot caught him in the ribs. Andros's men knelt, their hearts pounding like miniature machine guns. *Jesus! Save us!*

*Will the radicals behead us with their swords or shoot us in the back?
Which is more painful?*

Boots and gun barrels pummeled Karam as he curled into a fetal
position with his arms protecting his head.

The night blurred into a frenzy of blows, grunts, cries, and prayers.

Be strong. Endure it for Jesus. Jesus bore much more for me, he
whispered, bracing against the sharp blows. *Jesus help us!*

At the rendezvous location, John paced the floor. He checked his phone.
Hour after hour passed with no trace or word of his students. *My boys
are in trouble. Somewhere. . . .*

*Was this idea to train pastors a huge mistake? Am I getting Syria's
future church leaders captured and killed?*

*Lord, cover Your warriors with Your wings. These men and boys
are risking their lives to learn more of You to teach Your flocks.*

"Stand up! Hands in the air!" the masked gunman snapped. "You run
and you're dead."

Karam observed the bloody faces and arms of his comrades, cringing
in pain as they pulled themselves upright.

"Explain yourselves."

"We are on the way to a class we are taking." Andros stood erect,
meeting the gaze of the ISIS captors. His voice carried a confident ring
while carefully avoiding mentioning their text would be the Bible taught
by pastors from America.

"You're not going! Turn around and head back the way you came.
Don't look back. And don't even think about trying anything. Unless you
want a bullet in your back."

"Now that you've beaten us, can't you please let us go through?"

"Shush!" Andros hissed, wanting to tackle the boy to shut him up. But the boots and guns descended on the beaten bodies of the group again.

"Absolutely not! Get moving and head back the way you came before we start shooting!"

Shame washed over Karam like a cold, muddy rag as he limped toward the massive ditch. *What real man let someone else beat him up?*

"'If we suffer, we will also reign with Him,'" Andros encouraged softly as the men struggled through the massive ditch, mud and dirt mingling and smearing the bloody bruises.

Beyond the sight of the guards, the students huddled to analyze their options. They cleaned and dressed their wounds as they deliberated.

"Going home is not an option," they all agreed. "The smuggler said the border is more lightly guarded several hours away. It's worth an attempt."

The fourth attempt was as unsuccessful as the other three border attempts.

"There is one final option," a local hinted. "But it's a swamp considered so impassable that it's poorly guarded. The mud is said to be knee-deep. It's crawling with poisonous snakes. Guarded by several towers. Only the fittest should attempt it."

Andros surveyed his team, looking into each of the eyes, seeing the glint of courage.

"Count me in."

"Me too."

"I'm going."

"Alright, let's do it. But only the younger guys. You senior leaders are too valuable and vulnerable. For the sake of the churches, someone needs to survive. And the youngsters are much more likely to make it through."

The group huddled for prayer. The older men slapped the youngsters on the shoulders, urging them on.

The boys caught a ride to the outskirts of the marsh. Under the shroud of darkness, they plunged into the swamp.

Sticks in hand, Karam and his buddies slogged through the decaying vegetation floating on dark, fetid waters, sinking into the sticky mire up to their knees. Swirls of fog escaped toward the black tree branches wafting a pungent, sulfuric odor. The muck sucked at their shoes as they stumbled over decaying logs. Or snakes.

In the murky darkness, the strange noises—the croak of a frog, the dripping of water, splashes, the slurp of mud, the screech of bird hunting, the burps of air breaking the surface—reminded them they were not alone.

Their eyes barely registered the blazes of light across the night sky illuminating a pair of watch towers before the crack struck them like a slap. Their ears rang with the echo. The odor of burning powder wafted through the darkness.

"Forward!" Andros yelled as the bullets hissed past their heads. "Don't turn back!"

The boys slurped and sloshed frantically, plunging through the slime. No one slowed to find the tennis shoes swallowed by mud as flashes of fire and sharp cracks exploded through the blackness.

Once on solid ground beyond the bursts of gunfire, they collapsed, panting and groaning. After a long, cold night, daybreak brought glimmers of warmth and hope. The golden light caressed the land, igniting the birds into a chorus of melodies.

"We've got to find a public restroom to wash up, first off," the men determined, trying to brush the decaying leaves, slime, blood suckers, and algae from their scraped legs.

"And then to find a store to replace our shoes."

Their damp, musty clothing clinging to their backs, the guys limped weary but triumphantly into the rendezvous room. John grabbed them in a giant hug. The black eyes, bruised faces, and arms told the story.

"Brave soldiers of the Cross!" he cried, gently clapping them on the back.

"It looks like you lost your backpacks along the way," John observed after hearing their stories. "Here are a few tablets and pens. I'll see if I can find a few Bibles. Be ready to switch activities at the knock of the door. Pull out some games. Hide the papers and Bibles. Hopefully we won't need to relocate, but we do need to be vigilant and stay beneath the radar.

"You probably think I had it easy. I just had to fly in on a comfortable airline seat while you fought through the swamps, were beaten and dodged bullets. But let me tell you something. I know what it is like to be beaten up every day in junior high school for being a Christian by a guy named Vergie and his gang. And friends, I spent some time in a jail cell for Jesus, not knowing if and when I would get out. I didn't understand what it was all about back then, but maybe it was for today."

The men's hearts bonded with John's in that moment. *Here's a man we can trust.*

The fellows took in the truths like a caravan of thirsty camels who'd trekked the scorching Silk Road and were storing up for the next arid days of desert travel.

Pencils flew across the tablets.

"Pastor John, can you repeat that again? We don't want to miss a single word."

John taught from the Epistles, Galatians, and Romans. He taught leadership and godly marriage, carefully showing the men the rules of Bible interpretation, the principles of the Scripture, and the power of bathing their sermons and churches in prayer.

John taught the men to carefully observe, interpret, and make applications. He taught them to see the Scriptures from the context and culture the writer wrote from. And then to interpret what God was saying, forming a bridge to the application. There could be many applications but only one interpretation.

"Prayer is the powerhouse of a dynamic sermon and victorious life," he taught.

He read from Acts 14:22, "Encouraging them to continue in the faith, saying that through many tribulations we must enter the Kingdom of God."

The more John taught and answered the endless questions, the more he realized the urgent need for training.

These young Christians from Muslim and Kurdish backgrounds have no concept of cherishing a woman, he realized.

"Brothers, we must love our wives and serve them, never hitting or speaking harshly," John explained kindly. "If you don't know how to respond to your wife, think of Jesus, the humble servant washing the disciples' feet.

"If you want to be a pastor, I Peter 5:3 says we must be a servant and not act like a boss, lording it over people. Let me tell you something. My dad is the senior pastor for five churches, but he became a servant to them, opening up the church, turning on the heat before the service, cleaning the building, and even cleaning the toilets, besides visiting all the believers who needed encouragement."

The men laughed uncomfortably at the thought of a man, especially a senior pastor, cleaning the toilet! But the smiles and nods showed John they got it.

He surveyed the group thoughtfully. *There are more challenges than I dreamt. And there was Karam, only sixteen. Why did his church send such a youngster?*

"Okay, guys. That's it for the day." John stretched after six intense hours of lecturing. "Relax, study for tomorrow. You guys came out of a war zone. Go shopping for your wives, or your moms, and just enjoy yourselves a bit."

"Pastor John," Karam interrupted. "I don't mean to be disrespectful, but we did not endure beatings, risk bullets, and snake-filled swamps simply to relax and go shopping. Isn't there more you can teach?"

"Yes, Pastor John. We risked our lives to get here, and now we want to learn everything we can."

"Okay, okay, guys," John consented with a chuckle. "But take a quick break."

The students returned moments later, pressing around John again with notebooks, pens, and Bibles.

After John went to bed, Karam and his friends dialogued and discussed the truths they were learning until they dozed off in exhaustion at three in the morning.

Karam's got a brilliant grasp of Hebrew and Greek. He learns quickly. Maybe the church that sent him knew what they were doing after all.

John prayed passionately over these brave young warriors of the Cross, before sending them out to risk another border crossing, and to return home to the darkness, mortar fire, and persecution of the war.

"Father, this is our season of harvest. We cry out to You to be an advocate for these dear brave leaders. Encourage their hearts. Make them a voice of hope, healing, and restoration for the Kingdom of God in Syria. We pray You would give them strength to represent You and bring hope in the darkness.

"Lord, hide Your servants behind the Cross in humility and surrender. Bring fire from Heaven so they can stand firm for the Gospel in the midst of hardships. We defeat fear in the name of Jesus. In Your name we pray, amen."

John watched the men leave, praying, wondering. *What does the future hold for them back in the war zone?*

John continued mentoring the men long-distance after they returned home. Karam became the leader of his congregation by the time he was eighteen. Doctors and trained professionals sat in his audience. In the proliferative growth of believers in new churches without trained leaders, whoever had the most Bible knowledge was appointed leader, no matter their level of education, and in Karam's church it was him.

Bold and fearless, Karam regularly preached the Gospel in front of mosques throughout the countryside, calling the Islamic worshippers to consider the loving Isa who died for them. Repeated arrests, interrogation, and torture did not deter the fervent leader.

"We know you are attending classes with John Samara!" the secret police yelled, beating Karam until almost every bone in his body broke beneath their boots and weapons. "We know John's name and we know his wife's name is Mero. . . ."

But Karam refused to buckle beneath the blows and the broken bones. *I will never stop sharing the Good News of Jesus, who died for me.*

Eventually, with his life at risk, Karam was forced to leave the country and seek asylum. Yet, wherever he went, he continued to spread the hope of Jesus. Pastor John's teachings filled his heart with courage: "Suffering will lead to glory if we keep our focus on why we suffer."

FROM PERSECUTOR TO PROCLAIMER

"But love your enemies, and do good . . . and your reward will be great,
and you will be sons of the Most High,"

Luke 6:35

"Prayer is a shield for the soul, an offering for God, and a whip for Satan."
—John Bunyan

"In spiritual warfare, never forget that you are fighting from a position of
victory, secured by the blood of Jesus."
—John Eldridge

John studied the stranger worshipping in the Jesus of Nazareth Church.
John watched the tears on the man's cheeks, his uplifted hands, and
eyes closed in worship. *I don't remember seeing him here before.*

Something about the man sent an involuntary chill through John's
heart.

"When we meet under the Cross around the communion table, we
understand the true meaning of the victory that took place on the Cross."
Rami's low, resonant voice carried across the packed auditorium. "And
around that communion table we understand the real meaning of the
power of the Cross to unify us, forgive, and make us one body.

"God has answered our prayers and protected us many times, but
Philippians 1:29 says, 'For it has been granted to you that for the sake of
Christ you should not only believe in him but also suffer for his sake.' Many
Christians expect a normal life and comfort, and when suffering comes,
they are shocked. But we should expect suffering in the Christian life."

Around the courtyard, Syrians, Turks, and Iraqi Muslim background
believers and Alawite bent over basins of warm water, tenderly washing

the feet of those who should have been archenemies. And then the mosaic of believers clasped hands in a large circle around the circumference of the courtyard.

From the depths of their shattered, war-scarred hearts, the brothers and sisters passionately sang the Lord's prayer from the deep yearning of their souls: "Our Father which art in heaven, Hallowed be thy name. . . ."

"Forgive us our debts as we forgive our debtors. . . ."

The voices swelled triumphantly as they collectively lifted clasped hands and tear-brimmed eyes heavenward. "Thy Kingdom come . . ."

Oh glory. God's Kingdom was coming! And His Kingdom would bring peace, justice, and healing.

Before going back into the rubble-strewn, bullet-scarred streets, the sisters wrapped each other in a warm embrace, kissing each other on one cheek and then the other before parting, wondering, *Who will be missing when we meet again?*

The brothers thumped each other on the back, cheering each other, strengthened and fortified to face the intense battle against the spirit of darkness and hate.

It was during one of those services, when John was visiting Damascus, that he noticed a man he did not recognize raising his hands and worshipping with apparent deep feeling and passion. After the service, the man stood in the background, as the brothers gathered around John.

"Bring us up to date, John. What's happening with you and the ministry you lead?"

The men gathered chairs around John, and the stranger pulled up a chair as well.

"I am so excited at what God is doing. The churches in the West are partnering with the suffering churches here in the Middle East and North Africa. Schools in refugee camps, building churches, rebuilding destroyed church buildings, relief distribution, crisis intervention, leadership seminars. . . .

"You know I went to the States for school. I felt like a refugee, an exile, but God was preparing me to be a bridge between the churches in the West and the suffering churches in the MENA region.

"We want to leave no footprint—we work out of a donated office, and the staff donate their time. When I brought a few businessmen to the Middle East, they heard of a woman living in a tent who cared for abandoned babies dropped outside her door. They wanted to support her, so we gave the money through the local church for the woman caring for ten abandoned babies. The donor is in the background and the church is the face of the gift, so in this way we come alongside and empower the local churches.

"After the earthquake in Syria and Türkiye, we immediately reached out to our pastors on the ground. They contacted pastors in Antakya, which was 90 percent destroyed, to find out the urgent needs. An arm of our organization arrived to care, to pray, and to share boots, coats, blankets, heaters, food, tents, diapers, meals. . . .

"And while screams of the buried filled the air, heavy equipment operators, rescue teams, and the Turkish Army stood by waiting thirty hours for directions. But the arm of our organization dove into the rubble with boots on the ground from the first hours after the devastating quake.

"There's an intriguing story of how God used the ministry in the crisis of the earthquake, if you have a moment."

"Absolutely John, we would love to hear what God is doing."

"Türkiye's most popular television station carried an interview with a Muslim woman telling 80 million viewers, 'It was not the mosque, not the United Nations, not the government who came and helped, rescued, and fed and gave us shelter. But the people of the Messiah came and were there for us. They gave us food, stood with us, and gave us shelter.'

"And now all around Türkiye, where less than 2 percent of the populace know Him, people are asking, 'Who are the people of the Messiah?' giving us a wide open door to minister."

"John, how powerfully God is using Ananias House."

"Our mission is built on the concept of following Ananias's model of reaching out to the persecutors so that they could become proclaimers like Paul," John finished with a broad smile.

"And that is me, John. I am the Persecutor who became the Proclaimer because of the love of Jesus." The stranger embraced John like a long-lost friend. "John!" he exclaimed with emotion. "Oh, John."

"Should I know you?" John asked with a warm, questioning smile.

"John! You don't remember me? I am Vergie, your classmate who kicked and beat you back in junior high." The saddened eyes looked away in embarrassment.

"Vergie!" Like a jolt of electricity, the old terror and trauma flashed through John. The old survival instinct to turn and run. . . .

John reached out his arms toward his former abuser, feeling no love, no forgiveness. But he wrapped his old classmate in a bear hug. And in that instant the love and forgiveness of God surged over his heart.

"What in the world are you doing at Jesus of Nazareth Church, Vergie?" John stepped back to take in the man Vergie had become. *What is he doing here?*

"It's quite surprising, John, isn't it? I used to beat you for following Jesus, and now here I am, in your father's church!

"John, I am so very sorry." Vergie dropped his head. "I grew up in the Orthodox church but never knew Jesus, but I saw Him in you. Can you ever forgive me for how I abused you almost daily for three years?"

John searched Vergie's tear-filled eyes. He saw the genuine grief, the torment. "Vergie, of course I forgive you! I am just thrilled to observe what God has done in your life. Tell me about your journey."

"John, when we kicked you and beat you up, you never retaliated. Never got revenge. We just saw the sad look in your eyes and heard your words and prayers of forgiveness. You didn't retaliate, John, but God did with His love. I felt this love and it drew me. And then, as I walked by this church, I heard beautiful singing coming through the windows. I stepped inside and that same love just reached out and drew me in, and here I am."

"From Persecutor to Proclaimer! Thank you, Jesus!"

ISA—RESTORING
THE HONOR

"Beloved, let us love one another, for love is from God, and whoever loves has been born of God and knows God. Anyone who does not love does not know God, because God is love."

I John 4:7

"The Cross is not a symbol of suffering; it is a symbol of victory. Suffering may be involved in the journey under the cross, but it is not the destination. The joy set before us is the destination."

—Rami Ibrahim

"When do you think your family will send your brothers to restore the family honor?" Abdul finally verbalized the question haunting him and Samira. "They feel shamed because we left their religion. You know they will come."

"They will try. No doubt. But Isa Jesus is watching over us. I won't worry. Right now, I have much better things to think about. Dalia is having a baby! I am going to be a grandma! 'Taita Samira,' 'Grandma Samira,' doesn't that sound lovely!"

Samira prayed often for her daughter, married to Nasir, a strict Muslim who did not permit Dalia to be in public without being covered from the burka with the eye netting to the tips of her gloved hands. When Dalia was talking to her mother, she needed to hang up the moment Nasir walked into the house. Samira prayed for the salvation of Dalia and Nasir.

Three months before the baby's due date, the wee child arrived. The chances of survival were slim.

"Your infant is failing to respond to treatment," the doctor informed the young couple. "I am sorry to tell you he is dying."

"The doctor said he's going to die!" Dalia cried to her mother.

"You must go to the hospital and pray to Isa Jesus for your baby!" Samira instructed. "Isa Jesus came to Ali in a dream and told him we would have a boy child and should name him Isa, and then the name Isa opened the door for us to come to Lebanon. And then Jesus healed your father.

"You must go pray to Him for your child!" she urged. "He is a powerful God!"

"But Mama, I am not allowed into his room! And I never prayed to that God. I don't know how to talk to Him!"

"Go to the door of the NICU and put your hands on the door," Samira instructed. "I will tell you the words to say."

Without telling anyone, the young mother walked into the hospital, placed her hand on the door of the NICU, and with her mother coaching her on the other end of the line, Dalia prayed, "Dear Jesus, Isa, please come put Your hand on my precious baby, and heal him. Amen."

Within twenty-four hours, the doctor called Dalia: "A miracle has happened! Your son was dying but has suddenly taken a turn for the better and will live. I can't explain what happened, but you can come and hold your son. He is no longer in critical condition."

Samira's daughter began to believe in this loving Isa-Jesus who cared about a mother's hurting heart and a fragile tiny infant that needed healing.

Word of Abdul and Samira's change of faith found its way back to the mansion in Saudi Arabia. Samira's family was furious. She had shamed them. The honor of their family was at stake.

When Samira heard her brother's voice at the door, she knew exactly why he had come. He had come to restore the honor of his family. And he would be carrying a sharpened knife in the sheath on his belt.

Samira breathed a silent prayer to Isa and then calmly spoke through the door's iron grate. "Dear brother, what a privilege to have you come so far to visit us! I ask one request of you. Before I open the door, I want you to promise me that you will not use your knife before you have given us twenty-four hours to hear our story, until you've attended one of our services with us and experienced what we experience."

The brother scowled angrily. *The very idea!*

But Samira would only open once he promised.

What would it hurt? He could listen and then restore the honor, catch the next flight to King Abdulaziz International Airport, and be back in Saudi Arabia before anyone knew what had happened.

Samira and the family welcomed her brother with the warmest hospitality, serving him all his favorite foods, constantly refilling his coffee cup, and piling his plate with baklava. He noted that his sister's food options had shrunk, but her hospitality had not.

Feeling embraced in love, the sheikh settled back to hear Samira and Abdul's journey. Ali shared about the Man in glowing white in the vision. Abdul shared about the border guard letting them into Lebanon when he saw the name Isa after he had already denied them entrance. The brother listened intently. And then they told of Abdul's miraculous recovery. And the healing of the premature grandbaby in Türkiye.

The uncle tried to process it all as he lay in bed. His hand reached for the blade of the knife; he knew he could silently accomplish his mission in the dark of the night as the family slept.

Then he thought of the love that had washed over him like the warm waves of the Arabian sea, overwhelming him and knocking him onto the sun-kissed sand. He thought of the miracles, the boy child, the entrance to Lebanon, the healings. He sheathed the knife once again.

I can wait. I will go to the Isa meeting of the people of the Book tomorrow to hear what is said, and then I will be in a better position to argue.

The sheikh from Saudi Arabia accompanied his sister and family to the service where the man would talk of this Isa Jesus. The sheikh watched curiously as the families lovingly greeted each other with hugs and kisses before sitting together on the floor to sing the most beautiful melodies he had ever heard.

"Jesus keep me near the Cross, there a precious fountain, free to all the healing stream, that flows from Calvary's mountain."

The Jesus followers sang of Him with such passion in their voices and love in their eyes; he had never experienced anything like it before. "Near the Cross, near the Cross, be my glory ever, till my raptured soul shall find, rest beyond the river!"

The words and melody melted the cold, hard heart. His eyes grew moist. What love. What hope. How different from the frenzied shrieks, bullets, and swords of ISIS who followed his Allah.

As the sheikh wept, Jesus came down and ministered to his heart.

"The soldiers came to take Jesus for trial," the pastor said. "Jesus's student pulled out his sword, and in trying to behead an attacker, he cut off the man's ear. Jesus said, 'Put your sword away,' and healed the ear. And then God's Son went willingly with the men He knew would execute Him, and He let them slaughter Him like a lamb to save the souls of the whole world."

The sheikh sat frozen. He had never heard anything like that. His Allah said words of hate and death and would never sacrifice his life!

"Is there anyone who wishes for us to pray for them?" the Isa pastor asked.

The sheikh from Saudi Arabia felt the knife handle at his belt. His family depended on him to restore honor. *I have a choice. Either I use the knife on these precious youngsters and their parents, or my brother will use it on me.*

The overwhelming love in this room contrasted starkly with the hate of the ISIS soldiers who, in the name of his Allah, abused, raped, shot, and killed. And threatened his nieces. The hair stood up on the back of his neck at the thought.

He chose.

"I came here from Saudi Arabia with my heart filled with anger and hate!" he sobbed. "I sharpened my knife to restore honor to my family and take the lives of Abdul and Samira for following their Isa Jesus, but Jesus has captured my heart with His love. I want to follow Isa!"

The sheikh's family met him when the plane landed in Saudi Arabia. "You did not restore our honor!" The sheikh saw the sheaths on their belts.

And then he replied with gentle confidence. "The honor's been restored. The blood has been shed. Another has done it for us."

Back in Lebanon, Samira prayed for the salvation of her family: her parents, her siblings, her daughter and son-in-law, and her grandbaby.

Abdul, Samira, and their younger children could not learn enough about the Isa Jesus who had come to Ali in a vision. When John and his friend Ervin brought a team from America to teach the young leaders of the church, Abdul and Samira invited them to their home, wanting to learn all they could from these teachers.

Ervin and John settled comfortably on the rectangular cushions on the floor, leaning against the wall, surrounded by Abdul and his family. Samira and the girls served rose water-flavored rice pudding made from their dried milk rations.

Ervin listened entranced as Ali told the story of the shining Man in White. Abdul and Samira told of the miracles they experienced and about the miraculous recovery of the grandbaby.

"How are your daughter and son-in-law?" John asked, savoring his espresso cup of spiced coffee.

"We just received a message saying our son-in-law, Nasir, is now 'one of us!'" Abdul announced. "He was a radical follower of Allah, but Isa melted his heart!"

"Hallelujah! Thank you, Jesus!"

"And what of your brothers, Samira?"

"Ah, Mr. Ervin, you need to know, after my first brother came to convert us back to Islam or to restore the honor, my second brother came.

And now, Pastor Ervin, my second brother is in prison in Saudi Arabia for following Isa!"

"Unbelievable! How amazing—your brother embraced your faith instead of killing you and went to prison for his faith!"

"What about Aleppo?" Ervin asked Abdul. "What is happening to your property you left behind?"

"Sadly, I am told our lovely home is now a broken shell. The windows and doors were blown out with the bombing. Thank God we left when we did."

"You left everything."

"We left everything," Abdul affirmed. "I had dairy equipment, land, cows, goats, cheese-making equipment, and a large, comfortable home. It was not easy. Even our favorite cow had tears when we said goodbye to her. Brother Ervin, we lost everything, but it was worth it. We found Jesus."

Samira and the girls refilled the rich cardamom-spiced coffee in the tiny cups. Samira's son Ali put his arm around his wife and shared, "We want so much to have a child, but that honor has not been given to us."

"Ali, God can answer that prayer!" John exclaimed. "Mero and I waited eight years for a child. Then Pastor Ervin poured oil on our heads, and his church gathered around and prayed for us and now Mero is expecting our baby! We can pray for you and your wife right now, Ali!"

"Oh please, we would like that," Ali responded, leading his young wife to her knees in the circle's center.

"Samira," John asked, "Do you have some olive oil I could use? The book of James says when you are sick, you should call for the elders and have them pray and anoint you with oil."

John and Ervin poured a little oil on the heads of Ali and his wife and laid their hands on the heads of the two, asking Jesus to please hear the prayers of this dear couple and to bless them with a child to raise for Him.

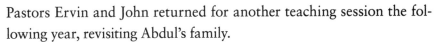

Pastors Ervin and John returned for another teaching session the following year, revisiting Abdul's family.

Samira and the girls served the guests rice pudding and the tiny porcelain cups of rich Turkish coffee as they sat in a relaxed circle on the floor.

"How is your family, John?" Samira wondered.

"Do you remember I told you how Ervin and his church anointed my wife and me with oil and prayed for us?" John asked. "Well, in November, God gave us a son whom we called Abraham."

"Beautiful, just beautiful." The family was so touched to hear of God's amazing gift.

A burka-covered woman seeming to be a family relative sat comfortably in the circle, listening intently to the conversation. The gold rings and bracelets evidenced wealth. Her youthful appearance would have placed her as a sister to Samira. But as the guests were introduced, they learned the woman was Samira's mother from Saudi Arabia.

"Where is Ali?" Ervin asked, missing Abdul's eldest son.

"Oh, he is at the doctor; his wife is not feeling well."

"I am sorry to hear that," Ervin replied with concern.

As Abdul and Samira shared their hearts, their love for Isa poured from their souls. "We are so thankful our children know the true God and want to serve him. Nothing could make us happier."

As Samira spoke, Ervin glanced at her bejeweled mother's response and was startled to see tears slipping down her cheeks behind the netted burka. The Saudi grandmother, too, was drawn by the irresistible power of God's love.

The door opened, and Ali entered with his wife. The visiting pastors rose to greet them. "I am sorry your wife is not feeling well and had to see the doctor," Ervin spoke compassionately, Pastor John translating.

"Not to worry!" Ali replied with a laugh. "The doctor said maybe baby!"

The room broke into applause for the blushing wife and her husband. And for Jesus, who loved deeply and cared intimately to draw this dear family to himself through a dream, miracles, and His love.

KIDNAPPED

"For I consider that the sufferings of this present time are not worth comparing with the glory that is to be revealed to us."

Romans 8:18

"As Christians, we believe in Divine providence. God is sovereign and is in control of every area. He can use suffering for His purpose. Suffering doesn't come from God, but God uses suffering for His purpose."

—Rami Ibrahim

"You will never leave this building alive." The radical Druze captor cracked his pistol on Rafiq's head.

The young pastor lay face down, motionless and bruised, on the cold floor, his hands painfully chained behind his back. His body tensed for the next blow.

"Your execution date is scheduled. We have a special torture squad just to deal with Christians like you!" the radical Druze finished with a savage kick.

God, I so wanted to attend the Ananias House leadership conference with John and Pastor Abraham next week! I've survived these last difficult weeks dreaming of rendezvousing with the other pastors from the Middle East and North Africa.

The mere thought of not connecting with other persecuted pastors who understood his journey, who cared, listened, and prayed over him, strangled the hope from his weary heart.

Lord, You know, the encouragement from that week gives me courage to keep preaching despite the threats by the radical Druze. And now the Druze have me beneath their boots, and the conference goes on without me.

Days before his scheduled departure, Rafiq stood in front of the crowded room, passionately sharing the hope of the Gospel with a room full of searching, hurting souls so wounded and disillusioned by the cruelties and losses of the war.

The attendees from the Druze sect had never heard such hope-filled words before. The verses from God's Holy Book seemed like a comforting flickering candle dispelling the hopeless darkness shrouding their lives.

"The Messiah already came!" The audience looked at each other with wide eyes and open mouths. "And when a believer in Jesus dies, he is taken to Paradise instead of being perpetually reincarnated like our old leaders taught."

As Rafiq spoke, the listeners absorbed every life-filled scripture the pastor shared like parched desert sand soaking up each glistening jeweled dew droplet.

The door burst open with angry shouts as a pack of inflamed radicals charged through the door, brandishing pistols, screaming obscenities and chilling threats.

Before Rafiq could think or pray, they had bound him and three other men, holding guns to their backs.

"Line up along the wall, you dirty prostitutes!" the leader screamed at the trembling women, terrorizing and harassing them. Wailing children clung to their mothers, sensing the spirit of evil invading the room.

"Males against the other wall! Move! Your filthy faces to the wall! Hands in the air!"

The gunmen prodded Rafiq and the three other captives toward the door with the muzzles of assault rifles and pistols.

Women sobbed silently into their burkas while the children clung to their skirts in terror.

"If you ever come back to a meeting like this again, we will *kill* you!" they threatened the cowering women who clutched their sobbing toddlers.

How could the hopeful light that had filled the room so quickly be extinguished with oppressive, dark evil? Just when they had begun to understand and to have a ray of optimism for the future.

Gunmen shoved the captives harshly into the backseat of a vehicle, thrusting them onto the floor so they could not see where they were taken, or be seen.

After a torturous ride careening from alley to alley, the car screeched to a halt. Gunmen threw open the doors, dragged the men out of the truck, and forced them into a small building.

"Lay on the floor face down." A harsh kick emphasized the words.

Feeling the muzzle of the gun on his back and a boot on his neck, Rafiq recalled the warnings. *Druze leaders feel threatened by those sharing the Gospel with "their" people and will fight against having their community drawn away from the Druze religion.*

Rafiq had known leading a church service in the Druze territory might cost his life. And now that the deputies of the radical Druze held him beneath their boots, he had no doubt that these trigger-happy extremists would zealously finish him off to purge the "infidels" from their village.

Please, Jesus! Your lambs! The girls! The women . . . My wife . . . The children . . . Let them kill me but spare the women and children!

How will I die? Beheading? Gunshot? Crucifixion? Torture?

"You will die. Unless you denounce Jesus."

"NO!" the four bound captives shouted from the floor. "We will never deny our Lord, no matter what you do to us!"

"Then get ready to die!" the radical terrorists screamed, shoving the barrels of AK-47s against their skulls. Like a pack of ravenous wolves, they descended on the Christians, smashing into their ribs with their boots, pummeling the men's backs, heads, arms, and legs with fists and guns.

A helpless, hopeless terror gripped Rafiq beneath the boots of his captor. *My future is in their hands.*

Words of a favorite song came to mind, comforting his thumping heart:

"The reins are in Your hand. You are ever faithful. The final word is Yours, no matter what others say."

The terrorists are not *in control,* the pastor whispered as a gentle peace enveloped his heart. *God, You are in control. You've got the reins in Your hands. The final word is* Yours. *If You are okay with me dying, then death will be a beautiful experience of seeing Jesus. Life is not about me. It is whatever brings You the most glory.*

And in that moment, all his dreams, the leadership conference, and all his possessions seemed to shrink until all that remained was the glorious awareness of the nearness of a mighty God who held the future in His omnipotent hands.

If God chooses this hour for my death, how precious to spend the last seconds suffering for Him—with His outstretched hands waiting just ahead.

Rafiq's tense limbs relaxed against the cold concrete in sweet surrender, blanketed in peace, no longer struggling or fearful.

As he lay in the darkness, a seed of hope began to sprout in his heart. *Maybe God wants me to live!*

"You are going to die! We will eliminate all of you filthy infidels!" the captors tormented the Christians.

The Spirit of God surged through the pastor like an electrical charge.

"No!" Rafiq shouted, jumping to his feet in a detonation of confidence and righteous indignation. "You will not kill us!" He stood fearlessly before his captors, his eyes ablaze.

"You are going to release us!" he thundered powerfully as the soldiers reared back in surprise. "We are going to continue telling people about Jesus! And they will tell people about Jesus! And then those people will tell others about Jesus until there are more of us than there are of you!" Rafiq finished passionately.

A captor raised his fist, smacking Rafiq brutally across the face, knocking him off his feet. The blows, kicks, and taunts continued.

But Rafiq focused on the awareness that God's hand was over all. God would be glorified.

As the night aged, the kidnappers wearied, and the beatings diminished. Eventually, snores escaped from the spent captors. But the tenderness of his bruises against the cold floor, and the uncertainty, kept Rafiq awake. He communicated with His Father and basked in the comfort of His nearness.

Jesus, my dear family . . . my beloved flock . . . Give me the strength to stay faithful. Precious Lord, be glorified.

The pale golden rays filtering beneath the door began pushing back the oppressive darkness. He remembered that it was resurrection morning.

The morning the stone was rolled away as the Lord burst from the darkness, breaking the chains of death forever! Light always wins in the end.

Let them shoot. The bullets will only catapult my soul far beyond their reach, to eternal bliss.

A wave of joy overwhelmed his heart, and his heart burst silently with the song:

> Lift your glad voices in triumph on high,
>
> For Jesus hath risen, and man shall not die.
>
> Glory to God, in full anthems of joy;
>
> The being He gave us death cannot destroy.
>
> But Jesus hath cheered the dark valley of sorrow,
>
> And bade us, immortal, to Heaven ascend.
>
> Lift then your voices in triumph on high,
>
> For Jesus hath risen, and man shall not die.

A phone vibrated in the pocket of one of the guards, who stirred sleepily to answer the call.

"Yeah?" he grouched.

"Get out here and help us right now!" The caller's yells carried across the cell. "We are losing the battle!"

In a flurry of exchanges, the terrorists leaped to their feet, grabbed the guns, and bolted from the building. Behind them, the door hung wide open, welcoming the morning rays to bathe the cell.

Painfully, Rafiq rolled to his side, watching as the truck sped around the corner and vanished into a cloud of dust and smoke.

Drawing himself to his knees, he crept cautiously to the door. Not a soul in sight. Only a couple alley cats.

"All clear! Let's run!"

Casting hasty glances in either direction, the four Christian leaders slipped as from their "grave" to the golden rays of the resurrection morning dawn.

"Vain were the terrors that gathered around Him, And short the dominion of death and the grave!"

What a joyous reunion welcomed the battered men as they limped into their homes. The miracle felt like a modern-day story torn from the book of Acts when Peter appeared at the prayer meeting after a miraculous escape from prison. The God of the first-century miracles still reigned.

Hours later, Rafiq caught a ride to the Ananias House pastor training conference, praying his captors would not hunt down his family in his absence.

Rafiq's wife shared his courage and passion for God. She was not hiding. Instead, she was figuring out how to slip out of town without being seen by the radical Druze threatening to shoot any female traveling to the women's conference in Damascus. Their threats did not keep the wife of the released pastor from hearing Amalee Samara speak about focusing on "The Joy Set Before Us!"

"ARMOR OF LIGHT"

"The night is far gone; the day is at hand. So then let us cast off the works of darkness and put on the armor of light."

Romans 13:12

"As Jesus carried the Cross, He was focusing on the joy—sitting at the right hand of the throne. As He walked toward Golgotha, He was not seeing the Cross, only people who would become saved and would be brought to the Kingdom of His Father—to suffer and bring others to the Kingdom."

—Rami Ibrahim

Only the slight tension of his facial muscles revealed the underlying uneasiness as Rafiq strolled into the pastors' training conference beyond the Syrian borders.

Lord, please protect my wife and my flock while I am gone. Don't let the wolves attack the precious lambs.

Did my wife get caught going to Amalee's women's convention?

Only those close to him knew about his capture, greeting Rafiq with triumphant high-fives and hugs.

As the men from Türkiye, Egypt, Syria, Lebanon, and North Africa walked into the conference room, a comet of awed joy flashed through John's heart. *These are men who risked all to follow Christ.*

"Let's gather in a circle to get to know each other better," he invited, surveying these battle-scarred men, relaxing in the safe haven of the conference room.

Many literally bore the scars of war, like the pastor with the bullet wound ripping the side of his face. Bomb explosions had robbed several men of the hearing in an ear.

"Since you don't all know each other, we will each tell a little about ourselves," John suggested, a warm smile illuminating his face as he drew the stories from businessmen, physicians, farmers, teachers, and a mathematician who had memorized Matthew, Mark, Luke, and John.

"I want peace so much that I named one of my daughters Tamar, a Muslim name, and the other Rachel, a Christian name," a pastor shared.

"One fact you might not know about me," Nabil revealed, "is that I once wore a burka." The men loved hearing how the pastor escaped under the very eyes of the ISIS soldiers beneath an ISIS wife's burka.

"I was trembling so hard the women told me to stop shaking or the ISIS soldiers would know I was not a woman," he shared with a laugh. "We have one caring, personal, and creative God!"

The fellow pastors laughed heartily, envisioning the scene.

"We escaped the ISIS guns and execution cross, resettling in another Christian community where we help lead a church," he finished.

"War took its toll on ISIS-targeted Christian villages," men shared. "Out of 2,000 Christians, in one town, only twenty elderly remain. The rest fled to other cities, refugee camps, or pulled on a life jacket and climbed onto an inflatable dinghy."

"My students are traumatized by bombs falling on the school playground," a schoolteacher bemoaned. "They witness their classmates dismembered and killed right before their eyes. Christian schools and churches are the prime targets of the radicals who hate what they stand for."

"This was my bus factory in Aleppo before it was bombed." Mikayel showed pictures on his phone. "And I had a toy factory as well. I was worth millions, but the bombs destroyed my means of income, and there were no resources to rebuild. During the siege, we had no water for 94 days except for the water we smuggled in from a well when the fighting died down. My house is 160 meters from the ISIS lines."

"And yet, Mikayel stayed," John added, clapping the pastor on the back. "He stayed living 160 meters from the ISIS lines, in a city destroyed by eight years of warfare, serving the church in radical obedience, radical humility, and radical generosity."

Abdullah, the former Imam's eyes glowed in triumph as he scanned the faces around him. "After three years, I finally came to the place where I can tell my wife 'I love you.' Instead of hitting Farida when she shames me, I can now say, 'I love you dear.'

"Farida told me she wants me to stay in this church because she knows as long as I am in this church where they teach me to love, I will not leave her and the family. For a while she was trying to take the children away from me, but when she saw my positive impact on them, she even let them come to church with me."

"Alleluia!" the pastors burst out in delight and praise.

"That's fabulous, brother! That is the way to have the same mind as Jesus had. Paul, the former terrorist Jesus struck down with a bright light on the Damascus Road, says in his book Philippians 2:5–8, 'Have the same mindset as Christ Jesus . . . who made himself nothing, taking the very nature of a servant'. . . . He humbled himself by becoming obedient to death—even death on a Cross!'"

"I'm Rafiq from Syria," the released pastor shared when his turn came, telling a little about his job, family, and church.

Zahir, a former follower of the Druze religion and Rafiq's fellow pastor, jumped to his feet. "Brother John, Pastor Rafiq didn't tell you that he and three others were captured by militant radicals last weekend. The radicals burst into a house church, kidnapped him, and traumatized the women. They were scheduled for execution.

"On Easter morning, the captors fled to join a battle, leaving the door open and unguarded for Rafiq to escape. And forty-eight hours later, he comes to this conference."

"Alleluia!" The room erupted with worship to their amazing God. "Thank you, Jesus!" "Glory!"

The men gave Rafiq high-fives and gentle claps on his shoulders, sensitive to wounds he might carry.

"Rafiq, why don't you come kneel in the middle here, and we brothers will gather around you." John gestured to the center of the auditorium.

The leaders from around the Middle East and North Africa surrounded Rafiq, laying hands on him, praying powerful prayers surging from passionate hearts of fervor for God and a deep connection with Him.

"We bless you, Lord, for the miraculous gift of Rafiq's release and his presence here at the conference."

"Cover his brave wife and children with your wings."

"Strengthen our brother Rafiq as he returns as a sheep to the wolves. And may those captors never torment our bother or his church again."

"And help the Druze community to learn to know the love of Jesus."

"I'd like to invite each of you to come to the center of the circle for all of us to lay hands on you and pray blessings over you," John invited. "Fawzi and Idris from Sudan, you've got a hard, lonely road with so much opposition, why don't you come next."

Fawzi and Idris knelt in the circle. As powerful prayers ascended for these lonely, battle-weary missionaries, the two men wept, lifting their hands toward God. They rose from that prayer circle heartened and strengthened for the intensity of the battle ahead.

As the men humbly shared stories between sessions, many did not reveal their personal crises, but their stories surfaced through their brothers who requested prayer for these pastors facing death sentences or who had just been released from prison.

As they took turns praying over each other, from deep within the souls of these Middle Eastern brothers rose a groaning to glorify God and advance His Kingdom. They were willing to pay the price.

None of their requests mentioned their material needs or comforts. Their prayers were all about God's Kingdom and His will being done.

A prayer Steve, the American counselor, heard intrigued him. "Bring revenge. Revenge on those who reported the girl for becoming a Christian, on those who captured and imprisoned her, on the guard that abused the girl. . . ."

"What do they mean by revenge?" Steve questioned.

"The best revenge, they believe, and what they are praying for is for the girl's captors to become saved, her family to become saved, and the prison guard who abused her to become saved. That is the best revenge!" John explained with a broad smile.

John and the American pastors Ervin and Steve could see the tense lines on the faces melting into relaxed smiles as the prayer, worship, and sharing wrapped the battle-fatigued warriors in healing safety, support, and hope.

Despite the recent capture, Rafiq exuded confidence and calm peace throughout the week, radiating the joy and strength of a true man of God.

Observing the banter and laughter between Rafiq and his friends, Steve asked John, "What's Rafiq laughing about? He just went through the trauma of kidnapping and beating; what's he finding so funny?"

"They are joking about a detail of the kidnapping. It's their way of coping. You will see that a lot in these men. Laughter is their tension reliever."

"Intriguing," Steve mused. "I work as a counselor in the US. I've observed when a person can no longer laugh, he loses his ability to cope.

"We've heard stories this week of former ISIS slaves coming into the church. How do you help these women work through the trauma of the denigrating abuse of being forced to serve the radicals all night long and then cook their food and care for their children during the day?"

"We could use thousands of counselors in this fractured Middle East," John replied. "But counselors are inaccessible. It's not an option. Our only option is prayer. As we pray over the hurting, broken people, God reveals himself in miraculous ways and brings healing and gives us the ability to overcome."

The conference attendees thrived like plants taken from the desert and placed into a greenhouse.

"We don't have time or resources to connect through the year. This week's fellowship is the invigorating highlight giving us courage for another year in the trenches," they revealed.

And they'll take what they learn and teach it in their home communities, John knew, recalling how he first taught the book of Galatians to a group of twenty-seven leaders in Egypt with short lectures and small group breakouts to answer questions and look up scriptures.

John assigned each pastor at that conference to go home and teach five other leaders Galatians as a prerequisite for returning the following year. Within three years, 2,000 leaders had been taught the book of Galatians.

Phones began vibrating across the conference hall. The pastors pulled out their phones and began exclaiming over the text messages from their wives back in Damascus.

"Alleluia! My wife made it safely to the Damascus Women's Conference! No bullets!" Rafiq burst out.

"Mine too! She didn't even get shot at!"

"They say 250 women packed into that chapel listening to Pastor Abraham's wife Amalee teach about focusing on 'The Joy Set Before Us!'"

"Glory!"

Their dear, brave wives needed the fellowship and refreshment every bit as much as the wounded warriors.

As the conference progressed, world news reported, "US ships off the coast of Syria prepare an attack on the Syrian regime in retaliation for the chemical bombs dropped on civilians in Douma. Hospitals had treated over 500 patients smelling of chlorine, suffering from corneal burns, foaming of the mouth and convulsions. Dozens died of suffocation."

The Syrian pastors checked their cell phones between classes, growing edgy at the news of potential US attacks.

"Jesus be with our wives, our children, and church families in the line of fire! Intervene! Change the course of the projected action!"

Mercifully, the planes remained secured to the aircraft carrier, allowing the pastors to focus.

As he observed the pastors and heard about their churches, John could see the prolific growth of believers across the Middle East coupled with the challenges his father talked about.

"We see scores of Druze coming to God in our community," one brother remarked. "But the real persecution comes from the local Orthodox priests feeling threatened by our growth."

"We used to have six Christians in our city, but now our church is so packed we need a new building."

A North African leader shared the picture of his baptism with Steve. "But please don't put it on social media, or I could be killed."

"These people are the new generation of Anabaptists," Steve told Ervin. "They risk their lives to be baptized just like our ancestors did 500 years ago."

"And we must do what we can to decrease their risk," John put in. "If someone had heard us pray the Lord's Prayer at the restaurant, they could have tracked down each of those men in our group and imprisoned them. And furthermore, they could go to jail if your number was found on their phones."

"I constantly travel under sniper fire to share the Gospel," a pastor admitted. "But God has kept me safe. The heart of our church is our prayer meetings."

"Prayer is the greatest need for the leaders of God," Pastor Abraham agreed. "We need prayer to strengthen, guide, and give wisdom."

Pastor Abraham found these precious men to be sponges, eagerly soaking up any wisdom and encouragement he had to share.

The dignified elderly pastor shared one of his life mottos from Philippians 1:21: "For to me to live is Christ, and to die is gain," giving the students a glimpse into the power propelling the successful man. Fearless of death, the man lived life full throttle for God.

"My second life motto is, 'I can do all things through Christ who strengthens me,'" he shared from Philippians 4:13.

As Dad kneels on his living room floor in those nightly prayer sessions, God empowers him with courage and wisdom, John thought, observing his father with admiring eyes.

"If you are going to be a successful shepherd, there are two things you must do," Abraham taught the men.

1. You need to be a man of prayer.
2. You must be a man of the Word.

"You are responsible for leading and feeding your flock. There is no other way to succeed but to be a man of prayer and a man acquainted with the Word.

"Furthermore, there are three vices that will ruin a pastor."

1. Pride
2. Money
3. Lust

These nuggets of wisdom and encouragement as well as the precious jam sessions with fellow warriors would help carry the pastors through the next intense months when many of them looked death in the eye.

What crises lie ahead for these brave battle-scarred warriors of Jesus? John wondered as he glanced around at the men urging each other on like football players in a huddle before the final game.

Yacoub, the youthful pastor with a brilliant mind and a fiery heart for God, caught John's attention. "Yacoub is working on memorizing the whole New Testament," Abraham told John.

John quizzed Yacoub, asking him to quote random chapters he requested until John grew weary. The youth quoted them all precisely.

What's ahead for this young man? Will he replace my father and be the next leader of the Syrian churches?

But Yacoub would need those scriptures he had memorized when kidnapped by the Druze. God knew what lay ahead for these courageous warriors. But God would be with them as they focused beyond their suffering to the joy at the end of the journey.

Like Mikayel, living in a war zone, the men asked each morning,

"Could this be the day?" And then others would respond, "This could be the day I die."

Living on the cusp of eternity, the pastors seemed to live with their ears against the heartbeat of God, a continual other-world-consciousness, constantly asking:

Lord, how can I please You today?

Who would You have me speak to today? For salvation? For encouragement? For prayers?

Which route shall I take today?

What is on Your heart for me today?

Who are the teachers and who are the students? Ervin wondered, learning so much from their brothers on the front lines.

As Ervin stood before the group, preparing to share his presentation, he surveyed the faces before him with reverent admiration. *These are the mighty men of God, not loving their lives unto death. Men who hazard their lives, facing obstacles, kidnapping, and death threats,* he realized. *I am humbled to be in their presence.*

As he looked into the eyes of those seasoned soldiers of the Cross who all had their death-defying moments, he sensed their need for encouragement rather than profound doctrinal teaching. He began to tell the leaders the story of Nokseng.

"Welsh missionaries took the Gospel to a tribe of headhunters in Northeast India. An Indian named Nokseng and his wife and family received Christ and shared the Gospel with the villagers.

"The pagan chief seethed about this new religion, calling Nokseng, his wife, and two sons to come before him.

"'Renounce your religion!' the enraged chief demanded, 'Or I will kill your sons.'

"Inspired by the Holy Spirit, Nokseng replied resolutely: 'I have decided to follow Jesus, no turning back, no turning back.'

"'Shoot his sons!' the chief ordered. Arrows sliced through the air, felling the two lads.

"'Renounce your beliefs, or we will kill your wife!'

"'The Cross before me, the world behind me, no turning back,' Nokseng responded passionately.

"The archer released the arrow, and Nokseng's wife fell at his feet.

"'One more chance to renounce your faith, or we kill you too.'

"'Though no one joins me, still I will follow, no turning back, no turning back!' Nokseng's voice rang out triumphantly just before the arrow cut him down.

"The scene of a family who would die for their God stabbed the heart of the pagan chief as he surveyed the arrow-pierced bodies lying in pools of blood.

"In a moment of overwhelming conviction, he questioned his own beliefs and the power behind a family ready to die for a man who lived so long ago. He desired that kind of conviction. He wanted to experience that kind of faith.

"'And I too will follow!' the smitten chief burst out.

"And a revival swept through the village of headhunters. The tribesmen, too, decided to follow Jesus. 'No turning back!'"

Tears slid down the battle-scarred cheeks of the pastors in Ervin's audience who had faced bullets, kidnappers, and missiles for Christ. Their hearts resonated with the account.

"And that is the story behind the song, 'I have decided to follow Jesus,'" Ervin finished. "Let's sing it together."

A bit of heaven seemed to descend on that meeting room as those men lifted their voices with emotion-laden conviction: "I have decided to follow Jesus, no turning back, no turning back."

Those seasoned warriors sang with an intense, heartfelt passion deep in their souls, keenly aware of what the commitment could cost. "The Cross before me, the world behind me. . . . No turning back, no turning back."

The fire of their souls propelled the words heavenward, tugging tears from their eyes and pushing goosebumps on their arms. "Though no one joins me, still I will follow. . . . No turning back, no turning back."

The men sat silently, reflecting, internalizing the commitment that if asked to face the AK-47s Rafiq faced, they would not turn back.

Rafiq's phone vibrated. A text from his wife. His hands grew clammy as he opened the message. His eyes widened with question as he stared at the photo of the remains of a mangled vehicle, an obvious missile target. *Who. . . . What. . . .*

Quickly he scanned the message: "Habibi, three of your kidnappers were killed in this attack. The fourth is seriously injured. Maybe the attack was the result of mistaken identity. Maybe an opposition force. . . ."

Rafiq froze as he stared at the words on his phone. Goosebumps prickled on his arms.

God! Not only did You deliver Your shepherd from the wolves, but You dealt with the wolves, and You dealt with them while I was out of town, so I could not be blamed for the attack!

Lord, You really are in control! You are surrounding us with Your armor of light!

As the brave frontline warriors filed out of the doors, they seemed to pick up their crosses and follow their Savior under the shadow of the Cross, faces aglow with the dynamic resurrection power unleashed within them.

Their focus was not on the bullets, risks, and threats that lay ahead but *on the joy set before them.*

As the US team packed to leave, Steve sat down next to John's father. "Brother Abraham, you must be approaching seventy."

"He's approaching seventy-five," John put in.

"Wow. You don't show it," Steve remarked, surveying the trim, spry pastor with a head full of dark gray hair and a groomed mustache.

"But Pastor Abraham, there is a price on your head. Your life is constantly in danger. You and Amalee must be getting weary. Why don't you just come back to the US with us?"

Abraham didn't even hesitate. "Brother, you see suffering. We see harvest." His voice ringing with confident authority, and eyes flashing with passion, he finished, "I need to stay to bring in the greatest harvest I have ever seen in my lifetime."

How great is our God!

EPILOGUE

"My Jesus I Love thee; I know thou art mine

For thee all the follies of sin I resign. . . .

I will love thee in life, I will love thee in death,

And praise thee as long as thou lendest me breath. . . .

In mansions of glory and endless delight,

I'll ever adore thee in heaven so bright;

I'll sing with the glittering crown on my brow.

If ever I loved thee, my Jesus, tis now."

"And let us run with endurance the race that is set before us . . . who for

the JOY that was set before him endured the Cross."

Hebrews 12:2

Oh God, please no. John felt goosebumps explode across his arm as the icy fingers of terror gripped his spine. *Not Yacoub. Not abducted by the radicals.*

John's urgent list on the desk before him faded. His head dropped to his hands as the strength drained from his body.

The face of the promising, dedicated young pastor with the goal of memorizing the entire New Testament rose before him.

Yacoub's devoted wife. The baby. . . .

The texts from the North African pastors worshipping in forests to avoid detection paled in comparison to the phone call from his father.

Messages from the pastor facing violence in Pakistan while the church building went up in flames dimmed beside the urgent call from Syria.

John cancelled the online meeting with Barbara's team regarding the Ananias House's fifth year of women's conferences in the MENA region.

The emails about the leadership training with the team heading to North Africa along with the messages from the teachers at the refugee camps lay buried beneath the urgent messages from the Middle East.

"Radical Islamists nabbed him as Yacoub walked out of a church service he led in the radical neighborhood." Abraham's voice broke. "They took him, John."

"'We will hang him if you don't pay the three billion pounds ransom by tomorrow,' the caller said. The treasurer told him it is impossible. Even if we sold the church building, we couldn't afford the ransom. And paying would encourage more abductions. The kidnapper then called me. By God's grace I spoke to him with such authority that he didn't dare ask for money.

"And then they sent a picture of his back fileted by the whip. Not an unbloodied spot, John!

"He must be so in pain that he has no strength to stand. I pray God heals his wounds and he is lifted up spiritually so that he can share testimony to the kidnapper and that the smile on his face will be a testimony for the evil people Satan is using."

Together, John and Abraham prayed, "Lord, we come before You, asking You to give wisdom to us men negotiating with the kidnappers. You know the government won't step in. It's just the church and the Druze. Yacoub's life is on the line.

"We saw the whip marks on his back. We pray that every cry and scream will speak to the Druze people. We pray for the men torturing and planning to hang him. We pray that they release him, and free them from the spirit of Islam. We pray they would release him tomorrow by the authority of scripture. We pray for Your glory to shine.

"We are interceding for Yacoub as he was planting Your church with his servant heart. We pray You would be with him, that he would know he is not alone, that there are thousands of people interceding. Encourage his wife and his daughter. Protect this young family sacrificially serving You. Be there with them; hear their cries for Yacoub. . . . I pray there would be no more pain and beating. Rescue him, reunite him with Your family.

"Encourage the church in Syria. You've been doing a great work for years but now is the time they need Your power."

Beneath the dark shades the Ottoman conquest had drawn over North Africa, faint glimmers of light began to glow again. Sheltered by tarps hidden in the forests, small groups lifted their hands in worship to the Creator God. To avoid detection, they could not lift their voices, but they could lift their hands.

At the Roman amphitheater on these North African shores in 203 AD, twenty-two-year-old Perpetua and her slave left their infants to step into the Roman Amphitheater dressed as brides to meet their Lord. As their blood dripped from the horns of the mad heifer to the arena sand, each red droplet seemed to become a spark of light spreading the hope of the truth to the 30,000 spectators and across the continent.

Now, centuries after the emperor lay in his grave and the amphitheater lay in ruins, Christianity survived. New sparks flickered across the dark continent in tiny house churches or forest gatherings. John, Ervin, Steve, and the team had come to fan those flames, gathering the leaders from across the Middle East and North Africa.

A few of the leaders were turned back at the border when guards discovered they were Christian. Those that survived the crossing worshipped the Lord in delighted abandon at the joy of not needing to keep their voices to whispers beneath forest tarps.

"It is so strengthening for us to experience your presence and hear of the prayers of our brothers and sisters in the West, showing us that we are not forgotten in our sufferings," the weary pastors wept.

"My wife and I can survive the persecution," a pastor shared. "But it is our children, our teens, that shrivel into silence, weary of the pain. Please pray for our teens."

"So true." The leaders around him nodded. "It's our children. . . ."

"My four-year-old son has black and blue marks where his teacher pinches him because I am a pastor," another leader said.

John cringed, thinking of his two young sons at home with Mero.

Somehow, in a Muslim majority country, my parents raised five frontline warriors. It was their prayers that brought us through, he realized, thinking of Nancy teaching art and working with Muslim women at pregnancy support centers; Joanna and her husband leading medical mission trips; Silva serving on the Ananias House board, and Sila and his family on the front lines in the Middle East.

The pastors continued to share their journeys. "My daughter was so harassed by her teachers that she became anorexic," a university professor and pastor told the group.

"'We will hunt you Christians, and find you and kill you,' the teacher taunted my daughter constantly.

"I had a talk with that professor, warning her, you had better be careful about messing with God's children. He takes that seriously.'

"And brothers, three months later, that antagonistic professor suddenly died!'"

The MENA leaders gathered around each other, praying for God to protect, heal, empower, and strengthen each of the attendees of the leadership conference.

John watched the men leave for the bus station heading back to the battle lines with a new confidence in their steps, strengthened to persevere, with the reminder they were not alone. Their brothers and sisters in America prayed for them.

How many of my brave warriors will survive till next year? They risk all to follow Jesus. And count it an honor to do so. Those who don't survive don't lose. They just receive their crown sooner than the rest of us.

When I came to America to study as a teen, it was not by choice, but I felt like an exile. I didn't realize God brought me to America to prepare me to be an advocate for the persecuted churches in twelve MENA countries, a bridge between the West and the East.

Thank You, Lord, for Dr. Ralph Freed, the missionary who braved the Syrian deserts a century ago, whose primary dialect was the gentle whisper of God. Whose wife tithed her time in prayer, praying two and a half hours a day. Thank you for the divine encounter with my great-grandfather in the desert, John prayed, thinking with gratefulness of how Dr. Freed shared the Gospel with his ancestor after his great-grandfather helped the missionary stranded in the desert.

Nearly 2,000 miles away, Martha and Barbara, with the Ananias House team, knelt to wash the feet of the weeping frontline women the team had discipled for five years.

"'Fear not, for I have redeemed you; I have called you by name,'" Martha quoted softly to the precious women from Isaiah 43:1–5. "'You are mine. . . . Because you are precious in my eyes and honored, and I love you. . . . Fear not for I am with you.'"

The team taught the forty-two hand-selected women precept upon precept from the scripture and through curriculum Barbara designed for the courses, leading the Muslim background women to healing from the abuses, as well as the traumas of war. In the only known mentoring program of its kind, Barbara's team met with the MENA women twice a year, discipling them via online video calls in between, in answer to Amalee's prayers for the women of the MENA region.

The women's team honored the five-year student with a celebration meal and graduation festivities, blessing the emerging butterflies returning to the war-torn countries. These brave women would lead Bible studies, teaching women of the love of Jesus in their home countries. And they would teach them to love their husbands crippled by their own backgrounds. And some would be beaten and thrown out of their homes.

"Nancy, if God opens the door for us to go to America, I am feeling in my heart we should go," Rami told his wife as they walked down the cobblestone streets of Old Damascus.

Noting a call from Texas on Rami's vibrating phone not an hour later, the couple's eyes locked.

"Southwestern Baptist Seminary is offering a scholarship for a Syrian pastor, are you interested?" Nancy's brother inquired.

"We are coming!" Rami responded, as Nancy nodded in affirmation.

"I don't see Crosses on the churches in the US. I fear the church is not under the Cross anymore," Rami told his wife and daughters. "I hear many pastors teaching seasonal messages and preaching on how to be saved, but I don't hear them teaching the whole Gospel, taking up the Cross, discipleship, and obedience.

"Dietrich Bonhoeffer wrote years ago, 'The church preaches a cheap Gospel.' And now, Professor Yarnell says, the church is teaching a cheap grace again."

Rami and Nancy's daughters Youanna and Priscilla, premed students in Ivy League universities, stood alone on the college campus, courageously sharing their faith.

"When I sat down for lunch in the university cafeteria," Priscilla told her parents, "one of the students mockingly announced, 'Here is the girl who is against abortion; let's all hear what she has to say!' And a crowd gathered to hear my answer."

"Girls, never forget, no matter what location or room you are in, you are a missionary," Nancy told her daughters. "If you are in a room, God has a mission for you there."

The crowd grew silent as Rami took the platform, his black hair neatly brushed back from his flashing dark eyes, a dark mustache and beard embracing his smile. The fire in his eyes and the passion of his deep voice coupled with his gentle humility revealed Rami to be a man of velvet and steel.

What will this frontline warrior from the Middle East's message be to us in America? the crowd wondered.

"Nehemiah 1 tells us the report came that those who survived the exile are in great trouble and disgrace. The wall was broken down and the gates were burned with fire. And this is the condition in the Middle East," Rami said.

"The walls are broken down; the gates are burned with fire and people are in great distress and disgrace. These are the last days. The war is raging, our people are in a desperate situation.

"So, what is the message of Nehemiah for us? Nehemiah 4:14 says: 'Don't be afraid of them. Remember the Lord, who is great and awesome, and fight for your families, your sons and your daughters, your wives and your homes.'

"When suffering and persecution and revival came to Syria, we felt God saying, '*Arise* and *fight* with prayer on the spiritual battlefield. Remember the Lord your God who is awesome and great.'"

Rami urged: "We need to fight through:

1. PRAYER
2. SURRENDER
3. FORGIVENESS"

Rami told stories of how God fought for them when they fought through prayer. When ISIS planned to attack the Christian community of Damascus, God foiled their plans. As the radicals poured out of the mosque all pumped up to attack the Christian community, the clear sunny day became cloudy, and large hail pelted the area, sending everyone rushing for cover. On another occasion, the radicals began fighting among themselves, were arrested, and never got to attack the Christians.

"Secondly, we fight by surrender, putting self on the altar," Rami continued. "After we surrendered our daughters, we had no more fear because we surrendered our most precious treasures on the altar. After surrender we live without fear, knowing it is a great honor to die for Jesus.

"Third, we fight through the power of *forgiveness*.

"We have the power of forgiveness because we received the forgiveness of Jesus.

"Brothers and sisters, it is hard to witness to Muslims because when you look them in the eye, you know good and well they are looking at you as the enemy and are thinking it would be a blessing to kill you. So we fight that spirit of hate through the power of forgiveness."

Rami urged, "Brothers and sisters, we must choose to stand in the front lines. Our job is to *stand* and *fight* and *pray* with our brothers and sisters and God will do miracles.

"Hebrews 12:28 says, 'Therefore, since we are receiving a kingdom that cannot be shaken, let us be thankful, and so worship God acceptably with reverence and awe.'

"The shaking of this earthly kingdom is a sign the heavenly one is near. Look, arise, and speak. Help us stand for Jesus. We all share the same mandate—we are all called to carry our Cross and follow Jesus."

The radicals hung Yacoub by his feet, with his hands tied behind his back, beating him with electrical cords every day.

Before the kidnapping, Abraham had scheduled the commissioning of the young pastor. Yacoub had been on a quest to memorize the New Testament, and those precious verses flooded back, encouraging his heart while his captors kept kept him blindfolded and beat him. For days on end, he could not tell whether it was day or night. The young pastor was sold numerous times.

"You must hate us, and wish for our death," his captors prodded him.

"No, I don't hate you," Yacoub responded. "I don't wish for your death or your harm. I just hate the spirit behind your actions."

Sunday morning, three weeks after Yacoub's abduction, Abraham stood in the front of the Jesus of Nazareth Church in Damascus with his arm around Yacoub, presenting the released pastor to the jubilant congregation.

"I believed it was possible for God to do a miracle, and to send an angel to rescue me," Yacoub shared. "When God delayed, I held on to the verse I had memorized in Psalm 27:14, 'Wait patiently for the Lord, be strong and courageous' (NLT).

"'I waited patiently for the LORD; He inclined to me and heard my cry," Yacoub quoted to the backdrop of the congregations' delighted "Alleluias."

"He lifted me up from the pit of despair, out of the miry clay;

He set my feet upon a rock, and made my footsteps firm.

He put a new song in my mouth, a hymn of praise to our God.

Many will see and fear and put their trust in the LORD.' Psalm 40:1–3 (BSB),

"God was saying, 'Wait for me, it is not my time.' I became frustrated because I was kidnapped, I knew my family was distressed.

"Dearest beloved, we keep quoting 'The Lord is my shepherd. I have all that I need. He lets me rest in green meadows. Even when I walk through the darkest valleys, I will not be afraid because you are close beside me.' Psalm 23:1,2,4 (NLT).

"Many times we repeat these verses, but I lived and experienced those verses. I said to the Lord, You are my Shepherd. I will not be afraid because You are close beside me.

"My kidnappers said, 'You wish to kill us, don't you?'

"I said, 'I don't wish you death or harm in any way. My battle is with the forces of evil.'

"God gave me this verse, 'Then call on me when you are in trouble, and I will rescue you, and you will give me glory.' Psalm 50:15 (NLT).

"The last day, God said to me, 'Just stand still and watch the Lord rescue you today.'"

"Amen! Amen! Alleluia!" the congregation burst out.

For security reasons, Yacoub did not reveal the details of his miraculous rescue. He only shared that the exact time Christians around the globe joined in a forty-eight-hour prayer chain, a man from outside of the country came in and unexpectedly rescued him from his captors—on the day God had promised.

"May God help me to stand firm in my faith in Him and be a living testimony of His work," he told the congregation, closing with a hymn of praise and surrender.

Approaching eighty, Pastor Abraham continued mentoring the MENA pastors and encouraging the churches, and traveled to Sudan in the midst of political turmoil to encourage Fawzi and Idris. Amalee continued her ministry of intercession.

Speaking from war-torn Damascus, Pastor Abraham shared his heart through an online video call to Christians around the globe.

"We praise God because this is *His* time, and this is *His* work and *His* church." The aging pastor's voice vibrated with passionate hope and his eyes glowed with fervor.

"We see Matthew 24's signs fulfilled, showing how close the Lord's return is. Praise God, He is coming! May the Lord unite all our hearts as believers worldwide because we are the one body of Jesus to pray one for another. Beloved brothers in the US, we pray for you often; please pray for us in the Middle East as well."

"What is the church experiencing under the moral collapse and the war?" John questioned.

"It's been a difficult time for the church, and for the whole country. In fact, every time a family member leaves their home, they don't know if they will return or not. But the believers know God is the protector." Abraham spoke with a steady voice, his dark eyes flashing above the graying mustache still distinguishing the elegantly aging face.

"Recently, I was going to church and always take a specific alley to get there, and the Lord told me, 'Change your route! Take a different way!'

"I was surprised because I always go that way to church. I started asking God, 'Am I going to meet someone? Do you want me to have an interaction with some person?'

"As I entered the other alley, an explosion shook the block as a missile exploded on the alley I usually take. A man came running around the corner toward me, bleeding, and yelling, 'Please! Please help me!' as he collapsed onto the street.

"I started yelling for neighbors to come help me. I could not carry him alone. As we lifted the injured man into the ambulance cart, he died in our arms.

"If I had entered the alley I usually take, the missile would have fallen right where I would have been. I would have been killed as our alleys are so small—there would have been no escape. But the Lord has an umbrella over us.

"We know that the Lord is in charge and in control of the whole universe. He doesn't allow anything to happen unless it is for the good of His children and His church—even sickness, even death. If He allows it, we know it will bring an ultimate good."

"So, Brother Abraham, why at nearly eighty years of age do you choose to stand in the gap on the front lines beside the pastors you mentored, encouraging them on, instead of living in comfort and safety with your children in America?"

"I would rather be under the bullets under God's will, than out from under the bullets, out from under God's will!" Abraham responded, his eyes alight with fire and his voice full of confidence.

"How can we pray for you, Dad?" John asked at the close of the online video meeting.

Abraham did not request prayers for safety, for the end of war, nor alleviation of suffering.

Instead, the battle-seasoned pastor powerfully replied, "Pray that the

Lord would unite the hearts of believers worldwide, so we are ready for His Second Coming!"

How great is our God!

"I am coming soon. Hold fast what you have, so that no one may seize your crown." Revelation 3:11

Thank you for taking the time to read this collection of historical events in the lives of modern-day believers in the Islamic world.

Thank you for caring about them and for your prayers on their behalf.

All the authors' proceeds from the sales of these books go directly to Ananias House to come alongside the suffering churches of the MENA region, training Christian leaders, discipling new believers, distributing Bibles, sharing crisis relief supplies, and supporting Christian education in these countries.

If you feel the Lord moving you to share toward the needs of these fearless evangelists, pastors, and believers, please visit the website at http://ananiashouse.org or send to Ananias House, P.O. Box 941292, Houston, TX 77094.

Thank You from the Kingdom.

And from the King, "Inasmuch as ye have done it unto the least of these my Brethren, ye have done it unto me."

Great is your reward in Heaven.

May the Lamb that was slain receive all honor and glory forever, Amen.

LIST OF CHARACTERS

THE SAMARA FAMILY:

Abraham Samara – Syrian patriarch who courageously pastored, planted churches, and trained leaders for sixty years.

Amalee Samara – selfless, gracious wife of Abraham, third grade school teacher and mother of five.

Nancy – eldest daughter of pastor Abraham, warrior woman, principal of a school for refugees, wife of Rami and mother of Priscilla and Youanna.

Rami Ibrahim – pastor with his father-in-law, Abraham Samara.

John Samara – eldest son of Abraham, studied in the US and UK, trains leaders and founder of Ananias House to bridge the Western churches to the MENA region. Husband of Mero.

Joanna – second Samara daughter.

Silva – third Samara daughter.

Sila – second Samara son, married to Charlotte, involved in oversees ministries.

OTHER CHARACTERS:

Abdul and Samira – a Syrian refugee family with prior involvement in al-Qaeda and a wealthy family in Saudi Arabia whose lives were changed by a dream.

Ali – the eldest son of Abdul and Samira.

Amar – a Christian boy abducted by radicals.

Mrs. Baghdadi – Silva's teacher.

Barbara – Ananias House director of women's leadership training.

Davit – son of Mikayel and Hannah forced to fight with the regime.

Ervin – an American pastor who teaches with John Samara in the Middle East and is an advocate for the suffering MENA churches.

Fawzi and Idris – Sudanese young refugees returning to their homeland to plant churches.

Hannah – wife of Mikayel.

Hassan family – the mother and daughters Sosa and Rahel were abducted and abused by radicals while the brother Lukose was forced to watch. Rahel falls in love with a young pastor.

Isa – the Arabic name for Jesus, used in the Qur'an. And the prophesied name for a child Abdul and Samira would have.

Javin – son of Mikayel, hit by sniper fire.

Karam and Andros – student and leader of the attendees smuggling across the border for the leadership conference.

Leyla and Zahir – former Druze, parents of a son with a birth defect. Zahir becomes a leader in the church.

Marc and Sarah – missionaries to Syrian refugees.

Mahir and Duniya – refugees with wealthy al-Qaeda connections. Duniya was a female Imam teaching women Islam.

Mariama and Elia – Silva's friends who were interrogated by the Mukhabarat.

Martha – wife of Ervin, Mero's "American mother," prayer warrior, gracious hostess facilitating meetings with the Samaras, team member in Ananias House women's ministry.

Mikayel – Armenian Aleppo businessman and pastor.

Nabil and Yasmine – Christian leaders in a town attacked by ISIS.

Nazir – the Middle Eastern pastor murdered for his faith.

Rafiq – a pastor kidnapped by Druze radicals.

Steve – another American pastor and counselor who has accompanied John Samara to the Middle East.

Vergie – John's junior high classmate who beat and harassed John nearly every day.

Yacoub – a gifted, committed young man with a wife and infant whose goal was to memorize the entire New Testament. He was kidnapped by Druze radicals.

Pastor Yosef – a pastor in the refugee camp coming from an affluent Alawite background.

GLOSSARY

Abaya – a long black cloak worn by Middle Eastern women

Allawite – A minority sect of Islam, the ruling class of Syria, with secretive religious beliefs including the concept that the five pillars of Islam are symbolic, and belief in Ali as a member of the trinity.

Baba – Arabic for dad

Burka – the most concealing of all Islamic veils, a one-piece veil that covers the face and body, often leaving just a mesh screen to see through

Druze – an Arab eclectic religious group adhering to an Abrahamic, monotheistic religion who believe in God and reincarnation. Most Druze religious practices are kept secret even from their members. Conversion to their religion or away from their religion is not permitted, and causes hostilities.

Falafel – a popular Middle Eastern street food, deep-fried balls made from chickpeas or fava beans with fresh herbs and spices served in pita sandwiches with pickles, hot sauce, tahini, and tomatoes, cucumbers, and lettuce.

Habibi – Arabic for my dear, my love, used for males

Habibti – Arabic for my dear, honey, or darling used for female

Hayati – an Arabic expression of love meaning "my life"

Isa – the name the Qur'an uses to refer to Jesus

Kaffiyeh – a traditional headdress worn by men from parts of the Middle East, fashioned from a square scarf, and usually made of cotton. The kaffiyeh is commonly found in arid regions, as it provides protection from sunburn, dust, and sand. An agal is often used by Arabs to keep it in place.

Jiddo and Taita – Grandpa and Grandma

Kaftan – a long tunic or shirt

Khalifa – ISIS judge, leader

Kibbeh – a national dish of Syria and Lebanon made of savory ground beef, onion, and bulgar croquettes stuffed with pinenuts, fried beef or lamb seasoned with coriander, pepper, nutmeg, cinnamon, and cardamom

Mukhabarat – Arabic term for intelligence agency, used in reference to secret police agents who spy on civilians

Rohi – my soul mate

Sfiha – a Syrian type of indiviudalized pizza made of soft flatbread topped with meat and spices

Shahada – The proclamation of Islamic faith, the most sacred statement in Islam. Reciting it is the gateway to joining Islam.

Shawarma – a flatbread sandwich including slices of lamb, veal, beef, or chicken roasted on a spit, served with garlic sauce, fries, and pickles

Shemagh – a traditional Middle Eastern scarf or wrap commonly used to shield the head and face from harsh weather conditions

Souk – a street market, bazaar, or open-air market stall

Sunni and Shia Islam – Though the two main sects within Islam, Sunni and Shia, agree on most of the fundamental beliefs and practices of Islam, a bitter split between the two goes back some fourteen centuries. The divide originated with a dispute over who should succeed the Prophet Muhammad as leader of the Islamic faith he introduced.

Sunnis believe that succession to the Prophet Muhammad (d. 632) rightly followed the line of his most able and pious associates. Approximately 75 percent of Syria is Sunni. ISIS are radical Sunnis.

Shiites and Alawites claim succession should have been based on bloodlines (giving the Alawites and Shiites a little common ground). While the the factions have generally lived in peace, the schism deepened in the late twentieth century, exploding into violence in many parts of the Middle East as extreme brands of Sunni and Shia Islam battle for both religious and political supremacy.

Suwar – chapters in the Qur'an, plural for surah

Tabbouleh – a cold salad made of finely chopped parsley, tomatoes, mint, onion, soaked uncooked bulgur, and seasoned with olive oil, lemon juice, salt, and sweet pepper originating from the mountains of Lebanon and Syria.

ACKNOWLEDGMENTS

I will always be grateful to our amazing God who showed His love and power in the Middle East, turning evil for good. I am grateful for His inspiration, and for bringing the fragments of this production together. I pray He is recording the many selfless investments made to bring these stories to print.

To the Samara family, not only have you lived courageously on the battlefront, but you have shared your journeys and memories so that the candles of the dark world might be lit with hope. Silva, knowing you graduated from my alma mater, Malone University, gave me an instant bond with you. Nancy and Rami, John and Mero, Sila and Charlotte, Silva, Priscilla, Abraham and Amalee, you selflessly shared your stories. John, you taught me so much about "living in the shadow of the Cross."

Janelle, the account you heard John share so inspired you, that you said, "Mom, I will cook and clean for you if you write those stories." You kept your promise, and prayed, encouraged, and reviewed.

Jerry, you supported my calling, prayed, listened to the stories, and urged me on, and flew us to meetings to make this book happen.

Ervin and Martha Barkman, you introduced us to John, hosted brainstorming meetings, served delightful meals, shared your journals and stories, reviewed and encouraged. Without you this book would not have happened.

My dear bosom college friend, Selana Shaheen, you introduced me to sfiha in the barn at Malone University, sharing the tasty meat pies your aunts had baked. Your Syrian heritage gave me an extra delight in writing these stories, as I recalled the unparalleled warmth of the hospitality of your precious family, your dear aunts, and of course Salem. Thanks for correcting, encouraging, and praying.

Mildred Martin, Gary Miller, Shirlene Hoover, Sarah Alimowski, Rhoda Wenger, Eric Bear, Vera Rose Campbell, Priscilla Ibraham, Silva,

Jana Kropf, Rosalind Byler, you tediously reviewed the stories, making this a stronger book and urging me to get it to press. Abigail Gehring, you are the best editor ever. I will always be grateful.

Our six children, you prayed, encouraged, and reviewed. Judith, your stories from Mosul first lit my fire to write about what God is doing in the Middle East.

Steve and Dorcas Stutzman, your passionate love for the MENA region and your insights breathed fresh life into this book, giving us courage to move forward to publication.

And my many faithful prayer warriors—you know who you are, Marie, Lori, Ruby, Lois, Martha, etc.—you fanned the flames of this project, and I am most grateful.

With a sense of responsibility to the brave men and women who have shared their stories, I have recorded each story as it was told to me. Every miracle, bombing, abduction, and imprisonment actually took place. Names have been changed, and at times locations are not disclosed to protect these courageous people who are still at risk. A couple stories are placed outside of original timing for the flow of the story—such as the chapter of the ISIS Prisoner—but the details are factual.

My life has been transformed by God's stories I have been privileged to work with, rekindling hope and courage in these intense days of final battle, helping us persevere, and focus on "the joy set before us." It's so near.

DH

MAPS

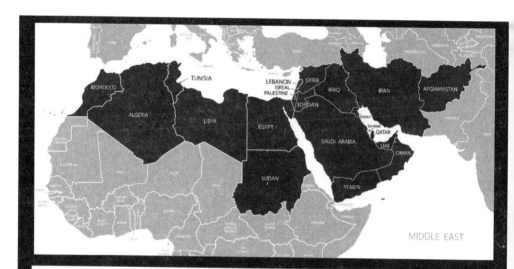

ANANIAS HOUSE

bridges the West with the MENA region (Middle East and North Africa) through spiritual and physical resources to strengthen the suffering body of Christ for generations to come through:

- **Bible Training** for pastors, men and women leaders
- **Crisis Relief** efforts through the church and long term sustainability
- **Evangelism, Discipleship and Bible Distribution** through frontline churches
- **Education** through Bible-based schooling in the Muslim world

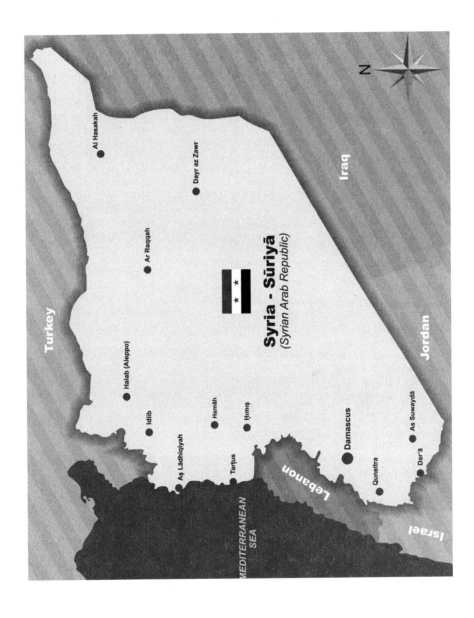